MODELING WITH TECHNOLOGY

Mindtools for Conceptual Change

MODELING WITH TECHNOLOGY

Mindtools for Conceptual Change

THIRD EDITION

David H. Jonassen
University of Missouri

Merrill
Prentice Hall

Upper Saddle River, New Jersey
Columbus, Ohio

Library of Congress Cataloging in Publication Data

Jonassen, David H.
    Modeling with technology : mindtools for conceptual change / David H. Jonassen.—3rd ed.
      p. cm.
    Rev. ed. of: Computers as mindtools for schools. c2000.
    Includes bibliographical references and index.
    ISBN 0-13-170345-5
     1. Computer-assisted instruction. 2. Computer simulation. 3. Change (Psychology)
    I. Jonassen, David H., Computers as mindtools for schools. II. Title.

LB1028.5.J612 2006
371.33′4—dc22

2005052745

Vice President and Executive Publisher: Jeffery W. Johnston
Executive Editor: Debra A. Stollenwerk
Assistant Development Editor: Elisa Rogers
Editorial Assistant: Mary Morrill
Production Editor: Alexandrina Benedicto Wolf
Production Coordination and Text Design: GGS Book Services
Design Coordinator: Diane C. Lorenzo
Cover Designer: Bryan Huber
Photo Coordinator: Valeric Schultz
Production Manager: Susan Hannahs
Senior Marketing Manager: Darcy Betts Prybella
Marketing Manager: Bryan Mounts

Photo Credits: Laura Bolesta/Merrill: pp. 3, 185; Anthony Magnacca/Merrill: pp. 12, 117, 133, 166; Patrick White/Merrill: pp. 27, 54, 71, 177; Liz Moore/Merrill: pp. 39, 91, 101, 149; Bill Burlingham/Prentice Hall School Division: p. 47; Silver Burdett Ginn: p. 81; David Young-Wolff/PhotoEdit: p. 194.

This book was set in Garamond by GGS Book Services. It was printed and bound by Courier Stoughton, Inc. The cover was printed by Courier Stoughton, Inc.

10 9 8 7 6 5 4 3 2 1
ISBN 0-13-170345-5

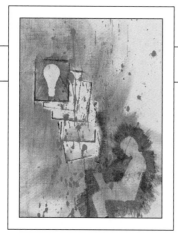

CONTENTS

PART TWO   Modeling Phenomena   37

CHAPTER 4   Modeling Domain Knowledge   39

CHAPTER 5   Modeling Systems   47

CHAPTER 6   Modeling Problems   54

CHAPTER 7   Modeling Experiences: Capturing and Indexing Stories   71

Note: Every effort has been made to provide accurate and current Internet information in this book. However, the Internet and information posted on it are constantly changing, so it is inevitable that some of the Internet addresses listed in this textbook will change.

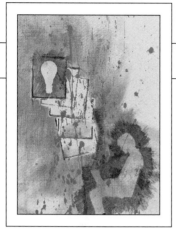

Education technologists have traditionally assumed that if you design, construct, and embed effective lessons in television or computers (i.e., technologies) and show them to students, students will learn the intended lessons. The role of the technology was to communicate ideas to learners, just like the most common role of teachers. The better the technology communicated ideas, the more students learned. However, students do not learn from technology; they learn from thinking. This third edition of *Modeling with Technology*, like the first two, focuses on how to use technology to help students to think more effectively.

To help students learn, educators must focus first and foremost on student learning, not on teacher or technology instruction. Educational technologists have spent decades trying to make technologies act like teachers, but technologies are lousy teachers. Rather than analyzing how technology can teach better, educators need to consider how students must think to learn most meaningfully. Technology-centric approaches to education ignore the sole purpose of technology in classrooms: to support meaningful learning. In a world where schools are systematically cheating on high-stakes tests to avoid censure or to attract dollars, students are being deprived of the most important purpose of education, learning how to learn effectively. Technologies have the potential to enhance, expand, and amplify learning if we reconceptualize the ways that they are used.

Therefore, this book is about learning, specifically meaningful learning. Schools and technologies too often engage and support memorization and the application of finite skills that can be measured on high-stakes tests. More meaningful forms of learning will enable students to better comprehend educational content and better perform on tests. This book assumes that meaningful learning requires at least four components: meaningful purpose, conceptual engagement, conceptual development, and methods and strategies that support these three components.

FOCUS ON MEANINGFUL LEARNING

Meaningful learning does not occur without a *purpose* or intention to accomplish a meaningful task. The most meaningful task that requires and engages meaningful learning is problem solving (Jonassen, 2004). Every learning activity in every class in every grade should engage students in problem solving because it leads to better understanding and better remembering ability. Unfortunately an educational revolution would be necessary to support problem-based learning everywhere.

Meaningful learning also requires *conceptual engagement*. When people intend to learn something to accomplish a task, they think hard about the components of the task and how they are interrelated. Learning to solve problems is conceptually engaging. Conceptual engagement is similar to such important educational concepts as cognitive engagement (Limon, 2001; Wolters, 2003) or mindful learning (Langer, 1997; Salomon & Tamar, 1998).

The result of conceptual engagement directed at intentional activity is *conceptual development*, also known as conceptual change. From an early age, humans naturally build simplified and intuitive personal theories to explain their world. Through experience and reflection, they reorganize and add conceptual complexity as they learn. Conceptual change occurs when learners change their understanding of the concepts they use and the conceptual frameworks that encompass them. "Conceptual change is the mechanism underlying meaningful learning" (Mayer, 2002, p. 101). The goal of learning should be conceptual change and development.

Meaningful learning requires *methods and strategies* that support intentional learning (and its self-regulation), conceptual engagement, and conceptual development. One of the most powerful strategies that support meaningful learning is learners constructing models of what they are learning. If you cannot build a model of what you think you know, then you do not really know it. This book is about using Mindtools (Jonassen, 1996, 2000) to support meaningful learning through model building.

Model building is among the most powerful strategies for engaging, supporting, and assessing conceptual change in learners. Building models is intentional and purposeful, and students love to do it because they have ownership of the models they produce. Building models is conceptually engaging. Building models supports conceptual change, and also provides evidence of conceptual change. Modeling with Mindtools is not the only way to use computers to support learning or the only way to engage conceptual change. There are many wonderful applications of computers and many conceptually engaging activities that teachers have used for decades. Nor is modeling with Mindtools a panacea for education; it will not revolutionize learning by itself. Rather, I believe that when educators are ready to innovate, modeling will support most forms of innovation.

ORGANIZATION OF TEXT

The first two editions examined the use of Mindtools for engaging critical thinking. The assumption was that Mindtools cannot be used without thinking critically. I continue to believe that. Mindtools are a useful approach for using technology to foster critical thinking. However, my conceptual framework for learning and technology has changed. This edition represents a fresh perspective, which is reflected in the organization of the text.

Part One of the book argues that meaningful learning naturally engages conceptual change. Because conceptual change is among the richest conceptions of meaningful learning, it should be the goal of schools at all levels. So how do we engage and support conceptual change in students? Certainly not by lecturing and not through standardized tests. Although there are many approaches and methods for supporting conceptual change, I believe that building models of the phenomena being studied is among the most effective methods. Therefore, Chapter 1 describes conceptual change and illustrates how building models helped me build richer models of the conceptual change process. Chapter 2 argues that conceptual change is fostered by model building, and explains model building and its rationale. Chapter 3 demonstrates that conceptual change can be assessed by model building and briefly describes methods for assessing models that students build. In this edition I rationalize the use of Mindtools as modeling tools that engage and support conceptual change.

Part Two represents the major change in the third edition. In the previous editions, Part One was followed by descriptions of how each technology tool could be used to engage critical thinking. In this edition, Part Two focuses on what can be modeled. Students can use Mindtools to model domain knowledge (Chapter 4) and the systems that organize that knowledge (Chapter 5). Students can use Mindtools to build models of the problems they are solving (Chapter 6), which results in better problem solving and better understanding of the knowledge that underlies problems. Rather than studying content, students can build models of people's experiences (stories) (Chapter 7). Students can use Mindtools to model how they are supposed to think in order to learn (Chapter 8). When students use Mindtools this way, they are self-regulating their learning experiences; that is, they are thinking metacognitively. Descriptions of the technology tools are deferred until Part Three.

The organization of the book is depicted in Figure P.1. Rather than reading this book linearly, identify your learning goals and classify them as domain knowledge, systems, problems, experiences, or thinking; then read the appropriate chapter. Part Three illustrates how different Mindtools can be used in modeling (Chapters 9–17). Think about how you want your students to model phenomena and which tools they should use. Then read the appropriate chapters to learn about those tools. Nine different kinds of Mindtools (databases, concept maps, spreadsheets, expert systems, systems modeling tools, teachable agents and direct manipulation environments, visualization tools, hypermedia, and computer conference) can be used to build models of the five different kinds of phenomena described in Part Two.

Use this book interactively. Move back and forth between parts to get ideas about how to engage your students in model building. Try different modeling tools with your students. Witness their conceptual engagement and reflect on the conceptual change processes they have undergone. You won't be disappointed if you relinquish control and allow your students to represent what is important to them.

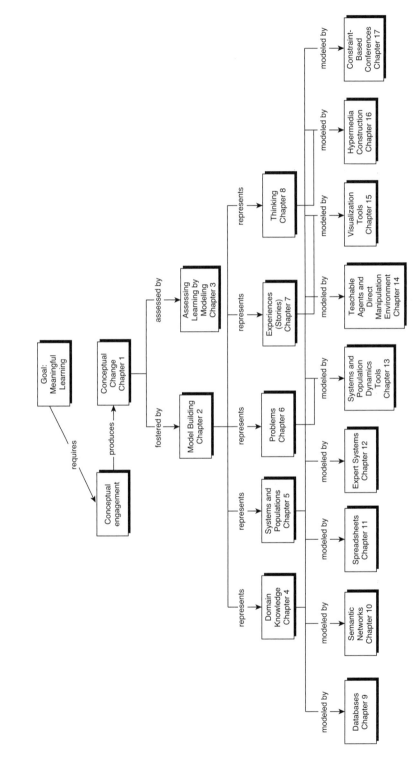

Figure P–1. Conceptual overview of this book.

FEATURES OF THE TEXT

Throughout this book, note these features:

♦ **A wide array of visual aids** support the concepts and tools discussed in each chapter. These include graphic examples, illustrations of models, and sample rubrics.

♦ **A coaching feature** in Chapters 9–13 and 15–17 gives examples of software and presents step-by-step classroom activities that can be used or adapted to help students create models.

♦ **A summary** at the end of each chapter reiterates the main points of discussion.

CAVEATS

Readers often ask for more detailed instructions on how to implement specific Mindtools in their classrooms than are possible to convey in a book. This book provides many examples of models that students have developed; these are offered as exemplars of the kinds of models that students can develop. Unfortunately, it is impossible to detail every step in the process or to provide examples that are relevant to every grade level and subject. To apply Mindtools, you must generalize the uses of the Mindtools illustrated in the book to your own classroom.

Learning how to use Mindtools to engage your students in constructing models depends on the problems you are solving, the tools you are using, the purposes of their use, the nature of your classroom, your background and beliefs, the school you work in, the available technology, and myriad other factors. Even with knowledge of all of those factors, it would be difficult to predict how well Mindtools will work in a specific setting. That is one of the enduring lessons of constructivism: It is impossible to predict the sense that anyone will make of any experience. What Mindtools share with all other constructivist pedagogies is an assumption of personal responsibility on the part of learners to construct their own interpretation of the use of specific Mindtools. That can result only from trying them.

Some readers request methods for using specific software to function as Mindtools. The software that you use depends on the technologies available to you, budgets, your personal biases, and so on. There are many software packages available, and they change frequently. New tools emerge daily and just as quickly disappear. There are also many texts (paper and online) that provide tutorials on how to use the software. If you want to use Mindtools you must make your own decisions about which software to use, how to best learn how to use it, and how to best support your students. Mindtools are a way of thinking about how to use technology to engage and support meaningful learning. You must construct your own understanding of what that means, which will depend on your school context, beliefs, educational history, school culture, and so on. I hope that you are able to construct and apply your own personal theory about how to use technologies as Mindtools. Best of luck.

ACKNOWLEDGMENTS

I would like to thank the following reviewers for their valuable feedback: Beverly Abbey, Austin College; J. David Betts, University of Arizona; J. B. Browning, Brunswick Community College; Irene Linlin Chen, University of Houston, Downtown; Kara Dawson, University of Florida; Kim Foreman, San Francisco University; Teresa Franklin, Ohio University; Khalid Hamza, Florida Atlantic University; Anne Hird, Bridgewater State College; Bob Hoffman, San Diego State University; Karen Ivers, California State University, Fullerton; Virginia Jewell, Columbus State University; Douglas R. Knox, New Mexico Highlands University; Natalie B. Milman, The George Washington University; and Desmond Rodney, Florida Atlantic University.

REFERENCES

Jonassen, D. H. (1996). *Computers in the classroom: Mindtools for critical thinking.* Columbus, OH: Merrill/Prentice Hall.

Jonassen, D. H. (2000). *Computers as Mindtools for schools: Engaging critical thinking* (2nd ed.). Columbus, OH: Prentice Hall.

Jonassen, D. H. (2004). *Learning to solve problems: An instructional design guide.* San Francisco: Pfeiffer/Jossey-Bass.

Langer, E. J. (1997). *The power of mindful learning.* Cambridge, MA: Harvard University Press.

Limon, M. (2001). On the cognitive conflict as an instructional strategy for conceptual change: A critical appraisal. *Learning and Instruction, 11*(4–5), 35–380.

Mayer, R. E. (2002). Understanding conceptual change: A commentary. In M. Limon & L. Mason (Eds.), *Reconsidering conceptual change: Issues in theory and practice* (pp. 101–111). Dordrecht, Netherlands: Kluwer Academic.

Salmon, G., & Tamar, A. (1998). Educational psychology and technology: A matter of reciprocal relations. *Teachers College Record. 100*(2), 222–224.

Wolters, C. A. (2003). Regulation of motivation: Evaluating an underemphasized aspect of self-regulated learning. *Educational Psychologist, 38*(4), 189–205.

David Jonassen is Distinguished Professor of Education at the University of Missouri where he teaches in the areas of learning technologies and educational psychology. Since earning his doctorate in educational media and experimental educational psychology from Temple University, Dr. Jonassen has taught at the Pennsylvania State University, the University of Colorado, the University of Twente in the Netherlands, the University of North Carolina at Greensboro, and Syracuse University. He has published 26 books and numerous articles, papers, and reports on text design, task analysis, instructional design, computer-based learning, hypermedia, constructivist learning, cognitive tools, and technology in learning. He has consulted with businesses, universities, public schools, and other institutions around the world. His current research focuses on constructing design models and environments for problem solving. Dr. Jonassen is Director of the Center for the Study of Problem Solving at the University of Missouri.

MODELING WITH TECHNOLOGY

Mindtools for Conceptual Change

PART ONE

Modeling for Conceptual Change

CHAPTER 1
  Meaningful Learning: Conceptual
  Change and Development

CHAPTER 2
  Model Building with Mindtools

CHAPTER 3
  Assessing Learning by Modeling

Meaningful Learning: Conceptual Change and Development

The increased emphasis on constructivism in the past decade has led educational researchers and theorists to focus the attention of educators on sense making and other conceptions of meaningful learning. From the myriad definitions of meaningful learning, research communities (psychology, learning sciences, science and mathematics education) have concentrated on the role of conceptual change (Limon & Mason, 2002; Schnotz, Vosniadou, & Carretero, 1999; Sinatra & Pintrich, 2003). Conceptual change has become one of the most common conceptions of meaningful learning because it treats learning as an intentional, dynamic, and constructive process. Conceptual change is rooted in theories of constructivism. Mayer (2002, p. 101) claims that "conceptual change is the mechanism underlying meaningful learning."

THEORY BUILDING

Conceptual change is predicated on the belief that humans are natural theory builders. Conceptual change theorists argue that from an early age, humans build simplified and intuitive personal theories to explain the external worlds in which they live. Through experience and reflection, they reorganize and add conceptual complexity to their theories as they learn. As theories mature, they gain strength and coherence. The conceptions (knowledge) that humans construct determine the sense that they can make of new information. Humans interact with new information to the degree that the information is comprehensible, coherent, and plausible according to their existing conceptual models. The cognitive process of adapting and restructuring these theories is conceptual change (Vosniadou, 1999).

Conceptual change occurs when learners change their understanding of the concepts they use and of the conceptual frameworks that encompass them. However, the amount and kinds of conceptual change depend on the learner's prior knowledge, individuality, usefulness of the content being studied, and context in which the content is being studied. Because of the complexity of the conceptual change process, different theories of conceptual change have been proposed. For some researchers (Smith, diSessa, & Roschelle, 1993; Siegler, 1996), conceptual change is an evolutionary process of adding concepts and reorganizing knowledge structures to include new concepts. This model of conceptual change is influenced by the theories of Jean Piaget, who taught that learners gradually accommodate existing knowledge into more coherent and well-organized knowledge structures.

Other theories claim that conceptual change is revolutionary (Thagard, 1992), perturbed by some external event that cannot be explained by prior knowledge. Revolutionary conceptual change occurs when information is inconsistent with learners' personal beliefs and assumptions (Vosniadou, 1994), so revision of conceptual frameworks (conceptual change) is necessary. When we encounter ideas that we neither understand nor believe, we are forced to change our conceptions if we are to accept the new ideas.

This chapter promotes one of the best ways to engage in and foster conceptual change, that is, to use technologies to construct models that represent learners' internal conceptual models. As learners build and alter their models, they are constructing knowledge by changing their conceptions of what they are learning.

This chapter also reviews theories of conceptual change. My colleagues and I constructed models of the theories to better understand them. In other words, I am practicing what I am promoting—modeling for learning. The following belief underlies this book: If you cannot build a model of what you are studying, then you do not understand what you are studying. A corollary states that to better understand what you are learning, you should build a model of it.

This book illustrates how a variety of technology-based modeling tools can be used as Mindtools to help learners construct models of what they are studying. Building models of subject content using technology-based modeling tools facilitates the process of conceptual change in learners. The models that learners build also provide evidence of their learning and conceptual change. A dynamic and reciprocal process occurs between internal conceptual models and the external models that learners construct.

The following sections of this chapter describe two theories of conceptual change and illustrate how model building was used to better understand the theories.

COGNITIVE CONFLICT

Conceptual change arises from the interaction between learners' experience and learners' conceptions while engaged in problem solving or some higher order cognitive activity. An important implication is that conceptual change is less likely to occur when students are memorizing information or attempting to understand ideas at a surface level in order to complete an examination. If learners are to be engaged in conceptual change, they must have a task that requires conceptualization.

One of the most commonly cited theories of conceptual change is cognitive conflict theory. According to this theory, when learners want to understand something and they experience a discrepancy between what they know and what they expect, a radical form of conceptual change may occur. When learners' current conceptions are unable to interpret their experiences or cannot be used to solve problems, cognitive conflict occurs (Strike & Posner, 1985). If learners become convinced that their current conceptions are inconsistent with the standards of the subject-matter domain, the learners may recognize the need to change their conceptions. They may admit that their theory is not really accurate. So conceptual change may result from cognitive conflicts when discrepant, dissonant, or anomalous data or events call into question learners' current understanding (Ferrari & Elik, 2003).

When learners are confronted with information that contradicts their existing conceptualizations, conceptual change may occur. The first step in the conceptual change process is the awareness of a contradiction (Luque, 2003), followed by awareness of a need for change. This may be the most difficult part of the conceptual change process. Learners who possess low domain knowledge have difficulty noticing contradictions between their own conceptions and scientifically acceptable ones, so they may not be aware of the need for change. Students with low interest and low domain knowledge are unlikely to engage in conceptual change. Experts, on the other hand, may recognize contradictions but be unwilling to give up their current conceptualization. Often experts are unwilling to change because they feel sure of what they know; they will change only when change is useful and relevant to achieving their goals. When learners are interested *and* possess understanding, they are more willing to change their conceptions (Luque, 2003).

Cognitive conflict is not always sufficient for causing conceptual change. When faced with anomalous or discrepant data or events, students often ignore, reject, exclude, or reinterpret anomalous data or hold the data in abeyance (Chinn & Brewer, 1993). Conflict must be supported by knowledge-building activities (Chan, Burtis, & Bereiter, 1997). One of the most powerful knowledge-building activities is model building.

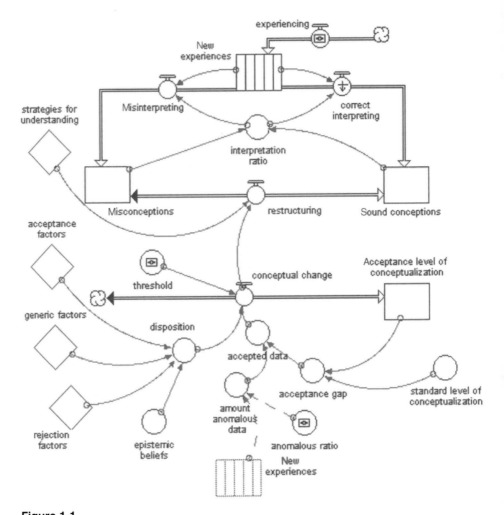

Figure 1-1
Cognitive conflict model of conceptual change.

To better understand the intricacies of the cognitive conflict theory of conceptual change, some colleagues and I constructed a model of the theory using the systems modeling tool, Stella (see Figure 1-1). Look at the boxes that represent entities and the arrows that depict flows. In this model, experiences that learners have flow into new experiences at the top of the model. Those experiences may be misinterpreted or interpreted correctly. Correctly interpreted conceptions become sound conceptions. Misinterpreted experiences become misconceptions, which must be restructured. Restructuring (small circle toward the top) is controlled by strategies for understanding (hidden in the diamond of that name) such as generating examples, analogies, or images. Restructuring is also affected by conceptual change (small circle just below restructuring). Conceptual change is a flow that is controlled by the learner's disposition to change. Disposition to change is a function of acceptance factors (hidden in the diamond of that name), generic factors, rejection factors, and epistemic beliefs. Conceptual change is also affected by the amount of accepted data, which is a function of the amount of anomalous data (a ratio of new experiences that are accepted).

This model is complex, but so is conceptual change. Stella and other modeling tools can be used to represent complex ideas. If students are to engage in meaningful learning, they must learn to wrestle with complexity. Teachers who oversimplify ideas to make them more easily communicable rob students of meaningful understanding. The power of Stella models is that they contain simple formulas that convey the strength of relationships among variables. After adjusting values, we executed the program underlying the model, and obtained the graphic output shown in Figure 1-2. The graphs show the growth of misconceptions and sound conceptions. We can change the values again and observe the effects on conceptual

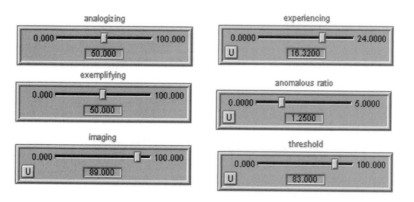

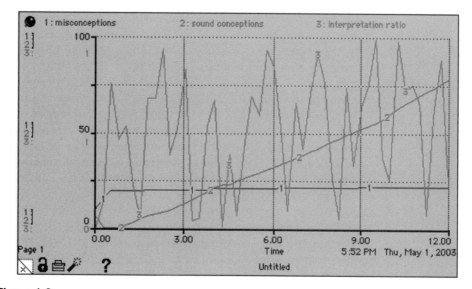

Figure 1-2
Value adjusters and output from running cognitive conflict model in Figure 1-1.

change in new graphs. In doing so, we are testing the accuracy of our model, which in turn tests the accuracy of the cognitive conflict theory. That's right, theories (even those in textbooks) are not always correct.

The process of constructing the model in Figure 1-1 required intensive negotiation about which factors in the change process are most important and how the process of conceptual change looks in an operationalized form. Building such models requires learners to articulate causal relationships among the entities represented in a theory. Causal reasoning is one of the most basic and essential kinds of thinking. Developing models of different theories of conceptual change also supports comparison-contrast thinking, another basic and essential skill in conceptual development. If you and your colleagues used Stella to construct a model of the cognitive conflict theory of conceptual change, your model would probably look and function quite differently from the model we constructed. When learners compare and contrast their models with those of others, the negotiations of differences of opinion (1) engage learners more deeply than just about any other kind of performance and (2) improve understanding of the theory by all engaged in the negotiations. Building such models is hard work. Because learners own the models they construct, they are more willing to engage in that hard work.

REVISIONIST THEORY OF CONCEPTUAL CHANGE

Strike and Posner (1985, 1992) regard conceptual change as a rational process in which theories are judged by "how successfully they solve their appropriate range of intellectual problems" (1985, p. 212). According to their theory, the intellectual problems or discrepancies in learners' conceptions do not simply emerge from experience; rather, they also depend on the nature of the learners' preconceptions and how those preconceptions impact data interpretation. Data are not just out there. Instead, data are interpretations of theories or models of the world that are semantically, culturally, and linguistically constructed. When we are confronted with data, we are also confronted by an already (socially) constructed reality that potentially can have a huge impact on our understanding. To know becomes less a measure of what we know or how we do things and more a matter of how many narrative layers we can reveal and accept for our own meaning-making process.

To better understand the revisionist theory of conceptual change proposed by Strike and Posner, my colleagues and I constructed the model of revisionist theory shown in Figure 1-3. Notice that the model appears quite different from the model in Figure 1-1. Revisionist theory is different from cognitive conflict theory. For Strike and Posner, the "explanatory power of mental models" for problem solving is the understanding of conceptual change. In the model (see Figure 1-3), minimally understood conceptions may be transferred to fully understood conceptions and then to accommodated conceptions depending on the level of explanatory power of one's conceptual model. Explanatory power is a function of plausibility, fruitfulness, dissatisfaction with existing conceptions, and other determinants for accommodation

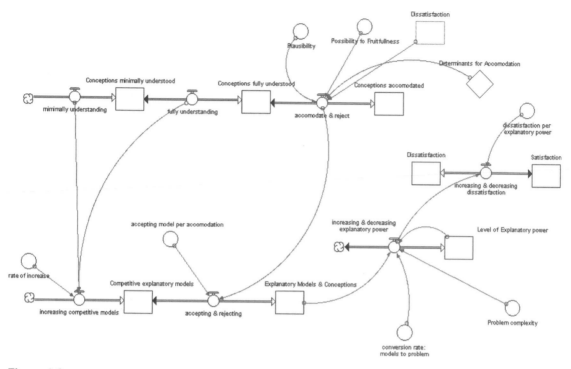
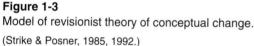

Figure 1-3

Model of revisionist theory of conceptual change.

(Strike & Posner, 1985, 1992.)

(shown in the upper right of the model). If existing conceptions are not sufficient to solve a given problem, dissatisfaction will increase.

When dissatisfaction is addressed, conceptual change begins to occur. There are two stages of understanding: (1) minimal and full understanding and (2) accommodation. The two stages reflect a distinction between understanding conceptions and using them. The repertoire of competitive conceptions available to solve a problem increases with better understanding, but existing conceptions will be changed only if accommodation occurs. The understanding and accommodation stages share common determinants such as dissatisfaction, plausibility, and possibility for fruitfulness. However, the accommodation process has an additional set of determinants: anomalies, analogies, past experience, epistemological commitments, knowledge for other problems, and so forth.

The purpose for presenting this model of revisionist theory as an alternative to the cognitive conflict theory of conceptual change was to illustrate how models can test learners' understanding. Now a comparison of Figures 1-1 and 1-3 provides evidence that the two proposed theories differ. When my students were building similar models to compare and contrast alternative theories, their goal was to construct a model of their own theory of conceptual change. That is the essence of constructivism.

SUMMARY

Conceptual change is one of the most meaningful conceptions of learning. All theories of conceptual change describe processes of conceptual reorganization in light of new information. One of the best ways to engage and support learners in conceptual change is to help them construct models of what they are studying using a variety of model-building tools.

To practice what we preach, my colleagues and I constructed two models while we were learning what conceptual change meant. The first model was based on the theory of cognitive conflict of conceptual change and the second model illustrated revisionist theory. The models improved our understanding and reflected our conceptual development. The models do not represent a reality out there; rather, they represent our conceptual models (i.e., our reality). That is the premise of this book.

We used a modeling tool called Stella to externalize our conceptual understanding. Like all models, those developed here are not complete, because our understanding involves more complexities than Stella models can represent. On the other hand, our conceptual models are less complex than reality, but they are reshaped through building external representations. Model building is a means to foster understanding and conceptual change.

REFERENCES

Chan, C., Burtis, J., & Bereiter, C. (1997). Knowledge building as a mediator of conceptual change. *Cognition and Instruction, 15*(1), 1–40.

Chinn, C. A., & Brewer, W. F. (1993). The role of anomalous data in knowledge acquisition: A theoretical framework and implications for science education. *Review of Educational Research, 63*, 1–49.

Ferrari, M., & Elik, N. (2003). Influences on intentional conceptual change. In G. M. Sinatra & P. R. Pintrich (Eds.), *Intentional conceptual change* (pp. 21–54). Mahwah, NJ: Lawrence Erlbaum.

Limon, M., & Mason, L. (2002). *Reconsidering conceptual change: Issues in theory and practice.* Amsterdam: Kluwer Academic.

Luque, M. L. (2003). The role of domain-specific knowledge in intentional conceptual change. In G. M. Sinatra & P. R. Pintrich (Eds.), *Intentional conceptual change.* Mahwah, NJ: Lawrence Erlbaum.

Mayer, R. E. (2002). Understanding conceptual change: A commentary. In M. Limon & L. Mason (Eds.), *Reconsidering conceptual change: Issues in theory and practice* (pp. 101–111). Dordrecht: Kluwer Academic.

Schnotz, W., Vosniadou, S., & Carretero   (1999). *New perspectives in conceptual change.* Amsterdam: Pergamon.

Siegler, R. S. (1996). *Emerging minds: The process of change in children's thinking.* New York: Oxford University Press.

Sinatra, G. M., & Pintrich, P. R. (2003). The role of intentions in conceptual change learning. In G. M. Sinatra & P. R. Pintrich (Eds.), *Intentional conceptual change.* Mahwah, NJ: Lawrence Erlbaum.

Smith, J. P., di Sessa, A. A., Roschelle, J. (1993). Misconceptions reconceived: A constructivist analysis of knowledge in transition. *Journal of Learning Sciences, 3,* 115–163.

Strike, K. A., & Posner, G. J. (1985). A conceptual change view of learning and understanding. In L. H. T. West & A. L. Pines (Eds.), *Cognitive structure and conceptual change* (pp. 211–231). New York: Academic Press.

Strike, K. A., & Posner, G. J. (1992). A revisionist theory of conceptual change. In R. A. Duschl & R. J. Hamilton (Eds.), *Philosophy of science, cognitive psychology, and educational theory and practice* (pp. 147–176). New York: State University of New York Press.

Thagard, P. (1992). *Conceptual revolutions.* Princeton, NJ: Princeton University Press.

Vosniadou, S. (1994). Capturing and modeling the process of conceptual change. *Learning and Instruction, 4*(1), 45–70.

Vosniadou, S. (1999). Conceptual change research: The state of the art and future directions In W. Schnotz, S. Vosniadou, & M. Carretero (Eds.), *New perspectives on conceptual change* (pp. 1–13). Amsterdam: Pergamon.

CHAPTER 2

Model Building with Mindtools

Science and mathematics educators (Confrey & Doerr, 1994; Frederiksen & White, 1998; Lehrer & Schauble, 2000, 2003) have long recognized the importance of modeling in understanding scientific and mathematical phenomena. However, modeling is useful in all other domains as well. Humans are natural model builders. We construct conceptual models of everything that we encounter in the world. The better that we understand any part of the world, the better are our models of that part of the world, whether it is English literature, political systems, or how an automobile operates. This book is about how to use Mindtools (Jonassen, 1996, 2000) to create models of the ideas that we are learning. This chapter describes the modeling process and how computer-based tools (i.e., Mindtools) can be used to construct models to represent what we know.

MODELING FOR CONCEPTUAL CHANGE

What are models? Lesh and Doerr (2003) state that models are conceptual systems consisting of elements, relations, operations, and rules governing interactions that are expressed using some external representational system. These models exist in the minds of learners and are embodied in the equations, diagrams, computer programs, and other representational media used by learners to represent their understanding. That is, there are models in the mind (mental or conceptual models) and there are external models that represent the models in the mind. The relationship between internal and external models is not well understood. I believe that there is a dynamic and reciprocal relationship between internal mental models and the external models that we construct. Mental models provide the material for building external models. External models, in turn, regulate internal models, providing the means for conceptual change (Nersessian, 1999). The construction of models using different technology-based modeling tools enables learners to tune their internal models.

The primary purpose of modeling is the construction and revision of conceptual understanding, that is, conceptual change (see Chapter 1). Building explicit models of internal conceptual models engages and supports conceptual change. When we build and test external models, our internal models benefit. Likewise, we could not build external models without the existence of internal models. The forms of representation afforded by different modeling tools enable learners to construct syntactically and structurally different models. Comparing and contrasting those different models is essential to achieving deeper understanding. Comparing and evaluating models supports the understanding (1) that every individual necessarily constructs a somewhat different model of the external world and (2) that the activity of modeling can be used for testing rival models. This two-part process is at the heart of conceptual change.

Historically, much of modeling research has focused on mathematics. Representing phenomena in formulas is probably the most exact way to model phenomena, but most of us do not think facilely with mathematical representations. Most of us build conceptual models using more qualitative representations, which are just as important as quantitative representations. Qualitative representation is a missing link when novices attempt problem solving (Chi, Feltovich, & Glaser, 1981; Larkin, 1983). When students try to understand a problem using only formulas, they reveal that they do not understand the underlying systems with which they are working. So, often students need help in constructing qualitative, as well as quantitative, representations of problems. Qualitative representations can both constrain and facilitate the construction of quantitative representations (Ploetzner & Spada, 1998).

Modeling is fundamental to human cognition and scientific inquiry (Schwarz & White, in press). Modeling helps learners express and externalize their thinking, and visualize and test components of their theories. In addition, modeling makes materials more interesting. Models function as epistemic resources (Morrison & Morgan, 1999): We must first understand what we can demonstrate in a model before we can ask questions about the real system.

MODEL CONSTRUCTION VERSUS MODEL USE

We can learn from models by building them and using them (Morgan, 1999). In building models, learning involves finding out what elements fit together in order to represent the theory or the world or both. Modeling requires making certain choices, and it is in these choices that the learning process lies. Morgan believes that we can also learn from using models; however, that learning depends on the extent to which we can transfer the things we learn from manipulating the model to our theory or to the real world. "We do not learn much from looking at a model—we learn a lot more from building the model and from manipulating it" (Morrison & Morgan, 1999, pp. 11–12). We learn from models by constructing them and by manipulating and experimenting with them.

Despite the cognitive benefits from building models, technology-based learning environments more often exemplify using models. Models commonly serve as the intellectual engine in software. For example, models provide the intellectual engine in microworlds and simulations, such as Geometric Supposer and SimCalc. These products, which were described in the first and second editions of this book, do not represent model building—the focus of this edition. In microworlds, the model is not explicitly demonstrated. Learners have no access to the model and they cannot change it, except to manipulate a set of preselected variables within the model. Learners can interact with these black-box systems, and they may infer the propositions embedded in the model to test hypotheses. However, research shows that interacting with microworlds and similar environments does not result in development and change of mental models (Frederiksen & White, 1998; Mellar, Bliss, Boohan, Ogborn, & Tompsett, 1993).

Why is model building so much more productive for learning and conceptual change than model using? When solving a problem or answering a complex conceptual question, learners must construct a mental model of the phenomena and use that model as the basis for prediction, inference, speculation, or experimentation. Constructing a physical, analogical, or computational model of the world reifies the learner's mental model. One reason that constructed models are so powerful is their intellectual autonomy. Models are autonomous because they are independent of theories and the world, which allows them to function as tools or instruments of investigation and a tool or instrument is independent of the thing on which it operates (Morrison & Morgan, 1999). So when students construct, manipulate, and test their own technology-mediated models, they learn more and change conceptually more than they do from trying to induce the underlying model in a black-box simulation. One of the most effective ways of engaging, supporting, and assessing conceptual change is to build and compare models that represent different kinds of knowledge. Model building is an engaging and important kind of learning for several reasons:

◆ Model building is a natural cognitive phenomenon. When encountering unknown phenomena, humans naturally begin to construct personal theories (models) about those phenomena.

◆ Modeling is quintessentially constructivist; learners construct personal representations of phenomena.

◆ Modeling supports hypothesis testing, conjecturing, inferring, and a host of other important cognitive skills.

◆ Modeling requires learners to articulate causal reasoning, the cognitive basis for most scientific reasoning.

◆ Modeling is among the most conceptually engaging cognitive processes that can be performed, which makes it a strong predictor of conceptual change.

◆ Modeling results in the construction of cognitive artifacts (externalized mental models).

◆ Modeling by students results in students who *own* the knowledge. Student ownership is important to meaning making and knowledge construction.

◆ Modeling supports the development of epistemic beliefs. Comparing and evaluating models requires understanding that alternative models are possible and that the activity of modeling can be used for testing rival models (Lehrer & Schauble, 2003).

◆ Modeling tools help learners transcend limitations of their minds—limitations to memory, thinking, or problem solving (Pea, 1985).

WHAT CAN BE MODELED

If model building externalizes mental models, then learners should use a variety of tools to model a variety of phenomena. Different models engage different kinds of thinking (Jonassen, 2000). This section briefly describes the kinds of phenomena that can be modeled using different modeling tools. Each category will be further exemplified in Chapters 4 through 8.

Modeling Domain Knowledge

Students can use a variety of computer-based modeling tools, such as concept mapping tools or systems modeling tools, to construct models of domain knowledge. For example, Figure 2-1 illustrates a single frame of an extensive concept map on plants that students built. As students study domain content in a course, they can continuously add to their concept maps (see Chapter 9). Those maps provide a means for representing the semantic structure of their domain knowledge. If students spend an entire year constructing a concept map that includes a couple thousand concepts, they will surely understand the domain better than they would by trying to memorize their notes. As with all other tools, comparing one student's concept map with those of others often results in conceptual change. Students see how other models represent and structure the same ideas.

Students can use a wide range of tools to construct models. Figure 2-2 illustrates principles of hyperbolas modeled in Cabri II, a geometry visualization tool from

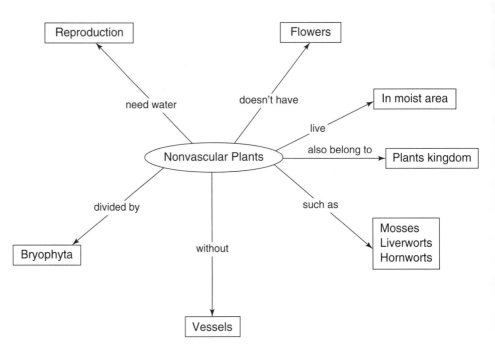

Figure 2-1
One frame of a semantic network on plants.

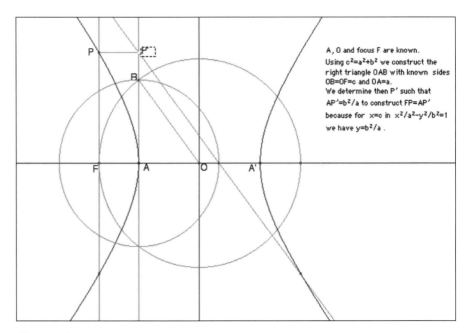

A, O and focus F are known.
Using c²=a²+b² we construct the right triangle OAB with known sides OB=OF=c and OA=a.
We determine then P' such that AP'=b²/a to construct FP=AP' because for x=c in x²/a²−y²/b²=1 we have y=b²/a .

Figure 2-2
Geometry model constructed using Cabri II.

Texas Instruments that provides functions similar to the company's graphing calculators. In each of these models (Figures 2-1 and 2-2), students are representing domain principles that they are studying. The modeling tools enable the students to describe and test their mental models of the phenomena. In both examples, however, the underlying model of the phenomena is implicit. The principles are exemplified in the visual representation, but the models are implicit. That is, the relationships among the variables are not explicitly stated.

Domain knowledge is often presented and understood in a linear fashion consisting of a series of facts and unrelated pieces. By modeling the domain and its structure, the linearity is jeopardized. Now elements are related to each other in complex associative maps (concept maps), causally related systems (spreadsheets and system models), or different forms of hierarchical representation (expert system or flexible hypertext system).

Modeling Systems

Another way of thinking about subject matter content is as systems (see Chapter 5). Rather than focusing on discrete facts or characteristics of phenomena, learners study content as systems, thereby developing a more integrated view of the world. Systems thinking involves understanding the world as process systems, feedback systems, control systems, and living systems. All of these conceptions share similar attributes. Systems are self-reproducing organizations of dynamic, interdependent parts. Systems are goal driven, feedback controlled, self-maintaining, self-regulating, and synergetic. When learners organize what they are studying into relevant systems that interact with each other, they achieve a much more integrated view of the world.

Systems and subsystems are defined by structural and causal relationships. Systems modeling tools (see Chapter 13) enable learners to build models that focus on systems and their internal interactions. Figure 2-3, produced by high school students, illustrates a model depicting the growth and maintenance of a deer population. The model shows that deer population is a function of factors that are part of the larger ecosystem, including reproduction rates, which are dependent on predation and hunting. Systems models show the interactions of components within any system.

Modeling Problems

To successfully solve virtually any kind of problem, the problem solver must mentally construct a problem space. A problem space is mentally constructed by selecting and mapping specific relations of the problem (McGuinness, 1986). Use of modeling tools to create visual or computational models externalizes the mental problem space of a learner. As the complexity of the problem increases, producing efficient models of the problem becomes even more important (McGuinness, 1986). Figure 2-4 illustrates the advice, factors, and rules for an expert system knowledge base (see Chapter 12) on how molar conversion problems are solved in chemistry.

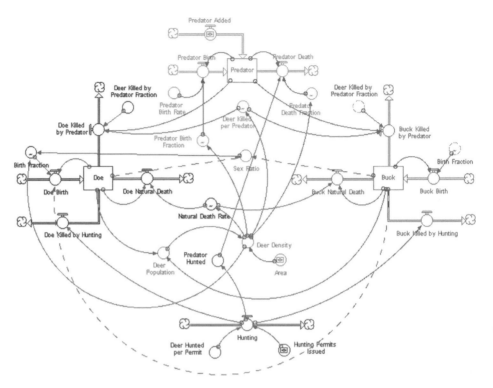

Figure 2-3
Systems model of deer population.

Students who reflected on the problem solution process were better able to solve this kind of problem.

Modeling Experiences (Stories)

Stories are the oldest and most natural form of sense making. Stories are the "means [by] which human beings give meaning to their experience of temporality and personal actions" (Polkinghorne, 1988, p. 11). Cultures have been conveyed most often through different types of stories, including myths, fairy tales, documentaries, and histories. Humans appear to have an innate ability and predisposition to organize and represent their experiences in the form of stories, because stories require less cognitive effort to understand than exposition (Bruner, 1990).

An alternative learning experience to studying content is to collect and study stories about people's experiences (see Chapter 7). Students can support conceptual change by modeling people's experiences, that is, by collecting stories about their experiences. Figure 2-5 shows a single record from a database of stories about Northern Ireland. The students who studied the conflict by collecting and indexing stories understood the conflict on a human level. Databases are the most common and logical means for storing the stories. The intellectual power of the activity lies in determining the indexes, then fitting excerpts from the stories into those indexes.

```
Context 'This knowledge base is intended to simulate the processes of
calculating molar conversions.'

D1: 'You know the mass of one mole of sample.'
D2: 'You need to determine molar (formula) mass.'
D3: 'Divide sample mass by molar mass.'
D4: 'Multiply number of moles by molar mass.'
D5: 'You know atomic mass units.'
D6: 'You know molar mass.'
D7: 'Divide mass of sample by molar mass and multiply by Avogadro's number.'
D8: 'Divide number of particles by Avogadro's number.'
D9: 'Convert number of particles to moles, then convert moles to mass.'
D10: 'Convert mass to moles using molar mass, and then convert moles to mol-
ecules using Avogadro's number.'
D11: 'Convert from volume to moles (divide volume by volume/mole), and then
convert moles to moles by multiplying by Avogadro's number.'

Q1: 'Do you know the number of molecules?'                A 1 'yes' 2 'no'
Q2: 'Do you know the mass of the sample in grams?'        A 1 'yes' 2 'no'
Q3: 'Do you know the molar mass of the element or compound?' A 1 'yes' 2 'no'
Q4: 'Do you know the number of moles of the sample?'      A 1 'yes' 2 'no'
Q5: 'Do you want to know the number of molecules?'        A 1 'yes' 2 'no'
Q6: 'Do you want to know the mass of the sample in grams?' A 1 'yes' 2 'no'
Q7: 'Do you want to know the molar mass of the compound?' A 1 'yes' 2 'no'
Q8: 'Do you want to know the number of moles of the sample?' A 1 'yes' 2 'no'
Q9: 'Do you know atomic mass units?'                      A 1 'yes' 2 'no'
Q10: 'Do you know the volume of a gas?'                   A 1 'yes' 2 'no'

Rule1: IF q2a1 AND q8a1 THEN D2
Rule2: IF (d1 OR q3a1) AND q2a1 AND q8a1 THEN D3
Rule3: IF q4a1 AND q3a1 AND q6a1 THEN D4
Rule4: IF q3a1 THEN D1
Rule5: IF q3a1 THEN D5
Rule6: IF q9a1 THEN D6
Rule7: IF qq3a1 AND q2a1 AND q5a1 THEN D7
Rule8: IF q1a1 AND q8a1 THEN D8
Rule9: IF q1a1 AND q6a1 THEN D9
Rule10: IF q2a1 AND q5a1 THEN d10
Rule11: IF q10a1 AND q1a1 THEN d11
```

Figure 2-4
Excerpt from expert system rule based on stoichiometry.

Modeling Thinking (Cognitive Simulations)

Many educators promote metacognition and self-reflection by learners; that is, they encourage students to reflect on their learning processes to better learn how to learn. Another kind of modeling entails developing models of thinking processes.

Figure 2-5
Entry in database on Northern Ireland stories.

Rather than modeling content or systems, learners model the kind of thinking that they need to perform to solve a problem, make a decision, or complete some other task. Learners can use computer-based modeling tools to construct cognitive simulations (see Chapter 8). Recall that Chapter 1 illustrated two different models of conceptual change; these were cognitive simulations of two theories of conceptual change.

MINDTOOLS FOR MODELING

This third edition is a reinterpretation of the first two editions of the Mindtools book (Jonassen, 1996a, 2000). In those books, I explained that Mindtools are computer-based tools and learning environments that have been adapted or developed to enable learners to represent what they know. They are knowledge representation tools that function as intellectual partners of learners, making the learners smarter than they are without the tools. In most partnerships, responsibility is assigned to the partner who is better able to perform specific functions. Unlike most other tools, computer tools can function as intellectual partners that share the cognitive burden of carrying out tasks (Salomon, 1993). When learners use computers as partners, they off-load some of the unproductive memorizing tasks to the computers, thereby allowing themselves to think more productively. Perkins (1993) believes that learning does not result from solitary, unsupported thinking by learners. So our goal should be to allocate to learners the cognitive responsibility for the processing that they do best, while we allocate to technology the processing that it does best. In intellectual partnerships, learners should be responsible for recognizing and judging patterns of information and then organizing that information (tasks that humans perform better than computers). Computers should perform calculations and store and retrieve information (tasks that computers perform better than humans).

Mindtools are generalizable computer tools that are intended to engage and facilitate cognitive processing; hence, they are cognitive tools (Kommers, Jonassen, & Mayes, 1992). Cognitive tools are both mental and computational devices that support, guide, and extend the thinking processes of their users (Derry, 1990). Mindtools do not necessarily reduce information processing (i.e., make a task easier); rather, their goal is to make effective use of the mental efforts of the learners. Mindtools are not "fingertip" tools (Perkins, 1993) that learners use naturally, effortlessly. In fact, learning with Mindtools requires learners to think harder about the subject-matter domain being studied than they would have to think without Mindtools. Students cannot use Mindtools without thinking deeply about the content they are learning, and if students choose to use Mindtools to help them learn, the tools will facilitate learning and meaning-making processes.

Mindtools represent a constructivist approach toward using computers (or any other technology, environment, or activity) to engage learners in representing, manipulating, and reflecting on what they know, not reproducing what someone tells them. When a Mindtool is being used, knowledge is constructed by the learner not provided by the teacher. Mindtools are just that: tools for engaging the mind.

Several classes of Mindtools are described in this book: semantic organization tools, dynamic modeling tools, visualization tools, and knowledge-building tools. Semantic organization tools include databases (Chapter 9) and concept mapping (Chapter 10). These tools help students to identify and convey the underlying semantic organization of concepts within any domain or system. The tabular structure of databases requires students to identify entities within a domain or system and compare and contrast those entities using a variety of fields. To build the data model, students must decide what relationships facilitate comparison-and-contrast thinking. They must then search for the information in a systematic fashion to fill the database. Students manifest those relationships in queries by searching and sorting the database. Intellectually, these processes require the integration and organization of a content domain.

Concept mapping or semantic networking tools (see Chapter 10) such as Semantica (semanticresearch.com) represent structural knowledge (Jonassen, Beissner, & Yacci, 1993), which is essential to conceptual understanding. Concept maps are used as a learning strategy for integrating domain knowledge as well as for assessing knowledge acquisition. Concept maps and databases support the explication of associative relationships among concepts in a domain.

Dynamic modeling tools enable students to represent dynamic, causal relationships among domain concepts. These tools include spreadsheets, expert systems, systems and population dynamics tools, and teachable agents and direct manipulation environments.

Spreadsheets (see Chapter 11) require learners to use existing rules, generate new rules describing relationships, and organize information by encoding numbers and formulas in individual cells. Spreadsheets are rule-using tools that require users to become rule makers (Vockell & Van Deusen, 1989). The rules that learners embed in their quantitative models can be used to analyze data from any kind of observation or experiment or to build simulations.

Expert systems (see Chapter 12) are artificial intelligence systems that formally represent an expert's knowledge as rules and facts. Students can use expert system editing systems, called shells (e.g., WinExpert or Knowledge Builder), to organize a formal set of rules that describe predictions, inferences, or explanations among phenomena. Building expert systems is a knowledge-modeling process that enables experts and knowledge engineers to construct conceptual models (Adams-Webber, 1995). This process requires identification of declarative knowledge (facts and concepts), structural knowledge (interrelationships among ideas), and procedural knowledge (how to apply declarative knowledge) that an expert (or at least a knowledgeable person) possesses.

A wide range of technology-based tools for representing dynamic systems (see Chapter 13) is available. Some tools (Stella, VenSim, PowerSim) use a simple set of building-block icons to construct maps of processes such as stocks, flows, converters, and connectors. Stocks illustrate the level of some thing; flows control the inflow or outflow of material to stocks; converters modify stocks and flows using coefficients, or represent factors themselves; and connectors establish a relationship between all of these entities. Using simple algebra, students can construct sophisticated models of any kind of phenomenon—models that can be executed in a simulation. Building systems models of phenomenon is among the most engaging and intensive learning activities possible.

A number of population-modeling environments are available (see Chapter 13). NetLogo and Agent Sheets are agent-based modeling tools for simulating natural and social phenomena over time. Modelers can give instructions to hundreds or thousands of independent "agents," all operating in parallel. This makes it possible to explore the connection between the microlevel behavior of individuals and macrolevel patterns that emerge from the interaction of many individuals.

A new genre of tools, teachable agents and direct manipulation environments (see Chapter 14), are emerging. These tools enable learners to represent dynamic relationships among concepts within a domain. For example, Interactive Physics enables learners to build and test experiments in mechanics. Generating new examples of physical phenomena is probably the most engaging and meaningful activity that students can perform.

Another class of tools consists of domain-specific visualization tools (see Chapter 15) that can be used by learners to visualize phenomena within different domains. Many of these tools support visualization of the atomic structure of chemicals. However, others, like Belvedere and QuestMap, help students visualize arguments.

Knowledge-building tools (e.g., hypermedia, see Chapter 16) provide open-ended systems for students to construct representations of their thinking. Many reports of the learning effects of student construction of hypermedia systems, Web sites, and multimedia programs have been published (see Jonassen, 2000). Hypermedia authoring tools, such as Storyspace (www.eastlake.com) or any Web authoring tools (e.g., Dreamweaver), enable students to easily organize and author rich hypermedia knowledge bases. Teachers can discover what rhetorical constructions, cognitive strategies, and social negotiations students engage in when constructing their hypermedia documents. Some special-purpose environments exist to support ethnographic investigations and interpretations by students (Goldman-Segall, 1995). Learning Constellations allows students to construct multimedia programs that include videos, pictures, and their own narratives about the topic of investigation.

A new breed of asynchronous conferencing tools are emerging. These tools scaffold different kinds of collaborative knowledge building by constraining the kinds of comments that students can contribute to discussion boards. Chapter 17 briefly describes the effects of using discussion boards such as FLE3 (www.fle3.com) and the system developed at the University of Missouri. These discussion boards model different kinds of reasoning in the structure of the discussion.

My purpose in this book is *not* to teach you how to use these various Mindtools. Rather, my goal is to convince you that constructing models facilitates intense cognitive and social activities that result in conceptual change. In order to do that, I present many examples of models that have been built by students. To discover which tools your students will adopt most readily, experiment with different tools for representing domain knowledge, systems, problems, experiences, and thinking processes.

Advantages of Mindtools

A practical reason for using computers as Mindtools for modeling phenomena is efficiency. Because Mindtools can be used in many ways in any course to engage meaningful learning, and because the cost per application is relatively low, the cost per student is extremely inexpensive. Mindtools can be used in much more of the curriculum at a lower cost than other currently available computer-based approaches to learning.

Not only do Mindtools provide cost efficiency, they also provide learning efficiencies. Each computer-based instructional program constructed by an individual software producer possesses a different set of outcomes and means for achieving those outcomes. Learning to use these individual software applications requires time and effort, which reduces the cognitive power that can be applied to the ideas being learned. Learning the procedures for using each program requires the teacher to study the software and related instructional materials for each lesson. Adaptation of each instructional program to the needs and abilities of each class is not an efficient use of teachers' time. In contrast, Mindtools require the development of learner skills in a limited number of programs that can be applied to a broad range of subject content. Mindtools simply represent a more efficient use of time and money for technology.

Limitations of Model Building

Although the case for using Mindtools in model building to foster conceptual change is strong, there are limitations of the modeling process.

Cognitive Load. Construction of models places a heavy cognitive load on learners. Sweller and Chandler (1994) found that integrating textual and diagrammatic information describing the same problem (known as the split-attention effect) placed heavy demands on working memory. Integration of multiple sources of information, a fundamental requirement of most modeling tools, is even more difficult and will likely impede many learners from constructing models. Mitigating this effect will require better-developed mental models for the tools, along with extensive practice. Model building is hard work that requires some devotion to the task.

Developmental Differences. Different kinds of modeling tools require different levels of intellectual development. I have found that first graders are competent at building databases and concept maps. However, use of expert systems and systems modeling tools requires at least nascent formal operational reasoning, as conceived by Piaget. Because some Mindtools appear complex, however, do not assume that students will be unable to use them. Students have surprised me many times with their capacities to comprehend software and produce amazing results. Experiment with different tools and give students the benefit of the doubt.

Fidelity. Many tacit misconceptions prevail about models. One is the identity hypothesis. Although one goal in building models is to reify ideas and phenomena, the models themselves are not, as many people tacitly believe, identical to the phenomena themselves. Models are representations of interpretations of phenomena in the world, not the objects themselves.

Another misconception about models relates to their stability. Models are usually synchronic representations of dynamic processes. Phenomena change over time, context, and purpose. Models often do not. Nevertheless, assuming that models are literal and immutable representations of phenomena will surely lead to misconceptions.

Phenomena in the world are typically far more complex than anything that can be represented by any model. Modeling always involves certain simplifications and approximations that have to be decided independently of theoretical requirements or data conditions (Morrison & Morgan, 1999).

As long as we recognize the limitations of models that we build, we will likely avoid overstating the meaning of our models.

SUMMARY

Among the best ways (not the only way) to use computers as support for meaningful learning (i.e., conceptual change) is to use technology-based modeling tools (i.e., Mindtools). Such tools help learners externalize internal conceptual models, modify their structure, and amplify their meaning by providing alternative representations. That is the essence of conceptual change. Modeling tools help learners transcend the limitations of their minds—limitations to memory, thinking, or problem solving.

Learners can build models of the domain content they are studying. They can model that content as systems or problems. Rather than studying didactic content, learners can collect and analyze stories of practice, or they can reflect and model their own learning processes.

Technology-based modeling tools function as intellectual partners of learners; the partners share the cognitive burden of carrying out tasks. The effects of modeling on conceptual change are dynamic and iterative. With each new model that students construct, they modify their mental models, which affects the nature of the external models that they build.

REFERENCES

Adams-Webber, J. (1995). Constuctivist psychology and knowledge elicitation. *Journal of Constructivist Psychology, 8*(3), 237–249.

Bruner, J. (1990). *Acts of meaning.* Cambridge: Harvard University Press.

Chi, M. T. H., Feltovich, P. J., & Glaser, R. (1981). Categorization and representation of physics problems by experts and novices. *Cognitive Science, 5,* 121–152.

Confrey, J., & Doerr, H. M. (1994). Student modelers. *Interactive Learning Environments, 4*(3), 199–217.

Derry, S. J. (1990, April). *Flexible cognitive tools for problem solving instruction.* Paper presented at the annual meeting of the American Educational Research Association, Boston.

Frederiksen, J. R., & White, B. Y. (1998). Teaching and learning generic modeling and reasoning skills. *Journal of Interactive Learning Environments, 55,* 33–51.

Goldman-Segall, R. (1995). Configurational validity: A proposal for analyzing ethnographic multimedia narratives. *Journal of Educational Multimedia and Hypermedia, 4*(2), 163–182.

Jonassen, D. H. (1996). *Computers in the classroom: Mindtools for critical thinking.* Columbus, OH: Merrill/Prentice Hall.

Jonassen, D. H. (2000). *Computers as Mindtools for schools: Engaging critical thinking.* Columbus, OH: Merrill/Prentice Hall.

Jonassen, D. H., Beissner, K., & Yacci, M. (1993). *Structural knowledge: Techniques for assessing, conveying, and acquiring structural knowledge.* Hillsdale, NJ: Lawrence Erlbaum.

Kommers, P. A. M., Jonassen, D. H., & Mayes, T. M. (1992). *Cognitive tools for learning.* Heidelberg, Germany: Springer-Verlag.

Larkin, J. H. (1983). The role of problem representation in physics. In D. Gentner & A. L. Stevens (Eds.), *Mental models* (pp. 75–98). Hillsdale, NJ: Lawrence Erlbaum.

Lehrer, R., & Schauble, L. (2000). Modeling in mathematics and science. In R. Glaser (Ed.), *Advances in instructional psychology: Vol 5. Educational design and cognitive science* (pp. 101–159). Mahwah, NJ: Lawrence Erlbaum.

Lehrer, R., & Schauble, L. (203). Origins and evolution of model-based reasoning in mathematics and science. In R. Lesh & H. M. Doerr (Eds.), *Beyond constructivism: Models and modeling perspectives on mathematics problem solving, teaching, and learning* (pp. 59–70). Mahwah, NJ: Lawrence Erlbaum.

Lesh, R., & Doerr, H. M. (2003). Foundations of a models and modeling perspective on mathematics teaching, learning, and problem solving. In R. Lesh & H. M. Doerr (Eds.), *Beyond constructivism: Models and modeling perspectives on mathematics problem solving, teaching, and learning* (pp. 3–33). Mahwah, NJ: Lawrence Erlbaum.

McGuinness, C. (1986). Problem representation: The effects of spatial arrays. *Memory and Cognition, 14*(3), 270–280.

Mellar, H., Bliss, J., Boohan, R., Ogborn, J., & Tompsett, C. (1994). *Learning with artificial worlds: Computer-based modeling in the curriculum.* London: Falmer Press.

Morgan, M. S. (1999). Learning from models. In M. S. Morgan & M. Morrison (Eds.), *Models as mediators: Perspectives on natural and social science* (pp. 347–388). Cambridge: Cambridge University Press.

Morrison, M., & Morgan, M. S. (1999). Models as mediating instruments. In M. S. Morgan & M. Morrison (Eds.), *Models as mediators: Perspectives on natural and social science* (pp. 10–37). Cambridge: Cambridge University Press.

Nersessian, N. J. (1999). Model-based reasoning in conceptual change. In L. Magnani, N. J. Nersessian, & P. Thagard (Eds.), *Models are used to represent reality.* New York: Kluwer Academic/Plenum.

Pea, R. D. (1985). Beyond amplification: Using the computer to reorganize mental functioning. *Educational Psychologist 20*(4), 167–182.

Perkins, D. N. (1993). Person-plus: A distributed view of thinking and learning. In G. Salomon (Ed.), *Distributed cognitions: Psychological and educational considerations.* Cambridge: Cambridge University Press.

Ploetzner, R., & Spada, H. (1998). Constructing quantitative problem representations on the basis of qualitative reasoning. *Interactive Learning Environments*, 5, 95–107.

Polkinghorne, D. (1988). *Narrative knowing and the human sciences.* Albany: State University of New York Press.

Salomon, G. (1993). On the nature of pedagogic computer tools. The case of the writing partner. In S. P. LaJoie & S. J. Derry (Eds.), *Computers as cognitive tools.* Hillsdale, NJ: Lawrence Erlbaum.

Schwarz, C. V., & White, B. Y. (in press). Developing a model-centered approach to science education. *Journal of Research in Science Teaching.*

Sweller, J., & Chandler, P. (1994). Why some material is difficult to learn. *Cognition and Instruction, 12*, 185–233.

Vockell, E., Van Dusen, R. M. (1989). *The computer and higher order thinking skills.* Watsonville, CA: Mitchell Publishing.

CHAPTER 3

Assessing Learning by Modeling

What is learned in most educational institutions is driven by what is assessed. Regardless of what educators profess to students, most students are strategic enough to realize that what is important is what is used to decide their grades. The tests, projects, and examinations that we require of students determine what and how they learn. We may claim that our goals for learners include becoming critical, independent thinkers. However, if the only way we assess their thinking is through multiple-choice recall, we are communicating a clearer expectation of how we want them to think than all of the mission statements and educational objectives produced by school districts. Most students will be able to think critically enough to realize that we are not serious about the lofty goals included in the curriculum guides and that their primary responsibility is to memorize material.

Unfortunately, assessment-driven learning is even more omnipresent in the current context of high-stakes testing. Too many schools are devoting too much of their time to preparing students to perform better on such tests, because failure results in censure and loss of funds. If this trend continues, the next generation of Americans will be doomed to mediocrity. An antidote to mediocrity is modeling. If students learn to model what they are learning, they will surely perform better on any test.

It is completely infeasible to relate the effects of modeling to every test used by every local, state, and national district, agency, or association. That would require tens of thousands of studies. Instead, let us examine how to assess student models and the cognitive residue from the modeling process.

ASSESSING CONCEPTUAL CHANGE WITH STUDENT-CONSTRUCTED MODELS

Chapter 1 argued that conceptual change is one of the most meaningful conceptions of learning. So if we want students to engage in conceptual change, then we need to assess conceptual change. Although there are many theoretical accounts of conceptual change (Limon & Mason, 2002; Schnotz, Vosniadou, & Carretero, 1999; Sinatra & Pintrich, 2003), no literature addresses how to effectively assess conceptual change. Researchers have analyzed student verbalizations while solving problems (Hogan & Fisherkeller, 2000), structured interviews (Southerland, Smith, & Cummins, 2000), and concept maps (Edmundson, 2000) to assess conceptual change. These methods are difficult and time consuming, and they require very specialized skills. I propose that the models students construct while representing domain knowledge, systems, problems, experiences, and thought processes (as described in Chapters 4 through 8) can be used to assess conceptual change. How do these models reflect conceptual change?

The models that students construct can and should be used to assess student understanding. The knowledge that is manifested in student models is usually deeper and more comprehensive than what can be assessed using traditional assessment methods, such as tests or essays. If students must engage in constructive, self-regulated, and critical thinking to use Mindtools to build models, then the products they create ought to provide better evidence of knowledge construction.

If learning is assessed through the models that students build, then it is important that learners use a variety of Mindtools. That is, educators should not rely on one kind of Mindtool for assessing all learning. For example, recently educators have tended to overstate the effectiveness of concept maps for assessments. Ideally, for each content domain being studied, students should construct two or more models, using a combination of databases, semantic networks, spreadsheets, expert systems, systems modeling, dynamic modeling, hypermedia knowledge bases, and scaffolded computer conferences. Why? One of the most important differences between experts and novices is that experts are able to represent their knowledge in different ways. In other words, experts have constructed different kinds of knowledge about their specialty. The more ways that you are able to represent what you know, the better you know it, thereby enabling more sophisticated application.

In Chapter 2 I explained that modeling building is complex and difficult work. I also claimed that the more complex that students' models become, the more complex and integrated students' understanding will be. However, complexity poses difficult assessment issues; that is, it is hard to adequately communicate assessment of complex models. A casual observation might indicate which models are better than others. However, teachers need to be able to convey their assessment in some comprehensible way to students. Chapters 9 through 17 provide some assessment rubrics that you may be able to use or adapt to assess different kinds of models. For example, assessing databases requires different rubrics than assessing expert systems. The rubrics discussed represent only a start. You must develop performance rubrics that address the domain that you teach. Generating rubrics is a difficult but necessarily interactive process.

ASSESSING LEARNING AND THINKING THAT RESULTS FROM MODELING WITH MINDTOOLS

If you use other forms of assessment (essays, problems, examinations, etc.) in addition to Mindtools models, make sure that they, too, assess knowledge construction and meaningful learning. If you have students use Mindtools to model phenomena but then administer tests of recall, students will easily infer that Mindtools do not count and will cease to invest serious effort in model construction.

The next sections provide rubrics for assessing the cognitive residue from building models. The following learning outcomes are analyzed: knowledge construction, self-regulation, collaboration, and critical thinking.

Assessing Knowledge Construction

Building models requires that learners construct their own knowledge. Therefore, it is important to assess the kinds and extent of knowledge construction by learners, not the regurgitation of ideas previously delivered to them. Genuine intellectual performance is inherently personalized, so the meanings students derive from knowledge construction experiences are personal and idiosyncratic. The personal theories of the world that students reflect in their models will differ, so it is important not to judge students' models or their understanding by similarity to a single model. Common knowledge need not always be the goal of education.

If learning is more like "contextual insight" and "good judgment" than it is like inert knowledge, we need to rethink our reliance on traditional assessment activities and methodology (Wiggins, 1993). Among the necessary changes are an emphasis on self-assessment by learners and the use of alternative forms of assessment that provide learners the opportunity to express what they know in the best way. Ask students to self-assess their models before they submit them; then you can assess the models. In most chapters, I include rubrics for assessing students' models. These are general rubrics for assessing the quality of the model produced by the Mindtool. In addition, you must apply domain-specific rubrics for assessing the quality and accuracy of students' domain understanding.

Figure 3-1 provides some general rubrics for assessing the quality of students' knowledge construction as reflected in their models.

Assessing Knowledge Construction

To what extent do students manipulate objects, make observations, and reason from those experiences?

Observation and Reflection

Students rarely think about or record the results of actions taken during activities.	Students often stop and think about the activities in which they are engaged.	Students share frequent observations about their activities with peers and interested adults.

Learner Interactions

Students manipulated none of variables or controls in the environment.	Students manipulated some variables and controls in environment.	Students manipulated all or nearly all variables and controls in environment.

Originality of Interpretations

Knowledge bases included teachers' ideas or textbook material with no original interpretation.	Knowledge bases included some original ideas but were based on teacher/textbook interpretations.	Knowledge bases included original ideas that were conceived, organized, and represented by students.

Curiosity/Interest/Puzzlement

Students engage in learning activities only because they are required, rather than having an intrinsic interest.	Learners' activities are frequently motivated by a sincere curiosity about the topic of study.	Learners are consistently striving to resolve the disparity between what is observed and what is known, operating on a sincere desire to know.

Constructing Mental Models and Making Meaning

Learners rarely create their own understandings of how things work.	Learners are often expected to make sense of new experiences and develop theories.	Learners routinely wrestle with new experiences, becoming experts at identifying and solving problems.

Figure 3-1
Rubrics for evaluating knowledge construction in students' models.

Assessing Self-Regulation

The purpose of assessing the outcomes of modeling with Mindtools is not necessarily to provide society with the information it needs to judge the individual who built the model. Rather, assessment of outcomes can provide learners with feedback that will enable them to comprehend how much they have learned so that they can better direct their learning. The use of Mindtools requires and fosters self-regulation by learners. Self-regulated learners set their own goals, determine their own activities, and regulate those activities in terms of the goals they have set.

Self-assessment fosters self-regulation. In self-assessment learners assess what they know (articulation) and how able they are to learn a particular skill or subject (reflection) for a purpose: to compare their base knowledge with what they need to acquire to meet their learning goals. To regulate their learning, learners must be able to self-assess their own knowledge growth.

The rubrics shown in Figure 3-2 can be used to evaluate the level of self-regulation that students exercise while modeling with Mindtools.

Assessing Self Regulation

To what extent do students articulate their goals and reflect on their accomplishments when using Mindtools? To what extent can learners explain their activities in terms of how they relate to the attainment of their goals?

Goal Directedness

Learners are often pursuing activities that have little to do with the attainment of specific goals.	Learners are generally engaged in activities that contribute to the attainment of specified goals.

Setting Own Goals

Learning goals are provided by educators.	Learners are sometimes involved in the establishment of learning goals.	Learners are routinely responsible for developing and expressing learning goals.

Regulating Own Learning

Learner's progress is monitored by others.	Learners are involved as partners in monitoring and reporting progress toward goals.	Learners are responsible for monitoring and reporting progress toward goals.

Learning How to Learn

Little emphasis is placed on metacognition. There are few opportunities to discuss the learning process with peers or educators.	The culture of the learning environment promotes frequent discussion of the processes and strategies (both successful and unsuccessful) involved in learning.

Articulation of Goals as Focus of Activity

Learners don't see the relationship between the activities in which they are engaged and specified learning goals.	Learners describe the activities in which they are engaged in terms that relate to the specified learning goals.

Mindtools Use in Support of Learning Goals

The use of Mindtools seems unrelated to the specified learning goals.	The use of Mindtools contributes to the attainment of specified learning goals.	The use of Mindtools makes a powerful contribution to the attainment of learning goals.

Figure 3-2
Rubrics for evaluating self-regulated thinking in students' model construction.

Assessing Collaboration

Mindtools are most effectively used collaboratively. Students who work together to negotiate their understanding will not only produce better models with Mindtools, but they will also learn more in the process. If students use Mindtools collaboratively, then why should they be evaluated independently? If the skills they are trying to acquire are best performed collaboratively, then removing collaboration during evaluation violates the most basic of assessment premises: The conditions, performances, and criteria for the assessment should replicate those stated in the learning goals and used during instruction. This premise provides a compelling reason for assessing the models that students produce, rather than evaluating students in a separate examination.

Assessing Collaboration

To what extent do students collaborate to construct their knowledge bases? To what extent are learners developing skills related to social negotiation learning to accept and share responsibility?

Interaction Among Learners

Little of the learner's time is spent gainfully engaged with other students.	Learners are often immersed in activities in which collaboration with peers results in success.

Interaction with People Outside of School

Students rarely seek information or opinions outside of school.	Students consistently seek information and opinions of others outside of school.

Social Negotiation

Little evidence that learners work together to develop shared understanding of tasks or of solution strategies.	Learners are often observed in the process of coming to agreement on the nature of problems and on best courses of action.	Learners collaborate with ease. Negotiations become almost invisible, yet the ideas of all team members are valued.

Distribution of Roles and Responsibility

Roles and responsibilities are shifted infrequently. Most capable learners accept more responsibility than the less capable.	Roles and responsibilities are shifted often, and such changes are accepted by both the most and least capable.	Students make their own decisions concerning roles and responsibilities, freely giving and accepting assistance as necessary.

Figure 3-3
Rubrics for evaluating collaboration in students' model construction.

The rubrics shown in Figure 3-3 can be used to evaluate the level of cooperation in which students model with Mindtools.

Assessing Critical Thinking

Modeling with Mindtools engages students in critical thinking, but there is no universal agreement on what critical thinking means. Therefore, critical thinking is difficult to assess. There are a number of tests of critical thinking, such as the Watson-Glaser test and the Cornell Test of Critical Thinking. However, they are not tied to specific learning outcomes, so they are probably not useful for assessing changes in critical thinking ability that may result from modeling with Mindtools. Norris (1989) contends that true critical thinking involves not only the ability to think critically but also the disposition to do so, and that it is unreasonable to attempt to measure judgment about when and how to think critically with a multiple-choice test. Furthermore, there is no evidence about what test takers actually consider when taking so-called tests of critical thinking. Are they actually thinking critically? Such tests are generic measures of thinking ability that research has shown to be too insensitive to the kinds of thinking engaged by Mindtools (Wang & Jonassen, 1993).

Critical thinking is context dependent. Thinking critically in different subjects (e.g., math, science, social studies) and in different real-world contexts engages

Do students evaluate information and ideas in their knowledge bases?	
Students use irrelevant, inaccurate, unreliable information, and do not judge quality of ideas or information.	Students discriminate relevant/irrelevant information, assess reliability and usefulness of information, identify criteria and judge merit of information, and recognize inaccuracies, untruths, and propaganda.
Do students analyze information and idea in their knowledge bases?	
Students cannot distinguish elements or classes of information, do not recognize or evaluate assumptions, and cannot identify main ideas or patterns of data.	Students examine and classify information normally, identify assumptions and positions, and determine essential ideas and patterns in data.
Do students connect ideas and understand relationships in their knowledge bases?	
Students cannot distinguish kinds of information, cannot makes inferences or determine causes and effects, and cannot describe relationships among ideas.	Students compare/constrast similarities and differences, evaluate arguments and logic, infer from generalizations to instances, infer from instances to generalizations, and identify causes and predict effects.

Figure 3-4
Rubrics for evaluating critical thinking in students' model construction.

different critical thinking skills or the same skills in different ways. For example, thinking critically to solve an engineering problem in a factory requires different thinking than solving a political problem at a city council meeting. Even transfer of critical thinking within a subject domain is difficult to assess. If transfer of learning fails to occur, you never know whether learners are unable to transfer critical thinking or if they simply lack subject-specific knowledge to be transferred (Norris, 1989). So, different measures of critical thinking would need to be developed for each context in which Mindtools are used to build models.

Critical thinking skills are stable and not easily altered. The development of critical thinking emerges over time and with lots of practice. You cannot expect to see significant changes in how someone thinks after he or she constructs a single model. Any detectable changes in critical thinking would require the construction of several models within a domain.

Despite the problems with assessing critical thinking, you may want to try. The rubrics shown in Figure 3-4 can be used to evaluate the critical thinking students use while constructing models with Mindtools.

SUMMARY

The premise of this chapter is simple. If you ask learners to build models with Mindtools, you are clearly encouraging knowledge construction, self-regulation, collaboration, and critical thinking; therefore, you should assess those outcomes. Assessing these higher order learning outcomes is difficult. You may have to abandon traditional assumptions about assessment, try different methods of assessment, relinquish some of your authority as a teacher by allowing students the opportunity to negotiate their goals and intentions and to self-assess, and to use multiple criteria when evaluating the outcomes of student learning. In doing so, you will allow your students to construct more flexible, meaningful, stable, and transferable knowledge than if you dictate the goals and products of assessment.

This chapter provides rubrics for assessing knowledge construction, self-regulation, collaboration, and critical thinking. By applying these rubrics, you will help your students become more insightful and self-reliant learners. That is sufficient for me.

REFERENCES

Edmundson, K. M. (2000). Assessing science understanding through concept maps. In J. J. Mintzes, J. H. Wandersee, & J. D. Novak (Eds.), *Assessing science understanding: A human constructivist view* (pp. 19–40). San Diego: Academic Press.

Hogan, K., & Fisherkeller, J. (2000). Dialogue as data: Assessing students' scientific reasoning with interactive protocols. In J. J. Mintzes, J. H. Wandersee, & J. D. Novak (Eds.), *Assessing science understanding: A human constructivist view* (pp. 96–129). San Diego: Academic Press.

Limon, M., & Mason, L. (2002). *Reconsidering conceptual change: Issues in theory and practice*. Amsterdam: Kluwer.

Norris, S. P. (1989). Can we test validly for critical thinking? *Educational Researcher, 18*(9), 21–26.

Schnotz, W., Vosniadou, S., & Carretero, M. (1999). New perspectives in conceptual change. Amsterdam: Pergamon.

Sinatra, G. M., & Pintrich, P. R. (2003). The role of intentions in conceptual change learning. In G. M. Sinatra & P. R. Pintrich (Eds.), *Intentional conceptual change*. Mahwah, NJ: Lawrence Erlbaum.

Southerland, S. A., Smith, M. U., & Cummins, C. L. (2000). "What do you mean by that?": Using structured interviews to assess science understanding. In J. J. Mintzes, J. H. Wandersee, & J. D. Novak (Eds.), *Assessing science understanding: A human constructivist view* (pp. 72–95). San Diego: Academic Press.

Wang, S., & Jonassen, D. H. (1993, April). *Using computer-based concept mapping to foster critical thinking*. Paper presented at the annual meeting of the American Educational Research Association, Atlanta, GA.

Wiggins, G. (1993). Assessment: Authenticity, context, and validity. *Phi Delta Kappan, 75*(3), 200–214.

Modeling Phenomena

CHAPTER 4

Modeling Domain Knowledge

For better or worse, educators evaluate students on how much they know. Teachers and professors want their students to know more. In subsequent chapters, I will argue that there are different kinds of knowledge, and so how you know something may be more important than how much you know.

The primary rationale that educators provide for having their students "acquire" domain knowledge is that domain knowledge is prerequisite to procedural knowledge (the knowledge of how to use domain knowledge). Most taxonomies of learning are built on the assumption that it is necessary to know about ideas before it is possible to apply that knowledge. This assumption has been questioned extensively by every contemporary and situated view of learning (see Jonassen & Land, 2000). In accord with those views, I believe that domain knowledge should be a corequisite (not prerequisite) for the effective use of domain knowledge. In fact, inaccurate or incomplete understanding of domain knowledge resulting from trying to acquire knowledge without using it may actually inhibit or interfere with learning (Alexander & Judy, 1988). Contemporary, situated learning theorists argue that domain knowledge that is acquired without applying it in some authentic context is meaningless.

Nevertheless, educators measure learning in terms of how much knowledge is acquired. This chapter argues that using Mindtools for building models of domain knowledge will help learners to acquire (comprehend and retain) that knowledge more effectively than most traditional learning methods. Mindtools represent a class of learning strategies. Educational researchers have long promoted use of learning strategies, such as note taking, summarizing, personalizing, or generating examples and analogies, for helping learners to better comprehend what they are studying. All of the Mindtools described in Part Three of this book can function as learning strategies. That is, when students use these tools to represent their understanding of what they are studying, they are elaborating on the information as presented and ascribing personal meaning to the ideas. Those actions are the essence of learning strategies. When students use Mindtools to build models of what they are studying, they will understand the subject matter better; and because they understand it better, they will retain it longer. So this chapter shows how some Mindtools can be used by students to build models of the domain content they are studying, thereby converting the information into domain knowledge.

MODELING DOMAIN KNOWLEDGE WITH DATABASES

Databases (see Chapter 9) are tools for analysis of content domains. While studying textbooks, CD-ROMs, lecture notes, library materials, or other information sources, students must analyze the content to identify the underlying themes that structure it. Those themes can be used as fields and examples can serve as records. The first example, produced by an elementary school class, is a simple database that includes social, political, and economic indicators from different countries (Figure 4-1). When analyzing content domains, students experience at least two levels of analysis. The first level occurs when students seek out and organize information in the

name	population	gnp i	pop density	tvs pe	infant mort.	defense bud	ave incom	literacy
Australia	16,646,000	220	5.4/sq.mi.	1/2.0	8.1/1000	2.7%	$14,458	99%
Brazil	153,771,000	313	47/sq.mi.	1/4.0	67/1000	.8%	$ 2,020	76%
Canada	26,527,000	486	6/sq.mi.	1/1.7	7.3/1000	2.0%	$13,000	99%
China	1,130,065,0	350	288/sq.mi.	1/12	33/1000	4.4%	$ 258	70%
El Salvador	5,221,000	4.1	671/sq.mi.	1/12	62/1000	3.9%	$ 700	62%u/40%r
India	850,067,000	246	658/sq.mi.	1/62	91/1000	3.8%	$ 300	36%
Iraq	18,782,000	34	104/sq.mi.	1/18	69/1000	32.0%	$ 1,950	70%
Japan	123,778,000	1800	844/sq.mi.	1/4.1	5/1000	1.0%	$15,030	99%
Mexico	88,335,000	126	115/sq.mi.	1/8.7	42/1000	.6%	$ 2,082	88%
Saudi Arabi	16,758,000	70	15/sq.mi.	1/3.5	74/1000	12.8%		50% (men)
Switzerland	6,628,000	111	406/sq.mi.	1/2.9	6.9/1000	2.2%	$26,309	99%
U.S.S.R.	290,939,000	2.5	33/sq.mi.	1/3.2	25.2/1000	17.0%	$ 3,000	99%
U.S.A.	250,372,000	4.8	68/sq.mi.	1/1.3	10/1000	5.7%	$16,444	99%

Figure 4-1
Social studies database produced by elementary school class.

cell type	location	function	shape	related cells	specialization	tissue system	associated pr	related disea:	other	growth
Astocyte	CNS	Supply	Radiating	Neurons,	Half of	Nervous			Neuroglia	No
Basal	Stratum	Produce New	Cube,	Epithelial	Mitotic	Epithelial		Cancer		Yes
Basophils	Blood	Bind Imm.E	Lobed	Neutrophil,	Basic,Pos	Connectiv	Histamine,			No?
Cardiac	Heat	Pump Blood	Branched	Endomysi	Intercalate	Muscle	Actin,	Athroscler		No
Chondrobl	Cartilage	Produce	Round			Connectiv	Collagen		Chondroc	Yes
Eosinophil	Blood	Protazoans,	Two	Basophil,	Acid,	Connectiv				No
Ependyma	Line CNS	Form	Cube		Cilia	Nervous			Neuroglia	No
Erythrocyt	Blood	Transport O2,	Disc	Hemocyto	Transport	Connectiv	Hemoglobi	Sickle Cell	Reticulocyt	No
Fibroblast	Connectiv	Fiber	Flat,		Mitotic	Connectiv	Collagen,	Cancer?	Fibrocyte	yes
Goblet	Columnar	Secretion	Columnar	Columnar	Mucus	Epithelial				No
Keratinocy	Stratum	Strengthen	Round	Melanocyt		Epithelial	Keratin			No
Melanocyt	Stratum	U.V. Protection	Branched	Keratinocy	Produce	Epithelial	Melanin	Skin		Yes
Microglia	CNS	Protect	Ovoid	Neurons,	Macropha	Nervous			Neuroglia	No
Motor	CNS(Cell	Impulse Away	Long, Thin	Sensory	Multipolar,	Nervous			Efferent	No
Neutrophil	Blood	Inflammation,	Lobed	Basophils,	Phagocyto	Connectiv	Lysozyme			No
Oligodend	CNS	Insulate	Long	Neurons	Produce	Nervous		Multiple	Neuroglia	No
Osteoblast	Bone	Produce	Spider	Osteoclast	Bone	Connectiv	Collagen	Osteopor	Osteocyte	Yes
Osteoclast	Bone	Bone	Ruffled	Osteoblast	Destroy	Connectiv	Lysosomal	Osteopor		no
Pseudostr	Gland	Secretion	Varies	Goblet	Cilia	Epithelial				No
Satellite	PNS	Control	Cube	Schwann,	Chemical	Nervous			Neroglia	No
Schwann	PNS	Insulate	Cube	Neurons,	Form	Nervous		Multiple	Neuroglia	No
Sensory	PNS(Cell	Impulse to	Long, Thin	Motor	Unipolar,	Nervous	Neurotran		Afferent	No
Simple	Digestive	Secretion,	Columnar		Cilia	Epithelial				No
Simple	Kidney	Secretion,	Cube		Microvilli	Epithelial				No
Simple	Lungs,	Diffusion of	Flat	Basal,		Epithelial				No
Skeletal	Bone,	Movement,	Long	Neurons	Neuromus	Muscle	Actin,			No
Smooth	Organ	Movement	Disc	Endomysi	Gap	Muscle	Actin,			No
Stratified	Epithelial	Protection	Columnar	Simple	Cilia	Epithelial				No
Stratified	Sweat,	Protection	Cube	Simple		Epithelial				No
Stratified	Lining	Protection	Layered	Basal		Epithelial	Keratin			No
T-	Lymphoid	Cell Mediated	Round	B,T Cells	Antigen	Immune	Lymphokin	Autoimmu		No
T-	Lymphoid	Cell Mediated	Round	Helper T	Graft	Immune	Antigen,Pe	Autoimmu	Killer T	Yes
T-	Lymphoid	Cell Mediated	Round	Killer T, B	Stimulates	Immune	Lymphokin	Aids,		No
Transitiona	Uterus,	Stretches	Surface		Expansion	Epithelial				No

Figure 4-2
Database of cells produced by biology students.

database. This is an analytical process. The second level is reflective and relational. Students ask questions about information in the database, such as, Do poorer countries have lower literacy levels? or If I knew nothing about any of these countries except for what is in the database, which one would I want to live in?

The database in Figure 4-2 was developed by biology students studying cells. Students identified each cell according to its functions, location, and so on. Building databases facilitates one of the most basic forms of cognition, comparison-contrast reasoning. Understanding how cells differ and the correlates of those differences enhances understanding.

MODELING DOMAIN KNOWLEDGE WITH CONCEPT MAPS

Concept maps can and should guide studying (see Chapter 10). For example, if students identified the 20 to 25 most important concepts in a chapter and constructed good concept maps with those concepts, they would likely perform better on any

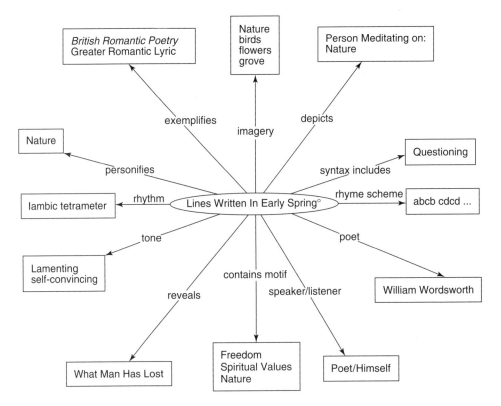

Figure 4-3
Screen from concept map on British romantic poets.

knowledge test than students who used traditional study methods. The concept map shown in Figure 4-3 is one computer screen from a much larger map produced by students of romantic poetry. Students studied different poems, and this screen describes "Lines Written in Early Spring" by Wordsworth. Other screens depict other poems, and yet other screens (Figure 4-4) elaborate on the concept of nature that provides imagery in many of the poems, including "Lines Written in Early Spring."

MODELING DOMAIN KNOWLEDGE WITH SPREADSHEETS

Spreadsheets (see Chapter 11) enable students to build numeric models of phenomena. Through building and executing equations with a spreadsheet, learners can build quantitative models. Figure 4-5 shows a simple spreadsheet for illustrating the effects of several variables on blood pressure; water intake, stress, internal temperature, sodium intake, and outside temperature. This model is relatively simple; nevertheless, it allows learners to construct a better understanding of causal relationships, which are the basis of almost all scientific reasoning.

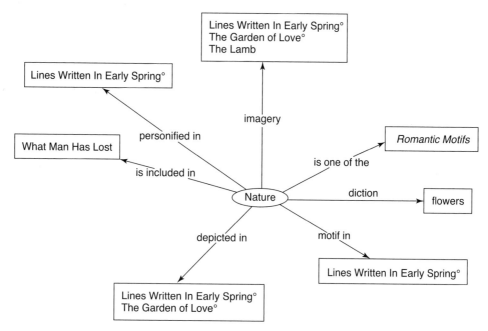

Figure 4-4
Another screen from concept map on British romantic poets.

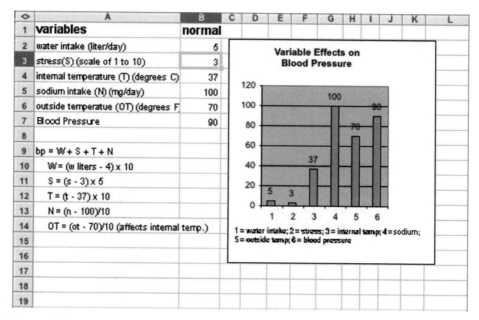

Figure 4-5
Spreadsheet indicating effects of variables on blood pressure.

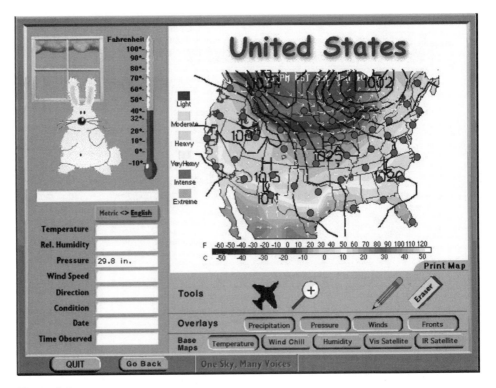

Figure 4-6
Weather visualization tool for children: One Sky, Many Voices—a science inquiry project
developed at the University of Michigan.

MODELING DOMAIN KNOWLEDGE WITH VISUALIZATION TOOLS

A wide variety of visualization tools (see Chapter 15) have been developed to support different kinds of investigations. Many learners (like myself) are visual learners; they have to see something before they understand it. For them, a picture may be worth more than a thousand words. A project titled Kids as Global Scientists produced a weather visualization tool called One Sky, Many Voices. The tool enables students to visualize local and national weather in many ways (see Figure 4-6); students have access to data about temperatures, winds, barometic pressure gradients, fronts, humidity, and so on. These data, which can be acccessed live via the Internet, enable students to make forecasts or resolve other related issues.

MODELING DOMAIN KNOWLEDGE WITH HYPERMEDIA

Hypermedia (see Chapter 16) are multimedia programs that are hyperlinked together. Hyperlinking of individual nodes or chunks of information can be used by learners to illustrate the complexity and interrelatedness of domains they are studying. Figure 4-7

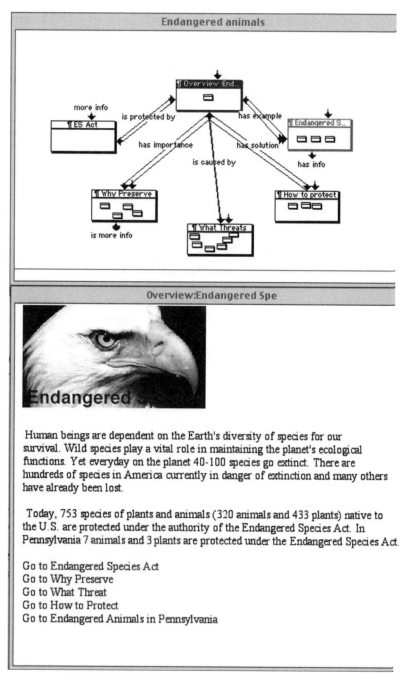

Figure 4-7
Frames from student-constructed hypermedia program on endangered species.

shows two frames from a hypermedia program on endangered species that students constructed. The upper frame shows a module titled Overview, which when opened shows the bottom frame. The bottom frame contains links to topics such as the Endangered Species Act and Why Preserve. Each link takes the reader to documents that contain pictures, text, and movies about endangered species.

The students who constructed this hypermedia program learned a lot more than they would have from merely viewing a hypermedia program. This program represents *their* understanding of endangered species. Their understanding was organized through a model that guided the construction of the hypermedia knowledge base.

SUMMARY

If you agree that knowledge is what we personally and collaboratively construct, then you should accept that student construction of knowledge bases will yield more meaningful learning. The Mindtools described in Part Three of this book are learning strategies that enable students to construct knowledge bases, that is, representations of their knowledge. Students construct their own domain knowledge from studying information that they have sought. Knowledge cannot be transmitted from the teacher to the student.

Students can represent their knowledge with the help of knowledge-modeling tools. Databases are tools that help students analyze content domain. Concept maps can guide the studying process. Spreadsheets enable students to build numeric models of phenomena. Visualization tools support students as they conduct varied types of investigations. Hypermedia allow students to see the complexity and interrelatedness of domains they are studying.

REFERENCES

Alexander, P. A., & Judy, J. E. (1988). The interaction of domain-specific and strategies knowledge in academic performance. *Review of Educational Research, 58*(4), 375–404.

Jonassen, D. H., & Land, S. L. (2000). *Theoretical foundations of learning environments.* Mahwah, NJ: Lawrence Erlbaum.

CHAPTER **5**

Modeling Systems

Among the most pernicious words in education, I believe, is *content.* Content is the stuff to be learned that is defined by the curriculum. It is the coin of the educational realm. Students are responsible for learning content in schools.

There are two major reasons why content learning is problematic. First, acquiring content is philosophically impossible in a constructivist perspective. Acquisition of content assumes that the content is some objective entity that can be passed from the teacher to the student, like the textbook that the teacher hands to the student. *Here is some knowledge; you can have it.* The most common metaphor for describing the content approach to learning is silos. In social studies, students acquire knowledge to fill up their social-studies silos. In math, students' math silos are filled up as knowledge is poured in. Constructivists, on the other hand, believe that knowledge is necessarily constructed by individuals and co-constructed by groups through their interactions with the world. What sense any person makes of an experience cannot be known entirely. However, some curriculum writers assume that if all students are exposed to the same content, they will all learn the same thing. At best, that is wishful thinking.

Second, content as defined by curricula is almost invariably organized in hierarchical lists of topics. Unfortunately, that conceptual organization is inconsistent with the ways that humans naturally tend to organize their experiences. What humans know best they understand epistemologically (knowledge in use) and phenomenologically (perceptions of the human experience). This distinction may appear to be philosophical hairsplitting, but it represents a serious psychological disconnect. Schools feed content to students in ways that do not naturally make sense.

Educators need not radically reconceptualize a curriculum to make better sense of it. Instead, one way (among many) that educators can organize a curriculum is in ways that reflect the world, that is, in systems. Rather than organizing concepts in structures that are defined by surface comparisons, why not organize concepts around how they naturally cohere in the world—in systems.

Systems are everywhere. They are integrated and interdependent aggregates of components that share a common purpose. Because they exist and strive for a common purpose, the components working together can accomplish more than they can separately (synergy). The work of the components is regulated by the system, so that the parts all focus on the goal of the system. Systems are regulated by feedback. When the output of the system is not achieving the goal, the system monitors that output and adjusts its operations accordingly. One of the most sophisticated and personally relevant systems is the human system. The human body (see Figure 5-1) is a synergy of subsystems: neurological, respiratory, circulatory, skeletal, and so on. The mere act of walking toward a goal engages complex, feedback-driven operations as the brain directs adjustments in gait and direction.

Systems may also be conceived of hierarchically. At the same time, most systems are subsystems of larger systems and suprasystems of subsystems. Your

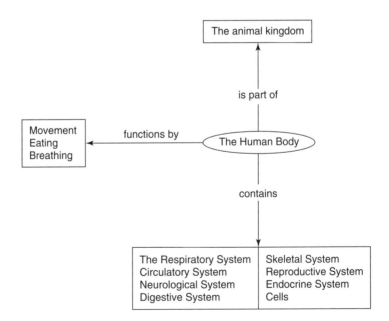

Figure 5-1
Systems of the human body.

school is a subsystem of a school district or university system, which is a subsystem of the state educational system, which is a subsystem of larger educational systems. Your school comprises many subsystems, including faculty, curriculum, classrooms, administration, and so on. Examining content in terms of how the concepts function together in the world may be a more effective way to organize content than lists of topics. If they are helped to think systemically, students will likely develop more useful conceptions of the world than they would from a list of topics.

This chapter describes briefly how Mindtools can be used to represent systems.

MODELING SYSTEMS WITH CONCEPT MAPS

Systems consist of interactive, interdependent components. Those components and the nature of their interactions can be represented in concept maps (see Chapter 10). Concepts, as described in Chapter 1, occur within conceptual systems. The conceptual systems that organize civil engineering, for instance, are different from those that organize religious studies. The conceptual frameworks differ dramatically.

Mathematics uses many different notation systems such as numerals, variables, and formulas. Systems of relationships that are conveyed by those formulas are known as functions. Figure 5-2 describes that system of functions.

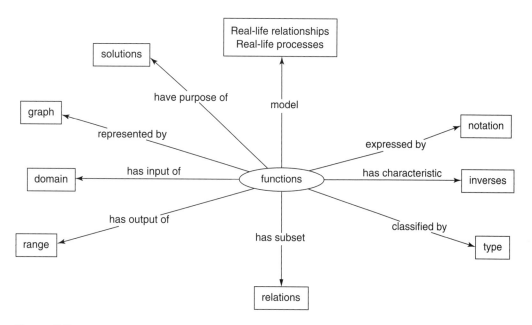

Figure 5-2
System of mathematical functions.

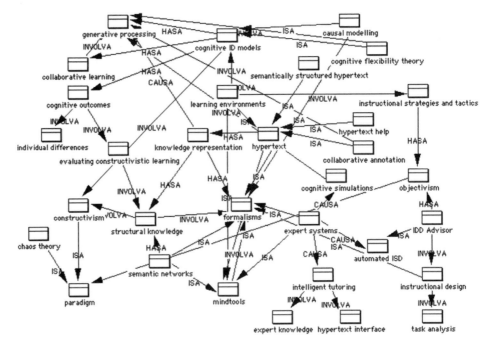

Figure 5-3
System of research issues.

Years ago, someone asked me to describe my research agenda. At the time, I was conducting research on many topics, all of which were interrelated and somewhat interdependent, ergo a system. Figure 5-3 is a concept map of that system of research. What is important to note is that the systemic interactions among research efforts enabled me to accomplish more than I could have by conducting separate research projects.

Concept maps are useful for identifying components, but they cannot represent the dynamic nature of interactions. For that, we need to construct models with systems modeling tools, which are described next.

MODELING SYSTEMS WITH SYSTEMS MODELING TOOLS

The most effective tools for modeling systems are systems modeling tools. A variety of computer-based tools for modeling systems are described more extensively in Chapter 13. These tools enable learners to construct dynamic systems models by describing the quantitative relationships among the components, then testing them by running the models. Figure 5-4 shows a systemic view of the spread of infections. Notice that people are shifted into subsystems, such as vaccinated people and

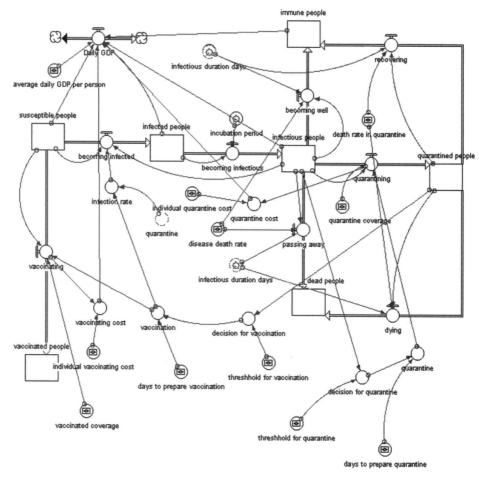

Figure 5-4
Systems model of infections.

infectious people, and that infectious people get well, are quarantined, or die. Any infection in any locale becomes a system.

Figure 5-5 is a simple systemic model of the overweight crisis in the United States. The population of overweight people is a function of the intake of fast foods, which is controlled by cravings for fast food, which is driven by food industry promotions and the desire for bigger profits. The major controlling process results from self-image. This student-developed model makes some naive assumptions that the teacher must question. Questioning or perturbing student models so that students adjust them is probably the most effective teaching act possible. As students improve their models and make them more complex, they are showing direct evidence of learning, so long as their changes are viable. In model building, the role of the teacher changes substantially from tradition. Rather than being the purveyor of knowledge, the teacher becomes the arbiter of acceptable knowledge and the

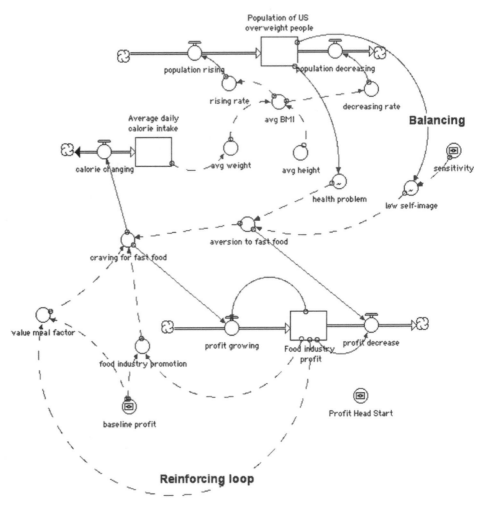

Figure 5-5
Simple systems model of overweight phenomenon.

perturber of that knowledge. Teachers should be asking questions such as these: What other factors might affect *X*? Are you sure that the relationship between *X* and *Y* is that strong? The teacher must have a well-developed conceptual framework in order to continually question that validity of student models. Such questioning can be the most rewarding of all teaching acts.

MODELING SYSTEMS WITH SPREADSHEETS

Spreadsheets are also effective for illustrating dynamic interaction among system components. Figure   shows one of a series of spreadsheets that predicts offspring from monohybrid crosses of plants that are homozygous and heterozygous for a

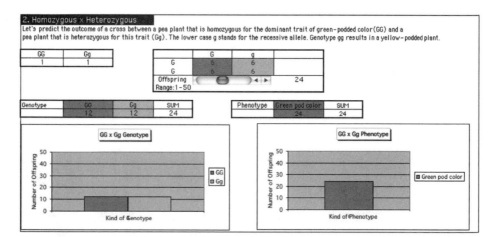

Figure 5-6
Spreadsheet model of monohybrid crosses.

dominant trait. The students who built this model also modeled the other conditions (homozygous × homozygous and heterozygous × heterozygous). Creation of dynamic representations of systems like this enables students to test their hypotheses.

SUMMARY

Traditional approaches to teaching content result in inert and useless knowledge in students because (1) knowledge cannot be conveyed (rather, it is constructed) and (2) content is conveyed to students in ways that are inconsistent with the ways that they naturally tend to think. An alternative is to construct representations of systems in the world (see Chapters 6 through 8 for other options).

Because of their inherent complexity and dynamic nature, systems are hard to model. Nevertheless, the end justifies the means, because systemic understanding is so much stronger than memorization.

A limited number of Mindtools can be used to model systems. Dynamic modeling tools such as expert systems (Chapter 12), spreadsheets (Chapter 11), and systems modeling tools (Chapter 13) are the most effective for modeling systems because they can be tested. Concept maps (Chapter 10) can represent system components and provide semantic descriptions of interrelationships among the components. Other Mindtools described in this book, such as direct manipulation environments (Chapter 14) and hypermedia (Chapter 16), enable learners to build systems models.

The most important outcome of efforts to represent systems is the kind of system thinking that may result. Getting students to understand the complexities among phenomena in the world and how the phenomena affect each other would represent a major accomplishment for any teacher or professor.

Modeling Problems

Chapter 5 argued that traditional, topic-based representations of content are inconsistent with the ways that humans naturally represent the world, so such representations are less understandable. Then Chapter 5 illustrated how learners could conceptualize the world as systems by using Mindtools to construct models of systems. Now Chapter 6 will show how learners can use Mindtools to reconceptualize content as problems. In our everyday and workplace lives, we most often encounter the world as problems, not as lists of content. So rather than learning social studies in terms of chronological lists, for example, why not learn social studies by representing the myriad problems found in newspapers and news magazines? Chapters 4 through 8 discuss five separate ways for representing the world. The more different ways in which learners think about and represent the world, the better they will understand the world. Problems are one of the most authentic ways of representing the world.

Among the most important skills in solving a problem is the ability to construct some sort of internal representation (conceptual model) of the problem (i.e., the problem space). The richer and more accurate a learner's representation of a problem, the better the learner's solution is likely to be. Personal representations of a problem serve a number of functions (Savelsbergh, de Jong, & Ferguson-Hessler (1998):

◆ To guide further interpretation of information about the problem
◆ To simulate the behavior of the system based on knowledge about the properties of the system
◆ To associate with and trigger a particular solution schema (procedure)

Most problems in schools are well-structured word problems found at the end of textbook chapters. These problems present numerical information about events in a shallow, story context. Most students solve these problems using a direct translation strategy; that is, they directly translate the problem into a formula and solve the algorithm. When students use this strategy, they often get the right answer without understanding the principles that are represented by the formula. They do not construct any qualitative understanding of the content they are studying. Developing qualitative representations of problems, however, is just as important, if not more important, than constructing quantitative representations. What good is to get the answer right if you do not understand what the problem was about?

This chapter shows how Mindtools can be used to construct qualitative and (in some cases) quantitative models of problems. Qualitative representations function to

◆ explain the meaning of information that is stated only implicitly in problem descriptions but is important to problem solution, and
◆ provide preconditions and constraints that determine guidelines for quantitative reasoning through numeric representations (formulas) (Ploetzner & Spada, 1993).

In fact, Ploetzner, Fehse, Kneser, and Spada (1999) showed that when in the discipline of physics, qualitative problem representations are necessary prerequisites to learning quantitative representations. When students try to understand a problem using only formulas, they do not understand the underlying systems in which they are working. The more ways that students represent problems, the better able they will be to transfer their problem-solving skills to new situations.

MODELING PROBLEMS WITH DATABASES

In solving problems, the problem solver's domain knowledge should be well organized and accessible. For example, nutritionists who are prescribing alternatives to drug therapies must understand the drugs they are replacing and their effects on humans. Figure 6-1 consists of related tables from a relational database (see Chapter 9) on drugs. The bottom table describes drugs; the middle table shows the presence of these drugs in natural substances; and the top table describes herbal alternatives to

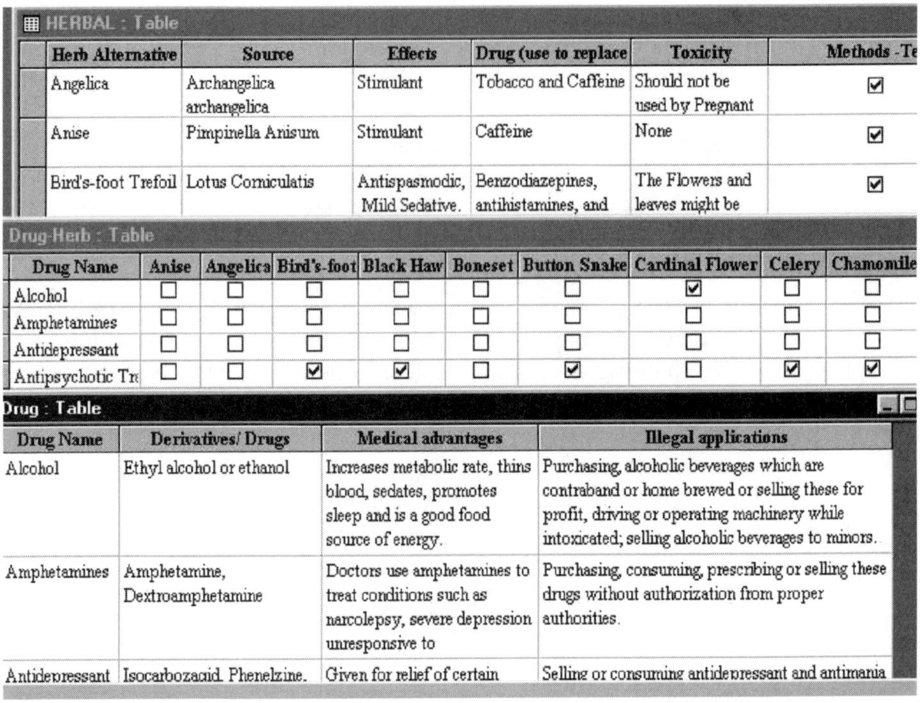

HERBAL : Table

Herb Alternative	Source	Effects	Drug (use to replace	Toxicity	Methods - Te
Angelica	Archangelica archangelica	Stimulant	Tobacco and Caffeine	Should not be used by Pregnant	☑
Anise	Pimpinella Anisum	Stimulant	Caffeine	None	☑
Bird's-foot Trefoil	Lotus Corniculatis	Antispasmodic, Mild Sedative.	Benzodiazepines, antihistamines, and	The Flowers and leaves might be	☑

Drug-Herb : Table

Drug Name	Anise	Angelica	Bird's-foot	Black Haw	Boneset	Button Snake	Cardinal Flower	Celery	Chamomile
Alcohol	☐	☐	☐	☐	☐	☐	☑	☐	☐
Amphetamines	☐	☐	☐	☐	☐	☐	☐	☐	☐
Antidepressant	☐	☐	☐	☐	☐	☐	☐	☐	☐
Antipsychotic Tr	☐	☐	☑	☑	☐	☑	☐	☑	☑

Drug : Table

Drug Name	Derivatives/ Drugs	Medical advantages	Illegal applications
Alcohol	Ethyl alcohol or ethanol	Increases metabolic rate, thins blood, sedates, promotes sleep and is a good food source of energy.	Purchasing, alcoholic beverages which are contraband or home brewed or selling these for profit, driving or operating machinery while intoxicated; selling alcoholic beverages to minors.
Amphetamines	Amphetamine, Dextroamphetamine	Doctors use amphetamines to treat conditions such as narcolepsy, severe depression unresponsive to	Purchasing, consuming, prescribing or selling these drugs without authorization from proper authorities.
Antidepressant	Isocarbozacid. Phenelzine.	Given for relief of certain	Selling or consuming antidepressant and antimania

Figure 6-1
Tables from a relational database on drugs.

drugs. Additional tables could be added, for example, to interrelate natural and artificial drugs in terms of their chemistry and pharmacology. Relational databases enable groups of students to create their own databases and combine them into a larger, classroom project.

The tables in a relational database can be searched, together, to answer queries. Queries are formal searches of the database that can be predefined in the database program. For example, Figure 6-2 shows the results of a formal query conducted in Access, a database program. Students constructed a query to search all of the tables for relevant information and to show only the records and fields necessary for answering a query about potential effects of ginseng.

MODELING PROBLEMS WITH CONCEPT MAPS

Another way of representing problems is through concept mapping (see Chapter 10). When groups of students are beginning to solve problems, such as molar conversion (stoichiometry) problems in chemistry, generation of a concept map can provide the organization required to solve the problem. Concept maps are a shorthand form for

What kind of abused drug could be replaced by Ginseng? : Se...

Drug Name	Derivatives/ Drugs	Ginseng
Amphetamines	Amphetamine, Dextroamphetamine	☑
Barbiturates	Amobarbital, Aprobarbital, Butabarbital, Mephobarbital¡K¡K	☑
Tobacco	Nicotine, Pyrrolidine	☑
Volatile inhalants	Products contain butyl and isobutyl nitrate. Nail polish remover, lighter fluids, cleaning fluids, ¡K	☑
Antidepressant	Isocarbozaqid, Phenelzine, Tranylcypromine.	☑

Record: 1 of 5

Figure 6-2
Formal query from drug database.

organizing and sequencing ideas. Figure 6-3 shows a concept map of all the concepts used in solving molar conversion problems.

MODELING PROBLEMS WITH SPREADSHEETS

Sometimes Mindtools can be used to build numeric models of a laboratory problem. For example, the spreadsheet (see Chapter 11) in Figure 6-4 supports a lab activity on blood analysis. Students collected data for each class member, arranged the data by gender (also arranged by descending white blood cell, WBC, in Figure 6-4), calculated averages by gender and by class, and compared an individual's values with the averages for his or her gender and for the class. The data collected in this experiment were white blood count, red blood count, hematocrit, and hemoglobin level. The spreadsheet was an integral tool in representing the problem quantitatively and in solving the problem. This model of blood analysis can also support qualitative questions such as these:

- Are there gender differences in blood components, for example, red and white cell counts or hemoglobin level?
- If white cell counts drop, what is the likely effect on red cells?

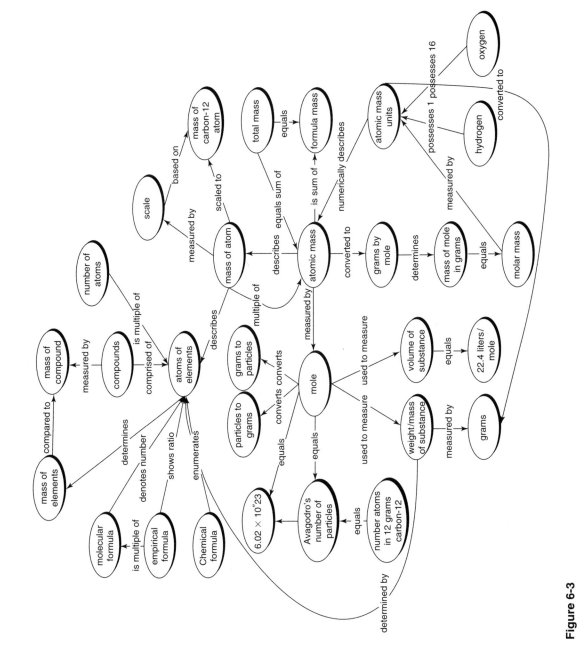

Figure 6-3
Concept map model of molar conversion problems in chemistry.

	A	B	C	D	E
1	SEX	WBC	RBC(X10E6)	HCT(%)	HGB
2	FEMALE	13760	11	42.2	15.25
3	FEMALE	9360	11.1	41.6	14.1
4	FEMALE	9000	1.3	43.4	17
5	FEMALE	9000	1.3	46.1	15
6	FEMALE	7960	3.7	34.1	15
7	FEMALE	7680	5.5	43.2	16
8	FEMALE	7080	4.4	41.6	14
9	FEMALE	6720	2.18	38.6	14.2
10	FEMALE	6600	4.5	57.1	17.5
11	FEMALE	6400	5.5	43.4	17
12	FEMALE	6240	3.42	52	19
13	FEMALE	5680	5.53	60	14.5
14	FEMALE	4980	4.74	44.6	15
15	FEMALE	4520	8.35	44.4	15.2
16	MALE	8968	5.79	42.2	15.5
17	MALE	7786	5.7	51.5	16.5
18	MALE	7760	3.4	50	15.7
19	MALE	7520	6.7	46.3	8.9
20	MALE	6600	3.73	49.1	19
21	MALE	6520	4.29	47	15
22	MALE	6450	6.5	47.2	16.5
23	MALE	6040	11	44	14.5
24	MALE	4600	5.7	46.2	14
25	MIN FEMALES	4520	1.3	34.1	14
26	MAX FEMALES	13760	11.1	60	19
27	RANGE FEMALE	9240	9.8	25.9	5
28	AVE FEMALES	7499	5.18	45.2	15.6
29					
30	MIN MALES	4600	3.4	42.2	8.9
31	MAX MALES	8968	11	51.5	19
32	RANGE MALES	4368	7.6	9.3	10.1
33	AVE MALES	6916	5.9	47.1	15.1
34					
35	MIN CLASS	4520	1.3	34.1	8.9
36	MAX CLASS	13760	11.1	60	19
	RANGE CLASS	9240	9.8	25.9	10.1
	AVE CLASS	7271	5.4	45.9	15.4

Figure 6-4
Spreadsheet to support lab experiment on blood analysis.

◆ If hemoglobin were administered to a patient, what is the likely effect on hematocrit readings?

Spreadsheets can be used to model nearly all phenomena in math and science. For example, consider the series of batteries problem in Figure 6-5. When the voltages on the left side of the model are reset, the values of the other variables in the figure change. Students constructed this simple model representing an experiment using Ohm's law. When students can construct original models representing principles or theories, you know that they understand the principles deeply.

The next example illustrates the use of a spreadsheet for solving subproblems. The process for developing new food products is complex, especially for fresh food products that are found in the produce section of supermarkets. Among the subproblems in product development is determining shelf life. Shelf life is negatively affected by the growth of pathogens. Figure 6-6 illustrates a simple,

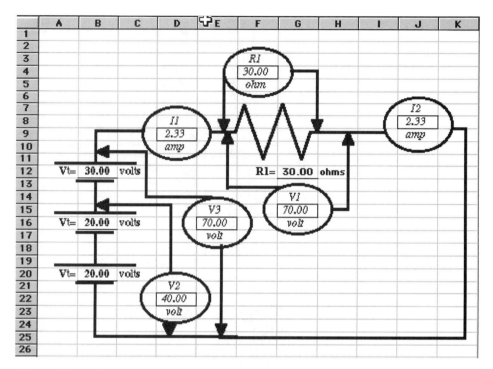

Figure 6-5
Battery series spreadsheet model.

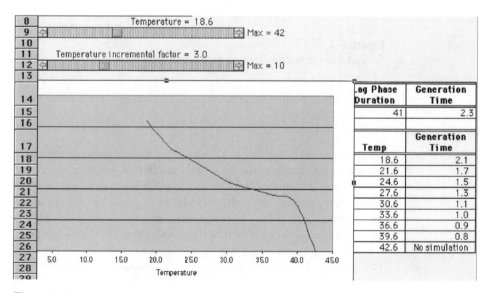

Figure 6-6
Pathogens experiment (courtesy of Julian Hernandez-Serrano).

student-constructed experiment on growth of pathogens. To run the experiment, you set the temperature and temperature change factor, then observe the effects on the growth of pathogens, as illustrated in the graph.

MODELING PROBLEMS WITH EXPERT SYSTEMS

Solving all problems requires some form of causal reasoning. The more complex the problem, the more sophisticated the causal reasoning must be. The knowledge base shown in Figure 6-7 was developed by a student using a simple expert system shell (see Chapter 11) called WinExpert, available with a wonderful book titled *How to Model It* (Starfield, Smith, & Bleloch, 1990; this is my preferred tool). The expert system attempts to represent the reasoning that President Harry S Truman may have used in deciding whether to drop an atomic bomb on Hiroshima during World War II. Although the content is gruesome and many factors were not considered, the expert system developed represents a deeper reflection on historical events than the typical memorization of names, dates, and places.

In the kind of rule base shown in Figure 6-7, decisions are usually stated first. This requires that the system designer identify goals before clarifying any of the decision factors. Next the designer identifies the decision factors in the form of questions that will be asked of the user. This is the essence of the design process. Writing questions that are simple enough for any novice user to answer is difficult. In this type of expert system, the designer next writes the rules, using IF–THEN (Boolean) logic to relate the decisions to the decision factors or questions. The rule base in this example consists of 20 rules that form the heart of the knowledge base. For example, the first rule states that IF the answer to Question 1 is yes AND the answer to Question 2 is also yes AND the answer to Question 5 is also yes, THEN the atomic bomb should be used as quickly as possible, primarily on military targets. The remainder of the rules specify alternative conditions that may have existed at the time.

Figure 6-8 is a set of rules selected from a knowledge base developed by students in a home economics class for advising classmates or the public on how to order more healthful foods from a fast-food menu. The need for more healthful diets has become a critical problem in the United States. The rule base was developed using a shell called McSmarts, which follows a different syntax from that of the rule base in Figure 6-6. In each rule, the advice is presented first; next, the conditions that will lead to that advice are listed.

Meteorologists predict the likelihood of different weather events. They engage in a diagnostic kind of problem solving that fairly accurately reflects the type of reasoning represented by expert systems. The next example of student-produced expert systems, shown in Figure 6-9, is excerpted from a knowledge base on predicting severe weather that was developed in a meteorology class. Only the decisions and factors are shown here because there are too many rules to display.

The three rule bases described are simple examples of how students can model the causal relationships in problems they are solving. When students become expert system designers, they have to become the authorities instead of the teacher (a role

Decision 1:   Atomic fission should only be used for peaceful purposes.
Decision 2:   The atomic bomb should be used as quickly as possible, primarily on military targets.
Decision 3:   Knowledge of the weapon's existence should be used as a threat to induce Japan to surrender.
Decision 4:   The atomic bomb should not be used, but research should be made known after the war ends.
Question 1:   Do you want to encourage the Japanese to surrender as quickly as possible?
Answers 1   Yes
          2   No.
Question 2:   Do you want to limit the loss of Allied and Japanese lives?
Answers 1   Yes
          2   No.
Question 3:   Do you want to use the weapon against the Germans?
Answers 1   Yes
          2   No
          3   Unsure.
Question 4:   Do you want to use the atomic fission research ONLY to create alternate sources of energy?
Answers 1   Yes
          2   No
          3   Unsure.
Question 5:   Do you want to increase the political power of the Allies during and after the war?
Answers 1   Yes
          2   No
          3   Unsure.
Question 6:   Will Japan surrender with continued conventional bombing of Japanese cities?
Answers 1   Yes
          2   No
          3   Unsure.
Question 7:   Was the Manhattan Project (atomic fission) begun primarily for future military use?
Answers 1   Yes
          2   No
          3   Unsure.
Question 8:   Do you want to end the Japanese march through Asia?
Answers 1   Yes
          2   No
          3   Unsure.
Question 9:   Do you want to use atomic fission as only a psychological weapon?
Answers 1   Yes
          2   No
          3   Unsure.
Question 10: How much longer should the war continue (from Spring 1945)?
Answers 1   3 months
          2   6 months
          3   1 year
          4   indefinitely.

Rule 1:
IF Question1=Answer1 & Question2=Answer1 & Question5=Answer1 THEN Decision2.
Rule 2:
IF Question3=Answer2 THEN Decision4.
Rule 3:
IF Question4=Answer1 THEN Decision3.
Rule 4:
IF Question4=Answer2 THEN Decision2.
Rule 5:
IF Question5=Answer1 & Question6=Answer2 THEN Decision2.

Figure 6-7
Expert system rule base on possible reasoning for the atomic attack on Hiroshima during
World War II.

Rule 6:
IF Question6=Answer1 THEN Decision4.
Rule 7:
IF Question6=Answer2 & Question1=Answer1 & Question8=Answer1 THEN Decision2.
Rule 8:
IF Question6=Answer3 THEN Decision3.
Rule 9:
IF Question7=Answer1 & Question1=Answer1 THEN Decision2.
Rule 10:
IF Question7=Answer2 THEN Decision1.
Rule 11:
IF Question7=Answer3 THEN Decision4.
Rule 12:
IF Question8=Answer1 & Question6=Answer2 & Question1=Answer1 THEN Decision2.
Rule 13:
IF Question8=Answer2 THEN Decision3.
Rule 14:
IF Question9=Answer1 THEN Decision3.
Rule 15:
IF Question9=Answer2 & Question8=Answer1 & Question7=Answer1 & Question1=Answer1 THEN Decision2.
Rule 16:
IF Question4=Answer1 & Question5=Answer1 & Question7=Answer3 THEN Decision4.
Rule 17:
IF Question10=Answer1 & Question2=Answer1 & Question6=Answer3 THEN Decision2.
Rule 18:
IF Question10=Answer2 & Question3=Answer1 & Question5=Answer1 THEN Decision2.
Rule 19:
IF Question10=Answer3 & Question6=Answer1 & Question8=Answer3 THEN Decision4.
Rule 20:
IF Question10=Answer4 & Question4=Answer1 & Question6=Answer3 THEN

Figure 6-7
(*continued*)

reversal that students enjoy), and this engages them in deeper thinking about the subject. Expert systems are perhaps the most appropriate Mindtool for qualitatively modeling causal reasoning processes.

MODELING PROBLEMS WITH SYSTEMS MODELING TOOLS

Systems modeling tools (Chapter 13) are used to model dynamic, feedback-driven systems. They are especially effective for modeling problems. Figure 6-10 illustrates a model of a simple stoichiometry (molar conversion) problem in chemistry; both quantitative and qualitative representations of the problem are presented. This model represents the problem qualitatively in the concept map. However, underlying each of the entities in the map are numbers and equations that enable learners to test their model. The graph below the model provides graphic results of those equations, which allow learners to check the accuracy of their equations.

Eat: Chunky chicken salad, diet soft drink, and low-fat yogurt cone
        IF YES: Question 1 Do you want a balanced, nutritious meal?
                (Meal will represent all of the basic four food groups.)
        IF YES: Question 2 Do you desire a low-fat meal? (<30% calories come from fat)
        IF YES: Question 3 Do you desire a low-cholesterol meal? (>84 mg)
        IF YES: Question 4 Do you desire a low-carbohydrate (sugar and starch) meal?
                (<30% calories come from carbohydrates)
        IF NO: Question 5 Do you desire a low-salt meal? (<650 mg)

Eat: Chunky chicken salad and 2% milk
        IF YES: Question 1 Do you want a balanced, nutritious meal?
                (Meal will represent all of the basic four food groups.)
        IF YES: Question 2 Do you desire a low-fat meal? (<30% calories come from fat)
        IF NO: Question 3 Do you desire a low-cholesterol meal? (>84 mg)
        IF YES: Question 4 Do you desire a low-carbohydrate (sugar and starch) meal?
                (<30% calories come from carbohydrates)
        IF NO: Question 5 Do you desire a low-salt meal? (<650 mg)

Eat: Garden salad and a diet drink
        IF YES: Question 1 Do you want a balanced, nutritious meal?
                (Meal will represent all of the basic four food groups.)
        IF NO: Question 2 Do you desire a low-fat meal? (<30% calories come from fat)
        IF YES: Question 3 Do you desire a low-cholesterol meal? (>84 mg)
        IF YES: Question 4 Do you desire a low-carbohydrate (sugar and starch) meal? (<30%
calories come from carbohydrates)
        IF YES: Question 5 Do you desire a low-salt meal? (<650 mg)

Eat: Hamburger, sm. fries, and dairy drink OR 6ct. McNuggets, sm. fries, and van. shake OR
Filet-o-fish, sm. fries, and van. shake
        IF YES: Question 1 Do you want a balanced, nutritious meal?
                (Meal will represent all of the basic four food groups.)
        IF NO: Question 2 Do you desire a low-fat meal? (<30% calories come from fat)
        IF YES: Question 3 Do you desire a low-cholesterol meal? (>84 mg)
        IF NO: Question 4 Do you desire a low-carbohydrate (sugar and starch) meal?
                (<30% calories come from carbohydrates)
        IF NO: Question 5 Do you desire a low-salt meal? (<650 mg)

Eat: McDLT and diet soft drink OR 6ct. McNuggets, side salad, and 2% milk OR Chunky chicken
salad and 2% milk
        IF YES: Question 1 Do you want a balanced, nutritious meal?
                (Meal will represent all of the basic four food groups.)
        IF NO: Question 2 Do you desire a low-fat meal? (<30% calories come from fat)
        IF NO: Question 3 Do you desire a low-cholesterol meal? (>84 mg)
        IF YES: Question 4 Do you desire a low-carbohydrate (sugar and starch) meal?
                (<30% calories come from carbohydrates)
        IF NO: Question 5 Do you desire a low-salt meal? (<650 mg)
Eat: Any food menu item of your choice
        IF NO: Question 1 Do you want a balanced, nutritious meal?
                (Meal will represent all of the basic four food groups.)

Figure 6-8
Expert system advice for more healthful eating from a fast-food menu.

SEVERE WEATHER PREDICTOR
This module is designed to assist the severe local storms forecaster in assessing the potential for severe weather using soundings. The program will ask for measures of instability and wind shear, as well as other variables important in the formation of severe weather. Instability and wind shear parameters are easily calculated using programs such as SHARP, RAOB, and GEMPAK. The other variables can be found on surface and upper-air charts.

ADVICE
The following output indicates the potential for severe weather in the environment represented by the sounding you used. A number between 1 and 10 indicates the confidence of the guidance. A higher number indicates a greater confidence.
Severe Weather (Tornadoes, Hail, and/or Straightline Winds)
Severe Weather Possible
Severe Weather Not Likely
Severe Weather Likely
Severe Weather Potential

QUESTIONS (Decision Factors)
What is the value of CAPE (J/kg)? < -6, -2 to -6, 0 to -2, > 0
What is the Lifted Index (LI) value (C)? 0, 0-25, 25-75, > 75
What is the Convective Inhibition (CIN) (J/kg)? 0, 1-3, > 3
What is the Lid Strength Index (LSI) (C)? > 450, 250-449, 150-249, 0-150, <150, < 0
What is the value of storm-relative helicity? > 6, 4-6, 2-4, < 2
What is the value of 0-6 km Positive Shear (s-1)?
What is the value of storm-relative helicity (m² s⁻¹)?, Left Entrance, Right Entrance, ☐ Right Exit, None
Which quadrant of the jet streak is the area of interest in? Cold Front, Dryline, ☐ Zone, Outflow Boundary, Nothing Significant
Is there likely to be a significant trigger mechanism? Yes, No

Figure 6-9
Advice and factors from an expert system predicting severe weather.

As will be shown in Chapter 13, systems can also be represented as populations. That chapter describes tools for modeling the growth of populations. For example, Figure 6-11 illustrates a tool, EcoBeaker, which can be used to model populations of bryozoan colonies after a hurricane. Each color on the chart represents members of different kinds of Bryozoa. As one kind grows, it takes over the other populations. Because bryozoan provide food for other animals, this model could help predict the growth of those other animals, which could also be represented using this tool.

MODELING PROBLEMS WITH VISUALIZATION TOOLS

Many scientific problems, especially in mathematics, are abstract and, therefore, difficult for many learners to comprehend. Mathmatica is a powerful suite of mathematical tools that are useful for visualizing experiments. Figure 6-12 shows the plot of the descent of a space shuttle. The formula is entered into Mathmatica, which then graphs it. Visualization makes the shuttle descent more understandable.

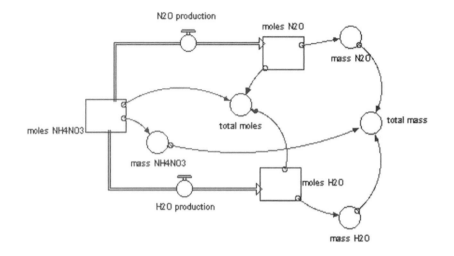

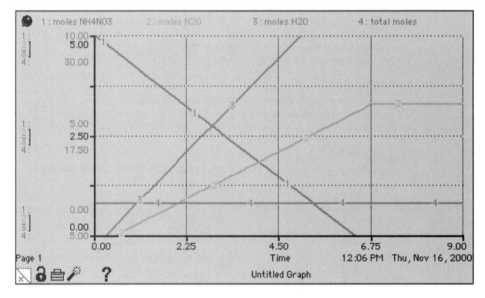

Figure 6-10
Systems dynamics model of stoichiometry problem developed using Stella.

Chemistry problems also present difficulties because many of the processes are not visible. There are a number of tools available for visualizing chemicals at the atomic level. Most students find it hard to understand chemical bonding because the complex atomic interactions are abstractions. The static graphics of these bonds that appear in textbooks may help learners to form mental images, but those mental images cannot be manipulated or conveyed to others. Tools such as MacSpartan enable students to view, rotate, and measure molecules in different views (see

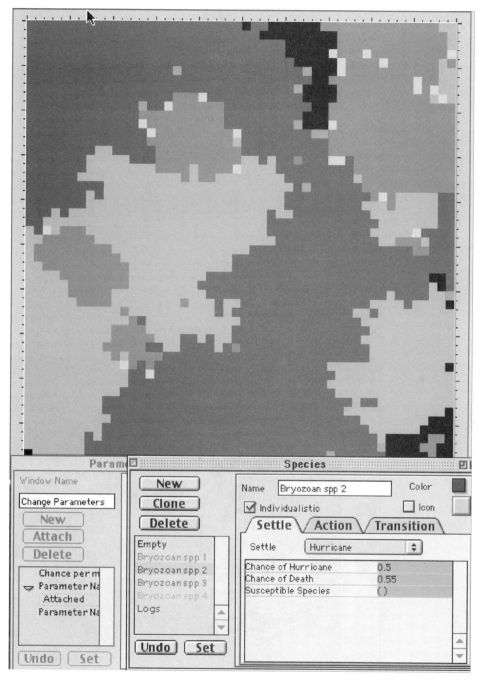

Figure 6-11
Modeling the effect of a hurricane on bryozoan using the modeling tool EcoBeaker.

```
Clear[v,t]

NDSolve[ {v'[t] == g ( v[t]^2 / 25000.0^2 - 1.0),
          v[0]==24000.0}, v[t], {t,0.0,1700.0}]


{{v[t] ->
    InterpolatingFunction[{0., 1700.},
      <>][t]}}


Plot[ Evaluate[v[t] /. %], {t,0,1700}]
```

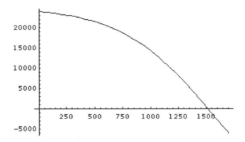

Figure 6-12
Descent path of space shuttle as graphed by Mathmatica.

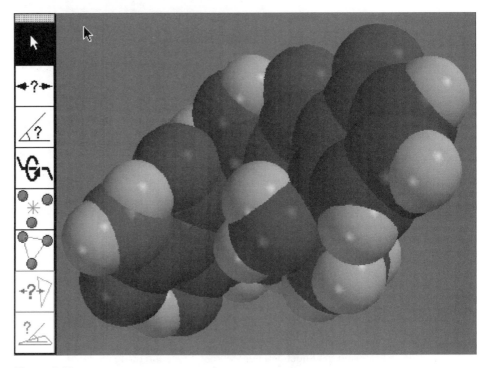

Figure 6-13
Display produced using MacSpartan tool for visualizing chemical compounds.

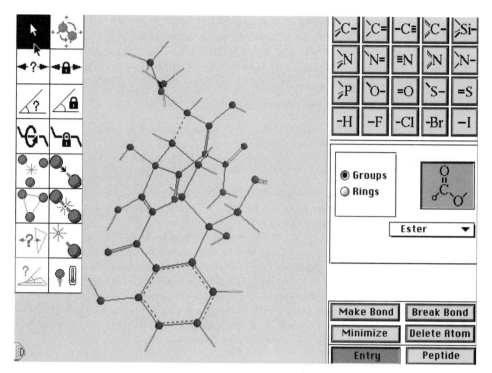

Figure 6-14
MacSpartan allows modification and construction of molecules.

Figure 6-13). Such tools also enable learners to modify or construct new molecules. In Figure 6-14, students can examine chemical bonds using the tools on the left or modify molecules by selecting new ions (at right) to bond. Visualization tools make the abstract real and help students understand chemical concepts that are difficult to convey in static displays.

Chapter 15 will describe how visualization tools can be used to model different phenomena.

SUMMARY

Qualitative representation of a problem is an essential process in understanding the problem conceptually. Learners need to develop conceptual understanding of the problems they are solving so that they can transfer their skills to new situations.

A variety of Mindtools can be used to qualitatively represent problems. Databases help organize the domain knowledge of problem solvers. Concept maps can also provide the organization necessary to solve a problem. Spreadsheets support model building for problems in mathematics and the sciences. Problem solvers in any subject area may be aided by expert systems, which are rule-based systems for modeling causal relationships. Systems modeling tools are especially effective for modeling problems. Visualization tools assist learners in solving abstract problems that are difficult to understand. These tools should be integrated with other problem-solving activities to achieve the greatest learning effects.

REFERENCES

Ploetzner, R., & Spada, H. (1993). Multiple mental representations of information in physics problems. In G. Strube & K. F. Wender (Eds.), *The cognitive psychology of knowledge.* Amsterdam: Elsevier.

Ploetzner, R., Fehse, E., Kneser, C., & Spada, H. (1999). Learning to relate qualitative and quantitative problem representations in a model-based setting for collaborative problem solving. *Journal of the Learning Sciences, 8*(2), 177–214.

Savelsbergh, E. R., de Jong, T., & Ferguson-Hessler, M. G. M. *Physics learning with a computer algebra system: Towards a learning environment that promotes enhanced problem representations.* (ERIC Document Reproduction Service No. ED421346)

Starfield, A. M., Smith, K. A., & Bleloch, A. L. (1990). *How to model it: Problem solving for the computer age.* New York: McGraw-Hill.

Modeling Experiences: Capturing and Indexing Stories

Chapters 4 through 6 showed how Mindtools can be used to construct models of subject content, systems, and problems. Chapter 7 focuses on an unusual, yet powerful, form of knowledge representation: stories. Although stories are not normally used in schools to represent ideas, stories are perhaps the most commonly used representation in informal and everyday settings.

ANALYZING STORIES

To be part of a culture, it is necessary to be connected to the stories that abound in that culture (Bruner, 1990). Telling stories is a primary means for negotiating meanings (Bruner, 1990), and stories assist us in understanding human action, intentionality, and temporality (Bruner, 1990; Huberman, 1995). Perhaps more importantly, stories help us to articulate our identity (Polkinghorne, 1988).

Stories can function as a substitute for direct experience. If we assume that we learn from experiences, then we should be able to learn from stories of other people's experiences. Many of our decisions are based on the experiences of other people. Some people believe that hearing stories is tantamount to experiencing the phenomena oneself (Ferguson, Bareiss, Birnbaum, & Osgood, 1991).

Stories are a primary medium for learning. Practitioners in many fields provide explanations to each other in narrative form. They work with case histories and use narrative explanations to understand why the people they work with behave the way they do (Polkinghorne, 1988). Schön (1993) found that architects, engineers, and psychotherapists encoded their experiences in narrative form by using case histories and narrative explanations. These practitioners offered stories to explain and justify their thinking and actions. For these practitioners, "storytelling represents and substitutes for firsthand experience" (p. 160).

The implication of the ubiquity of stories is that rather than studying content, students might analyze the stories and experiences of others for what they have to teach. If you replay and analyze most any conversation, you will find that it probably contains a series of stories. One person tells a story to make a point, which reminds other conversants of related events, so they tell stories, which remind other conversants of stories, and so on. Why do people use stories to support conversation? Because people remember so much of what they know in the form of stories. Stories are rich and powerful formalisms for storing and describing memories. So one way of understanding what people know is to analyze their stories, and one method of analysis is case-based reasoning (CBR).

CBR is a method of artificial intelligence for representing what people know. CBR claims that what people know is stored in memory as stories (Schank, 1990). In any new situation, people examine the situation and attempt to retrieve a previously experienced situation that resembles the current situation. Along with information about the situation, people retrieve the lessons that that situation teaches. New problems are solved by recalling similar cases and applying the lessons from those experiences to the new situations.

MODELING EXPERIENCES IN DATABASES

Students can engage conceptual change by modeling people's experiences, which is a form of ethnography. Students carry out this process by collecting stories about their experiences, indexing them, and storing them. After we collect stories, we must decide what the stories teach us.

People tell stories with some point in mind, so the indexing process tries to elucidate that point in a given situation. Schank (1990) believes that indexes should include the experience and the themes, goals, plans, results, and lessons from the story. Themes are the subjects that people talk about. Goals motivate the experience. Plans are personal approaches to accomplishing those goals. Results describe the outcome of the experience. The lesson is the moral of the story—the principle that should be taken away from the case. Indexing is an engaging analytical process, the primary goal of which is to make stories accessible. While indexing a story, we must continually ask ourselves under what situations we would be reminded of this story.

After determining the indexes for stories, students find excerpts in the stories that represent each index. The most commonly used tool for storing and accessing stories is the database (see Chapter 9). Each index becomes a field, and each story is a record. Recall the database in Figure 2-5, which recounts one of many stories that were collected by students studying the conflict in Northern Ireland. The database contains stories that have been indexed by topic, theme, context, goal, reasoning, religion, and so on.

When students analyze stories to understand issues, they better understand the underlying complexity of any phenomenon in terms of the diverse social, cultural, political, and personal perspectives reflected in the stories. Encountering diversity of beliefs provides anomalous data that may entail the need to change one's conceptual models of the world. From a CBR perspective, learning is a process of indexing and filing experience-based lessons and reusing those lessons in similar situations in the future. In the example of Northern Ireland, students learn about the horrors of religious conflict by examining the experiences of others.

Jonassen, Wang, Strobel, and Cernusca (2003) described the construction and implementation of a case library of technology integration stories shared by teachers. This library, Knowledge Innovation for Technology in Education (KITE), was funded by a PT3 (Preparing Tomorrow's Teachers to Use Technology) grant from the U.S. Department of Education (kite.missouri.edu). We interviewed more than 1,000 teachers and asked each to share with us a story about a use of technology in the classroom. After each story was submitted, we had to decide what the story taught us, so the stories were indexed. These indexes became the fields in an Oracle database.

Stories (see Figure 7-1 for an example) are retrieved from the database using a sophisticated search algorithm that compares the similarity of a query to all of the cases (records) in the database. Stories of teachers' experiences may be retrieved to help newer teachers learn about ways to use technologies in the classroom. Stories can also be accessed automatically to support a learning environment; for example, when a learner commits an error or asks a question, he or she is told a story instead of being presented with objective (right or wrong) feedback. If a new case "is instructive such that it teaches a lesson for the future that could not have been inferred easily from the cases already recorded, then record it as a case" (Kolodner, 1993, p. 12).

Databases are effective for collecting stories because they enable learners to search or sort on any field to locate similar cases or results. Sophisticated search algorithms are useful but not necessary to use a database of stories. A search based on multiple search criteria can provide helpful stories to learners.

Index	Content
General Context	
Teaching experience	17
Teacher technology experience/skill level	used consistently at home and in classroom;
Kind of school	junior high (7-8 or 7-9)
School location	suburban(major city)
Connectivity	link to world (WWW)
Location of technology resources	primarily in labs
Social economical situation of student	mixed (all classes)
Story Context	
Grade level of students	grade 8;
Subject/unit	science;
Course	
Goal in Story	
Planned activities in lesson	creating a student centered environment;
Level of learning outcome sought	designing a product, method, or process; modeling a system or object;
Standards	activity generally relates to more than one standard;
Story Activities	
Technologies used in lesson	internet searching, Web pages/linklist;
Reason for using technology	heard about it at a conference;
Nature of activities	creative, situated in captivating and challenging activities;
Difficulties run into	
Repair strategies	
Help/assistance used	none;
Role of teacher	facilitator, supporting collaborative problem solving; director, giving structured learning activities and explicit directions;
Role of student	explorer, discover concepts and connections; student, learning through structured activities; experimenter, trying out new processes;
Outcomes	
Observations	students performing required activity;
Assessment of learning	quiz; test/exam; subjective assessment (e.g. observation);
Lessons learned	

Figure 7-1
Story retrieved from KITE database.

LEARNING BY INDEXING

The process of indexing stories for storage in a database can be a powerful learning experience. In a series of studies (Atman & Bursic, 1998; Atman & Turns, 2001), students assumed the roles of researchers as they indexed the transcripts of problem-solving sessions. Rather than studying about how to solve problems, the students analyzed the written transcripts (stories) of problem-solving sessions conducted by other students. That is, they learned how to solve problems by analyzing how others solved problems.

Students were given the transcripts of problem-solving sessions in which other students were working in pairs to design a ping-pong ball launcher, a playground, or some other product. Participants in these sessions had been asked to think aloud (verbalize their thoughts) throughout their problem-solving process. The students who were analyzing the transcripts identified message units in the protocols and classified the purpose of each message according to the following categories:

- Identify need for solving problem
- Identify problem, constraints, and criteria
- Gather information beyond that provided in the problem statement
- Generate ideas for solutions
- Develop a model of the problems
- Determine feasibility of solutions
- Evaluate alternative solutions
- Make a decision
- Communicate decision and instructions to others
- Implement solution and draw implications

These categories were generated based on textbook descriptions of engineering design processes. Each student classified each message individually, then met with another coder to arbitrate differences among their classifications. Some differences were impossible to reconcile; nevertheless, agreement among student coders was high.

What is most significant about this process is that the students indexing the transcripts were learning about design by analyzing design activities (experiences), not principles or theories. Their analysis helped them to better understand the design process, appreciate the complexity and ambiguities implicit in the design process, and evaluate uses of alternative strategies for designing. I believe that indexing stories of practice is a powerful activity for helping students to learn how to become problem solvers.

MODELING EXPERIENCES WITH HYPERMEDIA

Another way of learning with stories is to tell stories about people. Those stories may be in the form of biographies and documentaries or ethnographies.

Biography

A few years back, my colleagues and I studied how students composed hypermedia stories of famous people, along with how they linked documents, how they used media, and how they socially constructed their knowledge. We asked these questions: How will students compose? How will they collaborate? How will they approach and deal with the new environment? How will they work through links and spaces? How will they use media? How will they deal with the constraints and potentials of the technology?

During the course of the study, seventh-grade students worked on biographies of famous historical figures. They collected multimedia artifacts—sounds, images, videos, and texts—which they digitized for use in constructing a Storyspace (my

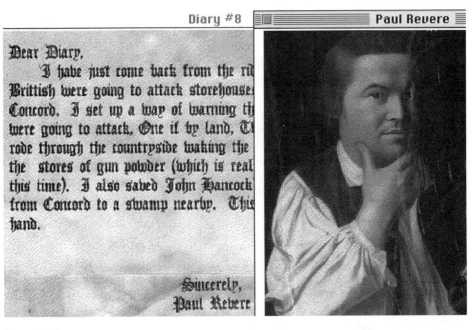

Diary #8   Paul Revere

Dear Diary,

    I have just come back from the ri[...] Brittish were going to attack storehouse[...] Concord. I set up a way of warning t[...] were going to attack. One if by land. T[...] rode through the countryside making the [...] the stores of gun powder (which is real [...] this time). I also saved John Hancock [...] from Concord to a swamp nearby. Th[...] hand.

        Sincerely,
        Paul Revere

Figure 7-2
Diary entry produced by seventh-grade students in a biography telling the story of Paul Revere.

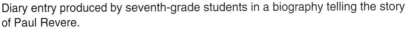

favorite hypermedia authoring system for students) multimedia document. In addition to using this hypermedia tool, each student developed skills in using the following tools: SoundEdit Pro for digitizing voiceovers and music; Adobe Premiere for digitizing video and creating original QuickTime movies; Adobe Photoshop linked to Desk Scan for digitizing images; and ClarisWorks for word processing.

    The student biographers chose personally relevant individuals, including John Kennedy, Colin Powell, Saddam Hussein, Paul Revere, Martin Luther, and Mother Seton. They brainstormed ways to present the projects such as dressing up as Martin Luther (homemade monk outfit and all), sitting Paul Revere atop a horse and filming part of the famous ride, and capturing part of the Kennedy assassination video from the movie *J.F.K.* One group decided to focus on a family tree to introduce their subject. The students chose to tell their biographies from the first-person perspective; all introduced their individual in a movie with first-person monologues. Students maintained some sort of first-person narrative throughout their hypermedia knowledge bases. One group chose to recount Paul Revere's life through a series of diary entries (see Figure 7-2).

    The students wrote scripts and narratives, scanned images, recorded and digitized sound, created movies, and planned and executed Story biographies, which were episodic models of the peoples' lives expressed through narratives. Research on reading has consistently shown that narrative forms of representation are much better remembered and understood than declarative forms. Most of the linking

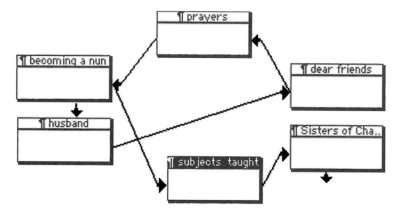

Figure 7-3
Web view of Storyspace document.

that the students did was implicit in the narrative structures in which their projects were presented.

Storyspace, the hypermedia program students used, also provides a Web view that graphically presents links between spaces. Figure 7-3 shows the topical organization of one group's project on Mother Seton. Each space (node on the map) in this Web view has two features: (1) the title of the space, which when clicked on reveals a window for writing text and media, called the writing space; and (2) the organizational space, in which subordinate spaces are represented by identical miniature boxes. The strings between nodes or spaces indicate author-generated hyperlinks between text or other media contained in each of the writing spaces. Not all of the links in a document are visible at one time, because each space can contain more spaces inside spaces inside spaces and so on. When the user double clicks in the organizational space, a new Web view of the next hierarchical level of spaces and links is displayed. A single click on the title of the space "becoming a nun" in Figure 7-3 reveals the writing space in which words, graphics, music, and video clips have been placed.

The level of student involvment in these biographical projects was incredible. Students came to school early and stayed late. They worked during their free periods and lunch periods. When they showed their projects to other students, teachers, and parents, their sense of ownership of the projects was overwhelming.

Ethnography

Conversational learners naturally seek opinions and ideas from others in order to become part of the knowledge-building and discourse communities. Reflective learners articulate what they are doing, the decisions they are making, the strategies they are using, and the answers they are finding, while reflecting on the meaningfulness of it all. Multimedia environments may be used to engage both conversational and reflective learning, in this case, through multimedia ethnography.

Figure 7-4
Perspectives available from Learning Constellations knowledge base.

Ethnographers are persons who investigate the customs, habits, and social behaviors of races and peoples. Ethnography has traditionally been used to research native, indigenous populations. Goldman-Segall (1992, 1995) developed a multimedia platform called Learning Constellations for supporting ethnographic investigations and interpretations by students. Learning Constellations allows students to construct multimedia programs, including videos, pictures, and narratives written by them, about the topic of investigation. For example, students of Goldman-Segall have used Learning Constellations to investigate the effects of clear-cutting in the rain forests of British Columbia and to examine the lives and histories of the First Nations of British Columbia.

Learning Constellations also allows readers to contribute their own interpretations of original stories or create their own stories. These stories come from multiple authors (Goldman-Segall uses the term *multiloguing,* rather than dialoguing) and are linked together in clusters or constellations of perspectives. These multilogues produce what Geertz (1973) calls "thick descriptions" of phenomena. The constellations of videos and stories that students produce represent larger and different patterns of meaning about the topics being studied (see Figure 7-4). "Layers build; stories change; patterns emerge; and inquiry becomes reflexive practice" (Goldman-Segall, 1995, p. 6). It is that kind of reflection that makes Learning Constellations a powerful multimedia experience.

Figure 7-5
Available perspectives provided by student ethnographies.

The student storytelling afforded by Learning Constellations leads to the social construction of knowledge. Students work together to investigate issues in multiple levels of conversation (see Figure 7-5). Students go out into the real world and investigate socially relevant problems. They collect evidence about those problems, usually in the form of video interviews and documentaries. They analyze, digitize, and assemble those videos into multiple-voice story chunks, called "stars," which include the videos and student annotations of them. These stars, produced and told by different people to represent their unique points of view, are assembled into larger groupings called "constellations." As other students or the public examine the students' multimedia database, they add their own views and annotations. Why? It is in "the process of making discoveries and the process of recursive reaction, within the data and among the users, that meaning of an event, action, or situation can be negotiated" (Goldman-Segall, 1992, p. 258).

When teachers have students design and film their own video narratives, they are creating a video culture in the classroom—not a passive culture of viewing video but a culture of constructing videos to tell a complex and important story. In becoming a video ethnographer, a student (1) becomes a friend of the camera; (2) becomes a participant recorder by training fellow researchers, teachers, and students on how to use video for observation; (3) becomes a storyteller by selecting video chunks and writing narratives; and (4) becomes a navigator by exploring the use of video in new situations (Goldman-Segall, 1992).

SUMMARY

Stories represent the oldest and most commonly used forms of sense making. Being part of a culture means knowing the stories in the culture. History is most naturally conveyed in the form of stories, and our understanding of events is best represented in the form of stories that convey the human experience.

The process of indexing stories for storage in a database is a powerful learning activity that helps students become problem solvers. Student construction of stories—for example, biographies and ethnographies—helps students to better understand phenomena. I am not arguing that stories should replace more declarative forms of representation, just that they should supplement them. Because storytelling is such a natural form of human communication, it can become a powerful tool of human learning.

REFERENCES

Atman, C. J., & Bursic, K. M. (1998). Verbal analysis protocols as a method to document engineering students' design processes. *Journal of Engineering Education, 87*(2), 121–132.

Atman, C. J., & Turns, J. (2001). Studying engineering design learning: Four verbal protocol studies. In C. Eastman, M. McCracken, & W. Newstetter (Eds.), *Knowing and learning to design: Cognitive perspectives in design education.* New York: Elsevier.

Bruner, J. (1990). *Acts of meaning.* Cambridge: Harvard University Press.

Ferguson, W., Bareiss, R., Birnbaum, L., & Osgood, R. (1991). ASK systems: An approach to the realization of story-based teachers. *Journal of the Learning Sciences, 2*(1), 95–134.

Geertz, C. (1973). *The interpretation of cultures.* New York: Basic Books.

Goldman-Segall, R. (1992). Collaborative virtual communities: Using Learning Constellations, a multimedia ethnographic research tool. In E. Barrett (Ed.), *Sociomedia: Multimedia, hypermedia, and the social construction of knowledge.* Cambridge, MA: MIT Press.

Goldman-Segall, R. (1995). Configurational validity: A proposal for analyzing ethnographic multimedia narratives. *Journal of Educational Multimedia and Hypermedia, 4*(2).

Huberman, M. (1995). Working with life-history narratives. In H. McEwan & K. Egan (Eds.), *Narrative in Teaching, Learning, and Research.* New York: Teachers College Press.

Jonassen, D. H., Wang, F. K., Strobel, J., & Cernusca, D. (2003). Application of a case library of technology integration stories for teachers. *Journal of Technology and Teacher Education, 11*(4), 547–566.

Kolodner, J. (1993). *Case-based reasoning.* New York: Morgan Kaufman.

Polkinghorne, D. (1988). *Narrative knowing and the human sciences.* Albany: State University of New York Press.

Schank, R. C. (1990). *Tell me a story: Narrative and intelligence.* Evanston, IL: Northwestern University Press.

Schön, D. A. (1993). The reflective practitioner—how professionals think in action. New York: Basic Books.

CHAPTER 8

Modeling Thinking by Building Cognitive Simulations

The previous four chapters focused on how to use Mindtools to model knowledge, systems, problems, and stories. The chapters described models of cognition, that is, different representations of what learners know.

This chapter promotes the use of Mindtools for modeling metacognition. The term *metacognition* encompasses a variety of activities and processes for becoming aware of one's cognitive processes (cognition about cognition, ergo metacognition). The processes involved in metacognition are normally thought to be monitoring one's cognitive processes and adapting one's cognitive processes using higher level executive processes. For our purposes, metacognition occurs when "one must stand back from a particular mental activity and comment on the activity rather than participating in it" (Reisberg, 1997). Metacognitive processes are important skills that are required for most higher order thinking processes. Many researchers have shown that good problem solvers differ from poor problem solvers in their use of metacognition (Davidson, Deuser, & Sternberg, 1994). Just as model building enhances cognition, model building can engage metacognition. Use of Mindtools to build models of cognition is an explicitly powerful metacognitive strategy.

CONSTRUCTING COGNITIVE SIMULATIONS

When we create models of cognition, we are constructing what are otherwise known as cognitive simulations. "Cognitive simulations are runable computer programs that represent models of human cognitive activities" (Roth, Woods, & People, 1992, p. 1163). They attempt to model mental structures and human cognitive processes. "The computer program contains explicit representations of proposed mental processes and knowledge structures" (Kieras, 1990, pp. 51–52).

The primary purpose of cognitive simulations is to reify mental constructs for analysis and theory building, that is, to manifest theories and models of human mental functioning. Recall Figures 1-1 and 1-3, which used the systems modeling tool Stella to represent two different theories of conceptual change. In all of my learning courses I require students to build cognitive simulations of the processes that we are studying. Rather than reading about cognition and learning, students construct simulation models. Cognitive simulations provide a medium for testing their models of learning theories.

Cognitive simulations were originated by Newell and Simon (1972) during the information processing revolution in psychology. Computers were being used to represent the way that humans processed information, and development of a runable computer model of those operations seemed to be the most scientific way to operationalize them. Cognitive simulations have always represented the junction of psychology and computer science. Earlier, the tools that computer scientists and psychologists used to build cognitive simulations were complex and computationally intensive. Most of the Mindtools described in this book, however, can be used by non-mathematicians to build cognitive simulations.

Traditionally, cognitive simulations were built to represent cognitive processes for the purpose of building intelligent tutoring systems. Such tutoring systems are complex computer programs that diagnose student understanding and adapt instruction to meet those needs. Cognitive simulations were built to represent how the expert thinks and how the learner thinks. The tutor uses a set of rules (see Chapter 12) to generate appropriate instructional interactions to reduce the discrepancy between the expert and the student. For example, while building an intelligent tutor, Roth et al. (1992) built cognitive simulations for identifying the cognitive activities involved in fault management under dynamic conditions in nuclear power plants.

DEVELOPING AN EXPERT SYSTEM TO SIMULATE REASONING

People who learn the most from intelligent tutoring systems are the ones who build them. So rather than having psychologists and computer scientists build cognitive simulations to control teaching programs, we, the teachers, ought to provide learners with tools to build their own simulations of their own activities. When they do, they are engaged in metacognition.

The implications of building cognitive simulations appear most obvious for courses in psychology, where learners are studying about cognition. In a seminar that I conducted some years ago, we were studying metacognition. After reading many papers and chapters, students all knew what metacognition was, but they did not fully understand how people came to use metacognitive strategies. So we (Jonassen & Wang, 2003) initiated a project in which the class would develop an expert system to simulate that reasoning process. The purpose of the project was to model how learners use metacognitive reasoning when learning in a defined context, specifically in this seminar itself. So we reflected on the processes that we all used to study for the seminar.

The procedure for building this rule-based cognitive simulation included identifying the range of learning strategies that can be used by learners (the outcomes). These include information-processing strategies such as recall, organization, integration, and elaboration strategies. Next, we identified the factors or variables that are needed to represent metacognitive decision making. This analysis led to a cognitive simulation with two rule bases: an executive control base and a comprehension-monitoring rule base. We used a commercial expert system shell (see Chapter 12) to enter, debug, and refine the rule bases (see Figure 8-1).

```
ASK: "Why am I studying this material?
Assigned = Material was assigned by professor
Related = Material is useful to related research or studies
Personal = Material is of personal interest"

ASK: "How well do I need to know this material?
Gist = I just need to comprehend the main ideas.
Discuss = We will discuss and interrelate the issues.
Evaluate = I have to judge the importance or accuracy of these ideas.
Generate = I have to think up issues, new ideas, hypotheses about the material."

ASK: "How fast of a reader am I?"
CHOICES: slow, normal, fast

ASK: "How many hours do I have to study?
None = Less than an hour
Few = 1 - 3 hours
Several = 4 - 8 hours"

ASK: "How many days until class?"
CHOICES Days: more_than_7, 2_to_6,less_than_2

ASK: "How do I compare with the other students in the class?
Superior = I think that I am better able than my classmates to comprehend the material.
Equal = I am equivalent to the rest of the class in ability.
Worse = I am not as knowledgeable or intelligent as the rest of the class."
```

Figure 8-1
Metacognitive factors in cognitive simulation of studying for a seminar.

The process of generating and testing a system of rules is complex. We originally began with 6 primary factors, which later grew to more than 20 to represent the complexity of the personal decision-making process. Because participants in the construction process of the knowledge base reflected on their own personal processes during the discussions, many different perspectives had to be accommodated in the rule bases. Initially, we intended to build an abstract model of metacognitive reasoning that could represent metacognition in different contexts. It became obvious that such a goal was not only impossible but meaningless, because metacognition could only be thought of in the context of a particular learning need.

The development process was highly iterative; it involved extensive discussions and intense self-reflections about our own methods. Development of the rule bases indicated the need for several overlapping or redundant factors, so eventually we combined the two rule bases into one. The merged rule base modeled the initial phases of engaging metacognitive processes, most of which normally take place before studying begins. Crucial elements of metacognition were identified through rule base construction:

◆ Depth of processing required by the subject matter
◆ Learner characteristics (prior knowledge, preferred learning style, etc.)
◆ Task variables (level of mastery required, difficulty of the material, time available, etc.)
◆ Kinds of support strategies that would facilitate maximum efficiency in studying (e.g., comfort of the studying environment and learner's energy level, attitude toward the task, and perceived self-efficacy)

After the expert system elicits this information from a user, the system describes the results—a set of study, metacognitive, and support strategies that would best facilitate the learning outcomes desired. This description represents a simulation of the thought processes that we believed (based on reading, understanding, research, and a lot of self-reflection) learners engage in when studying for a seminar. Inevitably, different groups of developers given the same task would generate different outcomes, factors, and rules. In the construction of simulations, there is no single right answer. It is instructive to contrast knowledge bases produced by different groups given the same topic.

The results of using an expert system to represent thinking processes have been varied. The students in my seminar who participated in constructing the cognitive simulation made significantly more contributions to the seminar discussion and had stronger opinions about the material.

A few other researchers have experimented with constructing cognitive simulations. Kersten, Badcock, Iglewski, and Mallory (1990) demonstrated the use of rule-based expert systems for simulating how negotiations progress. In a study reported by Law (1994), high school students used expert systems to simulate commonsense reasoning. Student reflection on their own thinking is the essence of metacognition. Expert systems provide a powerful formalism for thinking about and simulating how we think.

USING SYSTEMS DYNAMICS TOOLS TO SIMULATE THINKING

Systems dynamics tools (see Chapter 13) can also play a role in constructing cognitive simulations. Figure 8-2 is a Stella model of motivation. The model ties motivation to success and failure factors at the top of the model, and to several components of cognition—level of satisfaction, expectancy levels, relevance, effort,

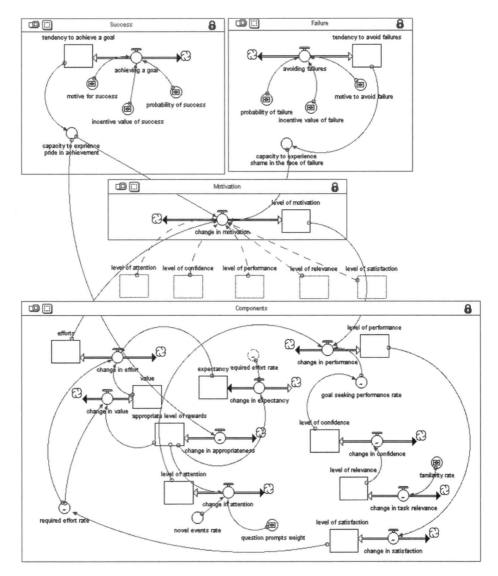

Figure 8-2
Stella model of motivation.

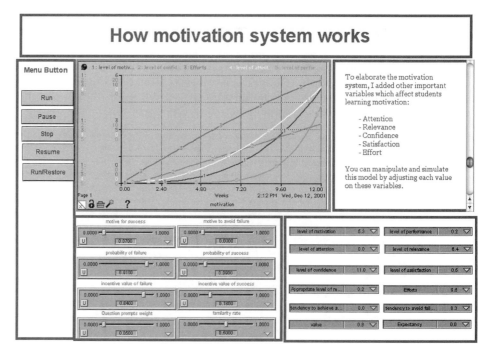

Figure 8-3
Simulation of motivation produced by model in Figure 8-2.

performance and so on—at the bottom of the model. In other words, the level of motivation in this person's model is controlled by achieving success and avoiding failure as well as by many expectancy levels. As described earlier, a good cognitive simulation is runable. Stella enables models that are built to be tested. Figure 8-3 illustrates the simulation produced by the model in Figure 8-2. Users may vary the levels of motives for success or failure such as probability of failure, incentive values, and so on and see the effects of their manipulations in a graph (e.g., Figure 8-3). They can run the simulation again and again.

One of the most powerful activities model-building learners can engage in is to compare and contrast their models with those of others in regard to assumptions, components, and relationships. For example, the Stella model shown in Figure 8-4 contrasts sharply with the model shown in Figure 8-2. The model in Figure 8-4 focuses on engagement and persistence, instead of success and failure (Figure 8-2) as performance indicators of motivation. The students who built these two models obviously constructed different theories about motivation. Which one is more accurate? Although these models share some conceptual characteristics, their differences are significant and merit extended discussions. Another powerful strategy is to require learners to find empirical proof to support their model. If the data are not consistent with the model output, then the model must be debugged. Changing the model to validate research results may be the most engaging activity that students can share.

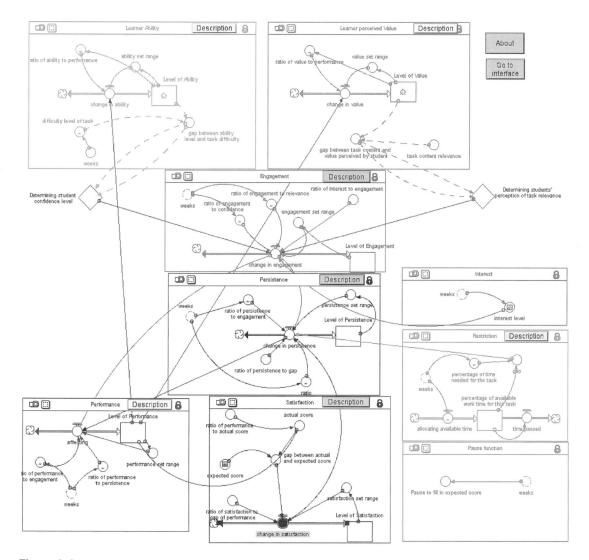

Figure 8-4
Alternative model of motivation.

SUMMARY

This chapter encourages modeling the ways that we think (i.e., metacognition) rather than the thinking processes themselves. Building cognitive simulations of learning activities necessarily engages learners in metacognition. Expert systems (IF-THEN rule systems) and systems modeling tools can be used to build and test student models of cognition. Expert systems are more qualitative representations than systems models, but they are simpler to learn how to use.

We need to conduct research to compare the effects of building cognitive simulations with other metacognitive activities such as journaling, think-alouds, and others. The reification of the thinking processes that is supported by model building will likely be shown to be more effective.

Not all of the Mindtools that will be discussed in forthcoming chapters will be equally effective for building cognitive simulations. The more effective tools are likely to be the dynamic modeling tools, like spreadsheets (Chapter 11), expert systems (Chapter 12), and systems modeling tools (Chapter 13), because they are runable. That is, once the model is built, it can be tested by running it. If the results support conceptual predictions, the model is probably fairly good. If the model produces unexpected results, then it needs to be examined for its assumptions or relationships. Debugging a conceptual model is perhaps the most conceptually engaging task that students can do. It is definitely worth the effort.

REFERENCES

Davidson, J. E., Deuser, R., & Sternberg, R. J. (1994). The role of metacognition in problem solving. In J. Metcalfe & A. Shimamura (Eds.), *Metacognition: Knowing about knowing* (pp. 207–226). Cambridge, MA: MIT Press.

Jonassen, D. H., & Wang, S. (2003). Using expert systems to build cognitive simulations. *Journal of Educational Computing Research, 28*(1), 1–13.

Kieras, D. (1990). The role of cognitive simulation models in the development of advanced training and testing systems. In N. Frederickson, R. Glaser, A. Lesgold, & M. G. Shafto (Eds.), *Diagnostic monitoring of skill and knowledge acquisition.* Hillsdale, NJ: Lawrence Erlbaum.

Kersten, G. E., Badcock, L., Iglewski, M., & Mallory, G. R. (1990). Structuring and simulating negotiation: An approach and an example. *Theory and Decision, 28*(3), 243–273.

Law, N. (1994). Students as expert system developers: A means of eliciting and understanding common sense reasoning. *Journal of Research on Computing in Education, 26*(4), 497–513.

Newell, A., & Simon, H. (1972). *Human problem solving.* Upper Saddle River, NJ: Prentice Hall.

Reisberg, D. (1997). *Cognition: Exploring the mind.* New York: Norton.

Roth, E. M., Woods, D. D., & People, H. E. (1992). Cognitive simulation as a tool for cognitive task analysis. *Ergonomics, 35*(10), 1163–1198.

PART THREE

Modeling Tools (Mindtools)

CHAPTER 9

Modeling with Databases

Database management systems (DBMSs) are computerized record-keeping systems. They were originally designed to replace paper-based information retrieval systems. DBMSs are, in effect, electronic filing cabinets that allow users to store information in an organized filing system and later retrieve that information. The advantages offered by computerized information storage include compactness, speed of entering information into the system (directly via the keyboard, bar code readers, scanners, or even voice), faster and easier access to information in the system, and easier updating of information in the system.

DATABASE MANAGEMENT SYSTEMS: COMPONENTS AND TOOLS

Database management systems consist of several components: the database, a file management system, database organization tools, and reporting (printing) functions. A database consists of one or more files, each of which contains information in the

Record	Field 1 Last Name	Field 2 First Name	Field 3 Address	Field 4 City	Field 5 State	Field 6 Zip
1	Smith	John	123 Maple Drive	Columbus	Ohio	54211
2	Buchanon	Peggy	4700 Oglethorpe	Moose	Oregon	90202
3	Fernandez	Jose	6325 VanBuren E	Los Angeles	California	95543
4	Richmond	Aletha	321 Aspen Way	Craig	Colorado	80437
etc						

Figure 9-1
Database structure.

form of collections of records that are related to a content domain, event, or set of objects (e.g., an individual's account information). Each record in the database is divided into fields that describe the class or type of information contained therein. The same type of information for each record is stored in each field. For example, the address database in Figure 9-1 contains four records, each with information about a different individual. These records are systematically broken down into fields (subunits of each record) that define a common pattern of information. The database in Figure 9-1 contains six fields: one for the last name, one for the first name, one for the street address, one for the city, one for the state, and one for the zip code. The content and arrangement of each field are standardized within the records, which enables the computer to locate a particular kind of information quickly.

Database-manipulation tools permit the user to organize and reorganize the information to answer queries. The primary tools are searching, sorting, and retrieving information. For example, you can use the file management capability of the DBMS to create a file that contains the class schedule of each student in a school. You could save that file, access it, and change it to reflect changes in schedules using the file management and editing capabilities of the DBMS. If a student were transferred to another class during fourth period, you would open the file, find the student's record in the database (by searching in the name field for that student's name), move across the record to the correct period, and change the information in the file.

Organization tools provide important functions in DBMSs. The search tool allows you to search through the database to find specific information. For example, you may search on the name field for a particular student's name because you know that the student's record contains information you need. For instance, you could search through the name field for "Smith." Search capabilities vary with each system, but most systems allow you to tailor your search using different requests. You could search the name field, for example, for records that EQUALS Smith. Such a search request would show every record that contains the word "Smith" and nothing more. Searching using CONTAINS Smith would produce every record that has the letters SMITH in it, though there could be additional letters, such as in Smith*son* or Smith*field*. EQUALS is a much more limiting search term, so it would be used if you wanted to refine your search. For example, you could search the database for all students scheduled into Mr. Brown's social studies class during fourth period. This information would be useful for printing grade sheets or interim reports.

Another common search feature is the NOT function. Searching a database field using NOT Smith would show every record in the database except those with Smith in the field. Most DBMSs support search methods that can search a date or number field for values greater than, equal to, or less than a particular value. Most DBMSs also permit you to identify multiple search criteria; that is, they allow you to search simultaneously on more than one field. For example, if you wanted to find all the Smiths in the eighth grade, you would make a search that identifies name field EQUALS Smith and grade EQUALS 8.

Another function that is important in the use of databases as Mindtools is the sort function, which enables you to rearrange the contents of the database in ascending or descending order according to one or more of the fields. For example, if you sorted on Field 1, Last Name, in the database shown in Figure 9-1, then the order of the records would change, with Buchanon appearing first, followed by Fernandez, Richmond, and Smith.

Essentially, DBMSs allow you to store information in an organized way and to locate or arrange the information in the database to help you answer queries about that information. The examples that have been used here to illustrate DBMS features all relate to administrative purposes (e.g., attendance, scheduling, student records). When using DBMSs as Mindtools, students use the same functions to analyze and enter subject-matter content into databases. The databases can then be searched and sorted to answer specific questions about content or to seek interrelationships and inferences among content subjects.

DBMSs also possess file management capabilities that allow users to create and define new database files. Once the data structure is defined, information can be entered into or deleted from the file. Any database file can be saved on a disk, deleted, copied, or saved under a new name. These file management functions enable users to make permanent copies of the information in the database.

The ease, capacity, and speed with which DBMS activities can be accomplished vary with each system. Many databases also possess security features and the capacity to integrate with other databases.

RELATIONAL DATABASES

The kind of database described so far in this chapter is referred to as a flat file or table, a two-dimensional organization of content into fields and records. Such databases use pointers (structural computer codes embedded in the file) to connect records in the database file. Early file management systems used to store and retrieve information in these flat files were weak compared with today's powerful DBMSs. For instance, in early systems the data model (organization of data into fields) could not be changed after the model was identified. If you wanted to add a new field to include a new kind of information, you had to start over by building a new database. In the past two decades of personal computing, database systems have become much more powerful and flexible. Most database programs have become more relational.

A relational database is a collection of relations or tables of different sizes and organization that are interconnected in a network-like manner based on the kind of data contained in the fields and records, not on pointers. Information contained in different files can be interrelated through key relationships, so that information does not have to be duplicated in more than one file. The order of rows and columns (records and fields) is insignificant. Relational databases permit more sophisticated organization and queries. They enable users to combine, compare, contrast, or otherwise interrelate information in several databases (tables). In comparison to flat files, relational databases can support a higher level of content analysis by more advanced learners.

MODELING WITH DATABASES

When students model phenomena with database management systems, they are required to integrate and interrelate content ideas into one or more matrices. Matrices are an effective way to represent information to support comparison-contrast reasoning. Schwartz (1971) found that matrix representations of information were substantially superior to groups, graphs, and sentences for representing problems, because matrix representations clearly define needed information, suggest orders of operations, and provide consistency checks for partial solutions. Matrices also reduce the load on memory (Polich & Schwartz, 1974).

Students who are building databases organize information by identifying the underlying dimensions of the content. For example, health students studying vitamin therapy might want to set up a database in which each vitamin is a record and the characteristics of each vitamin (e.g., dietary sources, physiology, metabolic effects) are the fields. The process of searching for information and creating the database—including deciding which fields are necessary, how large they should be, and how they should be ordered (creating the data model)—can be a meaningful instructional activity.

To build the data model, students must first decide on the appropriate content relationships. Then they must search for the information in a systematic fashion in order to fill the database. For example, Figure 9-2 shows a beginning database for vocabulary learning. Rather than memorizing definitions to learn vocabulary, students can compare and contrast vocabulary words in a database. They can also search and sort the database to generate a variety of comparisons and contrasts based on which fields are selected for searching and sorting. Intellectually, these processes require the organization and integration of a content domain.

A few examples have been reported in the literature where databases have been used as Mindtools:

◆ Goldberg (1992) recommended using databases to classify types of seashells.
◆ According to Rooze (1988–1989), databases have a value in teaching social studies; namely, creating databases places students in an active as opposed to a passive role. In preparing a database, students determine which information to

Vocabulary Chart

word	baseword	related words	definition	synonym	antonym	origin	part of speech	suffix	prefix
admiration	admire	admirer,	process of	respect		french	noun	ation	
contentedly	content	contentment,	in a satisfied way	complacently	disappointedly	french	adverb	ly	
cordially	cordial	cordiality	in a warm and	genially	coldly	mediev	adverb	ly	
description	describe	descriptive,	result of describing	explanation		latin	noun	tion	
digestion	digest	digestibility,	process of	devouring		latin	noun	ion	
explanation	explain	explanatory,	result of explaining	clarification		latin	noun	ation	
freedom	free		state of being free	liberty		old	noun	dom	
illegible	legible	legibly	not legible	unclear	distinct	latin	adjective		il
illiterate	literate	illiteracy,	with literacy	uneducated	learned	latin	adjective		il
illustration	illustrate	illustrator,	state of being	depiction			noun	ion	
immobilized	mobile	immobilization	without mobilization	disabled	capable		adjective	ize	im
impatient	patient	impatiently	not patient	eager	reluctant		adjective		im
inhuman	human	inhumanity,	not human	nasty	nice		adjective		in
invisibility	visible	visor, vision	without visibility	obscurity	discernible		noun	ity	in
irresponsible	response	responses,	not responsible	careless	careful		adjective	ible	ir
irresponsible	response	responsibly,	without	careless	careful		adjective	ible	ir
kingdom	king		domain of a king	realm			noun	dom	
leadership	leader	leadability,	skill of being a	dominance			noun	ship	
motherhood	mother	motherly,	condition of being a				noun	hood	
neighborhood	neighbor	unneighborly,	entire group of	area			noun	hood	
ominously	ominous			threateningly	promisingly		adverb	ly	
partnership	partner		state of being a	alliance			noun	ship	
permission	permit	permisability,	result of permitting	approval			noun	sion	
population	populate	depopulate,	result of populating	community			noun	ion	
suspension	suspend	suspend,	result of	delay	continuance		noun	sion	
tension	tense		state of being tense	anxiety			noun	ion	
unabridged	abridge	abridging,	complete	complete	shortened		adjective		un

Figure 9-2
Beginning database for vocabulary learning.

collect, and organize seemingly unrelated bits of information into meaningful categories. However, if students are to use the database effectively, the teacher must guide (not direct) the development of categories and search procedures. Rooze recommended strategies for concept development and data interpretation in the development and use of databases.

◆ Knight and Timmons (1986) recommended the use of databases to meet the objectives of history instruction.

◆ Pon (1984) described the use of databases as an inquiry tool to aid higher level thinking in a fourth-grade American Indian studies course.

◆ Watson and Strudler (1988–1989) described a lesson based on an inductive thinking model that teaches higher order thinking using databases. According to Watson and Strudler, building databases involves analyzing, synthesizing, and evaluating information.

EVALUATING DATABASES FOR MODELING

What makes an effective database? That depends somewhat on the ages and abilities of the learners who are constructing the database and the content they are trying to represent. Figure 9-3 presents a number of criteria for evaluating the databases that students construct as their knowledge and skills move from emergent to mastery. You will probably want to adapt these or add your own criteria as you evaluate your students' projects. In most cases, the quality of the database will be obvious.

Coaching Modeling with Databases

When should you use databases for modeling students' knowledge in the classroom? Databases are useful for supplementing the learning of concept-rich content, such as that in geography, social studies, and the sciences. They are especially useful when comparing and contrasting different forms, styles, functions, or approaches. For example, the uses of various chemical compounds, the demographics of different countries, and the stylistic elements used by authors in various literary periods are good candidates. Databases allow learners to examine the underlying structure of most course content.

Using databases and performing the kinds of content analysis required to build them will probably require new skills for many learners. Students should develop these skills carefully to meet this ultimate goal: to be able to independently analyze a new content domain in order to (1) determine the appropriate data model; (2) search for information in texts, videos, and other sources to fill in the database; and (3) use the database to create and answer relational queries about the information it contains. Teachers may need to support and guide students through some of the following learning activities and strategies to scaffold the development of database skills. Most students will develop database skills quickly.

STEP 1. Students query a completed database. To introduce students to the functions and organization of a database, you may want to prompt them by having them use an existing database to answer questions about the information contained in the database. Start with a familiar database, perhaps a database of personal information about the students in the class. Require them to search for information in the database (e.g., all students taller than 5 feet, 5 inches) or sort the database (e.g., arrange the class from youngest to oldest). Initially, students will need to be coached through these experiences. The activities familiarize learners with database functions and structure. They also serve as advance organizers or overviews for lessons, and they may facilitate generation of hypotheses.

STEP 2. Students complete existing data structures. Begin with a partially completed database and have students fill in gaps in the database by using their textbooks or going to the library to locate the necessary information. This activity provides students with some existing information for comparing new data and for generalizing. Later, require students to complete full records; that is, provide them with a blank database in which only the fields (data model) are defined. This activity stresses purposeful searching for information rather than general memorization of all information. If you observe textbooks that students have highlighted during reading, you will know that students do not understand how to discriminate important information from trivial information.

The activity of completing a database provides a model for searching and identifying the more important and relevant bits of information.

STEP 3. Students make a plan. Ask students to make a plan for the database. What are they interested in representing? What points do they want to make? What kinds of structure and information are required to make those points? What learning goals will they work toward?

STEP 4. Students adapt existing data structures or design new data structures for other students to complete. Start with familiar content and require students to adapt existing databases (e.g., the classroom information database) or design new databases that they can collaboratively complete. Here you are modeling the organizational skills required to develop data structures. Topics such as local sports teams, dating patterns, and television shows are popular.

STEP 5. Students create and complete data structures. Increase the complexity of the content by relating it to classroom studies. Then, starting with more concrete content (e.g., geographic or demographic features in social studies), have students in groups determine what fields are required. Selection of fields depends on what kinds of questions people have that need to be answered, that is, what kinds of information users may want from the database. Be certain to acquire a DBMS that allows you to add or delete fields after the initial design (some file management systems do not permit this). Compare the data models in class (each group of student will construct a different model) and discuss them in terms of how completely and accurately they reflect the content domain and how well they facilitate access to information. Do the fields allow for efficient searching? Do they represent the content faithfully? This step in modeling with databases is the most complete activity, because it requires learners to identify variables and information needs, build data structures, access information and complete the database, and search the database.

STEP 6. Students write queries for other students. Ask students to write difficult queries that require other students to use multiple search criteria to answer the questions. Students are often challenged by the prospect of constructing queries that are difficult for their fellow students or for teachers to answer. The activity is valuable because it requires learners to think about relationships among and implications of information contained in the database and the ability of the data structure to support various queries. Students will probably require a lot of coaching as they write queries, because these are difficult skills to develop.

STEP 7. Students extrapolate from databases. Encourage students to create new fields in existing databases to support other applications. For example, in a database of geographic information, the addition of political and economic fields of information to support geopolitical queries would be useful. Students may choose to restructure the databases to meet the needs of another class.

STEP 8. Students reflect on the activity. Reflection should not wait until the project is completed. Instead, encourage students to continuously review their progress on the project. Are we achieving our goals? What changes are necessary? How do we compare with other groups? Are we answering questions and making the points that we set out in our plan? After the project is completed, the students should reflect on the project as a whole. What have we learned about the content? What have we learned about database construction and how we represent knowledge? What have we learned about working with each other? You may choose to provide students with some or all of the criteria for evaluating student databases (presented in the next section) to use for self-evaluation. The activity of constructing databases engages meaningful thinking. Reflection cements the knowledge that learners construct.

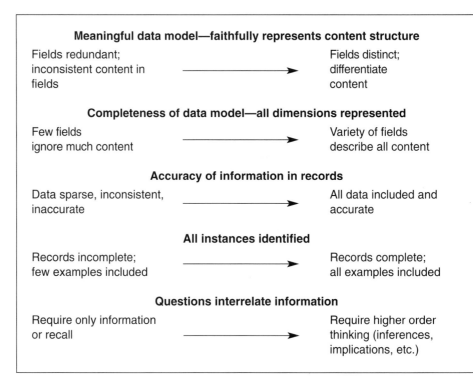

Figure 9-3
Criteria for evaluating student databases.

ADVANTAGES AND LIMITATIONS OF DATABASE MODELING

A number of advantages accrue to learners from using databases for modeling domain knowledge:

◆ The process of creating and manipulating a database is inherently constructive. Therefore, learners are (mentally) actively engaged in constructing representations rather than merely reading or responding to questions.

◆ Learners are actively building knowledge structures, because they are actively engaged in knowledge representation activities. Learners are required to define the nature of the relationships between concepts and to construct records and fields that map those relationships. This activity requires comparison-contrast thinking, which is one of the most basic and essential kinds of cognitive activity.

◆ Learners are exposed to a process of comparing concepts and relationships in the database that is greatly facilitated by the speed and reporting capabilities of the DBMS.

◆ Learners can search their databases in any number of ways, for example, to provide an overview of all types of cells or to compare particular characteristics of different cells.

◆ Learners can try to arrange information in ways that may make more sense to them.

◆ Learners engage in data entry that is easy and often automated in most systems.

Despite the advantages, some problems may occur when databases are used for modeling learner knowledge. Some critics may claim that these database activities produce nothing more than a tabular summary of information that is commonly available in textbooks. It is true that some textbooks provide tabular summaries. However, using databases to model content engages learners in constructing their own tables rather than memorizing those provided for them. The table that each learner constructs will be more personally meaningful, because it will contain the learner's concepts and relationships between those concepts. This generative processing of information is fundamentally different from memorizing tables.

Some teachers may be concerned that the interpretations of content produced by students may be too individualistic or idiosyncratic and that the divergent database representations may confuse students more than enlighten them. Personal knowledge representations, indeed, are individualistic. Students should be encouraged to compare their databases with other students. When they do, they will realize that other people see the world differently. Students can also collaboratively construct databases. Such databases become a medium for socially negotiating a common understanding. For this reason, collaborative database projects will probably be more productive than individual projects.

SUMMARY

Database management systems support the storage and retrieval of information in an organized manner. Structure is inherent in all knowledge, so if learners use a tool that helps them structure what they know, they will facilitate their own understanding. To develop and use databases, learners must analyze and comprehend the information that they store and retrieve. This analysis requires identifying the underlying structural properties of the information. Two important tools in the use of databases are the search function and the sort function.

Although databases are often used as organization and retrieval tools, they can also function especially well as Mindtools. When students construct and query databases, they are building and exemplifying structural models of the content they are studying, and they are using those models to compare and contrast relationships among information contained in their models. That is the kind of meaningful processing of information that students should perform more regularly in schools. The activity necessarily engages higher order thinking in learners, which results in better understanding.

REFERENCES

Goldberg, K. P. (1992). Database programs and the study of seashells. *Computing Teacher, 19*(7), 32–34.

Knight, P., & Timmons, G. (1986). Using databases in history teaching. *Journal of Computer-Assisted Learning, 2*(2), 93–101.

Polich, J. M., & Schwartz, S. H. (1974). The effect of problem size on representation in deductive problem solving. *Memory and Cognition, 2*(4), 683–686.

Pon, K. (1984). Databasing in the elementary (and secondary) classroom. *Computing Teacher, 12*(3), 28–30.

Rooze, G. E. (1988–1989). Developing thinking using databases: What's really involved? *Michigan Social Studies Journal, 3*(1), 25–26.

Schwartz, S. H. (1971). Modes of representation and problem solving: Well evolved is half solved. *Journal of Experimental Psychology, 91*, 347–350.

Watson, J., & Strudler, N. (1988–1989). Teaching higher order thinking skills with databases. *Computing Teacher, 16*(4), 47–50, 55.

CHAPTER 10

Modeling with Semantic Networks: Building Concept Maps

Semantic networks, also known as concept maps, are spatial representations of concepts and their interrelationships that simulate the knowledge structures that humans store in their minds (Jonassen, Beissner, & Yacci, 1993). These knowledge structures are also known as cognitive structures, conceptual knowledge, structural knowledge, and semantic networks. The semantic networks in memory and the maps that represent them are composed of nodes (concepts or ideas) that are connected by links (statements of relationships). In computer-based semantic networks, nodes are represented as information blocks and the links are labeled lines. Figure 10–1 illustrates one screen of a complex concept map on evolution produced with Semantica (www.semanticresearch.com). Double-clicking any of the concepts on the map puts that concept in the middle of the screen and shows all of the other concepts that are associated with it. Most semantic networking programs also provide the capability of adding text and pictures to each node to elaborate that concept, which makes the programs more like hypermedia representations (Chapter 16).

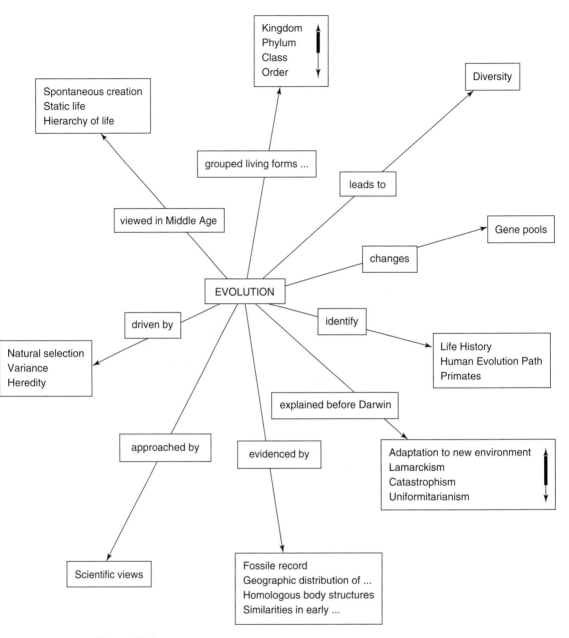

Figure 10-1
Single screen of a concept map on evolution.

Other concept mapping programs, such as Inspiration (www.inspiration.com), display all of the concepts on a single screen. The result is visual complexity, as illustrated in Figure 10–2, that is difficult for learners. A solution to this problem—one that is too common—is to require only simpler concept maps. The best concept

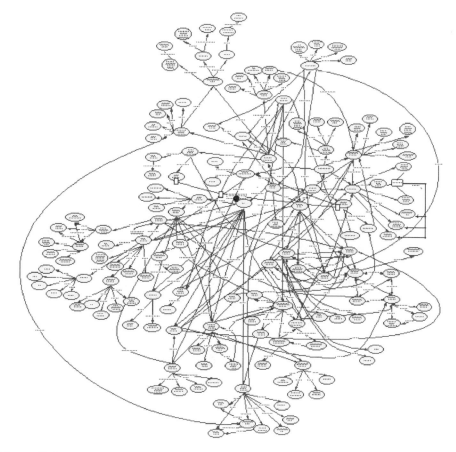

Figure 10-2
Screen from a concept mapping program that represents all of the concepts on
a single screen.

maps, however, are those that are built over the school year and contain a few thousand concepts. When students build complex concept maps, they begin to comprehend the interconnectedness of ideas in a knowledge domain.

Semantic networking, or concept mapping, is the process of constructing concept maps—of identifying important concepts, arranging those concepts spatially, identifying relationships among those concepts, and labeling the nature of the relationships among those concepts. These maps represent what learners know or are learning as multidimensional networks of concepts. Semantic networks and concept maps can be drawn by hand using simple artifacts such as cards and string or paper and pencil (see Jonassen et al., 1993, for descriptions and instructions). However, a variety of computer-based semantic networking software enables much easier (and arguably more powerful) production of concept maps. So semantic networking programs function as Mindtools for modeling the semantic organization content, problems, systems, stories, or thinking processes of students.

RATIONALE FOR SEMANTIC NETWORKS

The psychology of learning has often distinguished between declarative and procedural forms of knowledge. *Declarative* knowledge represents awareness of some object, event, or idea (knowing that). It enables learners to come to know, or define, ideas (verbal information or awareness of) and forms the basis for thinking about and using those ideas. However, merely knowing something does not mean that individuals can use that knowledge. Declarative knowledge is what you remember. *Procedural* knowledge is the knowledge of how to use declarative knowledge, that is, how to solve problems, form plans, and make decisions and arguments (knowing how). Procedural knowledge is what you know how to do.

Declarative knowledge and procedural knowledge are interdependent. Some procedural knowledge is acquired by learning how to apply declarative knowledge, and some declarative knowledge is remembered in the context of learning how to do something. Most of us possess a considerable volume of declarative knowledge that we cannot apply and really have no use for (except for answering *Jeopardy* questions); this is inert knowledge. On the other hand, we know how to do some things that we cannot adequately declare.

Semantic networks represent an intermediate type of knowledge, *structural* knowledge, which connects declarative and procedural knowledge. Structural knowledge is the knowledge of how the ideas within a domain are integrated and interrelated (Diekhoff, 1983). Awareness of those interrelationships and the ability to describe them are essential for higher order thinking. It is not enough to know *that*. In order to know *how*, you must know *why*. Structural knowledge provides the conceptual bases for knowing why.

Structural knowledge is also known as cognitive structure, the pattern of relationships among concepts in memory (Preece, 1976) or, more specifically, the organization of the relationships among concepts in long-term memory (Shavelson, 1972). Semantic networking activities have been shown to be an accurate means for representing cognitive structure (Jonassen, 1987). That is, semantic networking, as described in this chapter, helps learners map their own cognitive structure.

Jonassen et al. (1993) describe a number of reasons for studying structural knowledge using semantic networks:

◆ Structure is inherent in all knowledge, so understanding the structural foundations of any content domain improves comprehension.
◆ Structural knowledge is essential to recall and comprehension.
◆ When learners study, they necessarily construct structural knowledge along with declarative knowledge.

◆ Memory structures reflect the world; people naturally learn the underlying organization of ideas while learning.

◆ Structural knowledge is essential to problem solving and acquisition of procedural knowledge, so semantic networking will necessarily improve problem-solving ability.

◆ Experts' structural knowledge differs from that of novices; understanding these differences is facilitated by semantic networking.

Semantic networking tools are Mindtools for representing structural knowledge (Jonassen et al., 1993). Semantic networking aids learning by requiring learners to analyze the underlying structure of the ideas they are studying. The process of creating semantic networks engages learners in an analysis of their own knowledge structures, which helps them to integrate new knowledge with what they already know. As a result, the knowledge that is constructed can be used more effectively.

MODELING WITH SEMANTIC NETWORKS

Semantic networking tools are the most popular kind of Mindtool. They are used in schools all over the world. Likewise, building semantic models of content, problems, systems, and stories, and thinking with concept maps have been researched more than any other Mindtool activities. The usefulness of semantic networks and concept maps in schools is shown by their relationship to other forms of higher order thinking, each of which requires integrated knowledge of content. Consider these examples:

◆ Marra and Jonassen (2002) found that students who constructed concept maps of knowledge domains in preparation for building expert systems constructed expert systems with more rules and rule types, that is, more complex representations.

◆ Learners with better structural knowledge are also better problem solvers. "The students who had concept-mapping experience approached each problem by first sketching a map of the elements in the problem and were more decisive in choosing a point at which to begin their attack of the problem" (Okebukola, 1992). The concept mappers also focused more on the problem to be solved rather than irrelevant aspects of it.

◆ Basconals and Briscoe (1985) found that mean scores on problem-solving tests in a high school physics course were much higher for students who prepared concept maps in comparison with students who followed a traditional physics program in which concept maps were not used.

◆ Robertson (1990) found that the extent to which a learner's semantic networks contained relevant structural knowledge was a stronger predictor of how well learners would solve transfer problems in physics than either aptitude or performance on a set of similar problems.

◆ The similarity of learners' underlying cognitive structure with that of an expert is highly predictive of the learners' problem-solving ability (Gordon & Gill, 1989).

Thinking about the connections between concepts, evaluating their linkages by revising and reviewing the logical relationship among concepts, and planning how to organize concepts meaningfully provides valuable evidence of self-reflection and metacognitive reasoning. Concept maps assist learners to become aware of and control the cognitive processes of the task (Jegede, Alaiyemola, & Okebukola, 1990).

Semantic networks can also be used as tools for assessing what learners know. If we agree that memory is organized as a semantic network, then learning can be thought of as a reorganization of semantic memory. Producing semantic networks reflects those changes in semantic memory, because the networks describe what a learner knows. So, the semantic networks that learners generate after instruction reflect the growth of their knowledge structures. Semantic networks are beginning to be used to assess learning outcomes in schools and universities:

◆ Mansfield and Happs (1991) used concept maps to evaluate teaching outcomes and to monitor student progress in a geometry class.
◆ By use of Pathfinder networks (Schvaneveldt, 1990), concept maps have been related to course examination performance (Goldsmith, Johnson, & Acton, 1991).
◆ In a study examining generation of computer-based concept maps in a computer programming course, Feghali (1991) found that students who built maps scored better in course tests; however, the differences were not statistically significant.
◆ West, Pomeroy, Park, Gerstenberger, & Sandoval (2000) concluded that concept mapping is a valid measure of conceptual change and differences among groups.
◆ Senior nursing students significantly improved the quality of their concept maps over the course of the semester, which indicates an improvement in their conceptual understanding (Daley, Shaw, Balistrieri, Glasenapp, & Piacentine, 1999).
◆ In the assessment of knowledge integration, expert reviews of maps recommended using three criteria: comprehensiveness (breadth and depth of knowledge), organization (systematic arrangement), and correctness, that is, accuracy (Besterfield-Scare, Gerchak, Shuman, & Wolfe, 2004).

Coaching Construction of Concept Maps

Semantic networks are versatile tools that your students will learn to use quickly and will want to apply in a variety of situations. Some research has begun to focus on how to best integrate semantic networking with other educational activities:

• When students share concept maps and collaboratively construct them, they much prefer immediate feedback rather than computer-mediated communication (DeSimone, Schmid, & McEwan, 2001)

- Chang, Sung, and Chen (2001) found that scaffolding concept mapping by providing blank nodes and links resulted in higher scores on a posttest than providing feedback during concept mapping.

Consideration of the following sequence of activities will help you to integrate semantic networks in your instruction.

STEP 1. Students make a plan and set the perspective for analyzing a domain. Before beginning, students need to make a plan for the semantic network. What are they interested in representing? What points do they want to make? What kinds of information are required to make those points? What learning goals will they work toward? To answer these questions, the teacher and students must understand the perspective from which they are analyzing the content domain. For example, when studying concepts of Newtonian mechanics, such as speed, acceleration, mass, and force, high school students are likely to immediately relate those concepts to their automobiles and the feats they dream of performing in them. Although those may be acceptable and even relevant associations, it is also important to require students to "think like physicists" when analyzing the domain. If students were to analyze the same set of concepts but "think like poets," a substantively different set of associations would be generated. Personal knowledge structures are not static entities. They are dynamic and changeable, depending on the constructor's mood and frame of mind, recent events, and other factors. So help your students establish the proper perspective or frame of mind when planning for the activity.

STEP 2. Students identify important concepts. Understanding is made up of concepts, and we communicate through our shared understanding of concepts. So identification of the important concepts in a content domain is crucial not only to understanding that content, but also for collaborating on tasks. In textbooks, important concepts are often highlighted for learners. For example, they may appear in list form at the beginning or end of textbook chapters, or they may be highlighted in the text. Initially, you may want to analyze the textbook or supplementary materials and provide a list of concepts for the learners to define in the semantic network.

As students gain experience in semantic networking, they should become responsible for highlighting important concepts in textbooks, lectures, or supplementary materials. Rather than allowing students to highlight large sections of the textbook (producing pages of colorful text), suggest that they highlight only single words or short phrases that are essential to understanding the content, then use those for building semantic networks. You may want to focus a discussion on evaluating the relevance and importance of different concepts that might be included in the networks. Students could vote or argue for the inclusion of different concepts. In this approach, all learners start with the same list of concepts. However, the beginning list will likely be amended during the network construction process as students discover the need for additional concepts to adequately describe and elaborate the concepts already in the network.

STEP 3. Students create, define, and elaborate nodes. A node is created and labeled. For each concept listed in Step 2, pictures, descriptive text, and synonyms can be added to each node as appropriate. You may want to begin by supplying a network and requiring students to add details about the concepts in it. Or the students may be responsible for developing the list as well as for defining the concepts in it. Each node may be embellished with graphics or a picture. Some of the semantic networking programs provide primitive graphics tools for drawing images. Most allow the learner to add descriptive text to each node, so students can relate personal interpretations or beliefs about the concepts.

STEP 4. Students construct links and link concepts. After identifying the concepts in a domain that should go into the semantic network, the learner begins the more difficult and challenging part of the process: linking the concept nodes. The task of describing precisely the relationship between two ideas is much more difficult and engaging than it initially appears. The process of articulating those links requires learners to search through the range of possible relationships in order to define the relationship that exists in the context in which they are studying. Concepts can (and typically do) relate to each other in different ways, depending on the context in which they are being used. For example, thinking about the concept *speed* in the context of physics class implies a different set of relationships than studying the concept in the context of a drug education class. This variability is what contributes to the complexity of internal knowledge representations. Because concepts may be related to each other in several ways, it may be necessary to link the same two concepts with more than one relationship. Figure 10–3 presents a fairly comprehensive list of link types that may be used to connect nodes.

What characterizes a good link? Preciseness and succinctness, but more importantly, descriptiveness. Try to avoid using links such as "is connected to," "is related to," or "involves." They do not tell anything meaningful about the relationship. Be sure not only to link new concepts that are added to the network, but also to interlink existing concepts as much as possible. Attempt to pair each concept with every other concept in the network and decide if there is a meaningful relationship between them. If there is, create a link between them. The more interconnected your network is, the more meaningful your understanding of the content domain will be.

STEP 5. Students continue to expand the network. The linking process continues among all or most of the nodes in the network. While the linking is going on, new nodes or concepts are being added to the network to explain some of the existing concepts. Those concepts are linked, and additional

Symmetric Links

is opposite of	has synonym	is same as	is equal to
has sibling	is near to	is independent of	is opposed to
is opposite of	is similar to	is equal to	is same as

Asymmetric Links

Inclusion Relations (typically the most common)

has part/is part of	contains/is contained in
composed of/is part in	includes/is included in
has example/is example of	has instance/is instance of

Characteristic Relations (next most common)

has characteristic/is characteristic of	has attribute/is attribute of
has property/is property of	has type/is type of
has kind/is kind of	defines/is defined by
describes/is described by	models/is modeled by
denotes/is denoted by	implies/is implied by
has advantage/is advantage of	has disadvantage/is disadvantage of
has function/is function of	has size/is size of
is above/is below	is higher than/is lower than

Action Relations

causes/is caused by	uses/is used by
solves/is solution for	exploits/is exploited by
decreases/is decreased by	increases/is increased by
destroys/is destroyed by	impedes/is impeded by
influences/is influenced by	determines/determined by
enables/is enabled by	absorbs/absorbed by
acts on/is acted on by	consumes/consumed by
converted from/converted to	designs/designed by
employs/is employed by	evolves into/evolved from
generates/is generated by	modifies/modified by
originates from/origin of	provides/provided by
requires/is required by	regulates/is regulated by
sends to/receives from	

Process Relations

has object/is object of	has output/is output of
has result/results from	has subprocess/is subprocess of
has process/is process in	organizes/is organized by
has input/is input to	proposes/is proposed by
depends on/has dependent	concludes/concluded by

Temporal Relations

has step/is step in	has stage/is stage in
precedes/follows	

Figure 10-3
Possible links between nodes (Adapted from Fisher, 1988).

concepts are added to explain them. This process of augmentation continues in a cycle until the network builder feels that the domain is explained well enough. Interestingly, this process mirrors to some degree the natural pattern of knowledge acquisition. It is theoretically (although not practically) possible for learners to build networks consisting of all of the concepts they know are linked together. After building a large network students find it rewarding to realize how much they really know.

STEP 6. Students *reflect* on the process. Reflection should not wait until the project is completed. Rather, students should continuously review their progress through questions such as these: Are we achieving our goals? What changes are necessary? How do we compare with other groups? Are we answering questions and making the points that we set out in our plan? After the project is completed, students should also reflect on the project: What have we learned about the content? What have we learned about semantic network construction and how our networks represent what we know? What have we learned about working with each other? You may choose to provide students with some or all of the criteria for evaluating student databases (presented in the next section) to use for self-evaluation. The activity of constructing semantic networks engages meaningful thinking. Reflection cements the knowledge that learners construct.

It is absolutely essential for students to construct concept maps, *not* the teacher. Often teachers create semantic networks and present them to students as study guides. Students try to memorize them like they do their textbooks, which prevents them from thinking meaningfully about what they are studying. Brandt, et al. (2001) showed that teacher-provided concept maps failed to enhance learning of chemistry concepts. Although teachers benefit from constructing semantic networks about whatever they teach, it is crucial for students to construct the maps. In addition, teachers should not show students "the right structure for the network" (I have witnessed this many times). *There is no right structure.* The networks created by students will vary because students differ in so many ways (see Jonassen & Grabowski, 1993, for a lengthy description of individual differences and learning).

Students enjoy creating semantic networks. When my colleagues and I were working with students in a junior high school in north Denver, not even the winter flu season kept students away on the days they were assigned to the lab to create semantic networks. A number of students have written to me:

I was not looking forward to studying all that material. SemNet gave me an interesting and highly effective way to study some semi-boring stuff. I was surprised—it really did work. I remembered a lot of the material.

I found that my interest level was much higher when I could utilize it, not just do it because it is an assignment for a class. I like to look at it [semantic networks] as a tool that I can use and understand for tomorrow's problems. Thing is, I don't view them as problems, I see them as opportunities waiting to be solved.

ASSESSING AND EVALUATING SEMANTIC NETWORKS

Assessing Semantic Networks

The cognitive processes engaged by concept mapping are complex and cannot be adequately assessed using a single measure. Because there is a larger research base related to semantic networks, more criteria are available for assessing networks. The following list highlights some of the many criteria for assessing the quality of students' semantic networks:

- ◆ Note the number of nodes, because that indicates the breadth of the net.
- ◆ Note the number of distinct propositions (node–link–node combinations), because that indicates completeness.
- ◆ Determine the ratio of instances to concepts, because that is an indicator of how well integrated the concepts in the domain are (also known as embeddedness).
- ◆ Determine the centrality of each node, which is indicated by its number of direct links (concepts linked directly to it) and indirect links (concepts linked to other concepts directly linked to it). Centrality is a measure of the importance of concepts in a domain. Look at the rank ordering of centrality for the most embedded concept (number of paths two nodes away). Often, the concepts that you believe are most important (typically those at the highest level of abstraction) are not central to the network, at least according to this criterion.
- ◆ Note the depth (hierarchicalization) of the network, which is measured by the levels of nodes represented.
- ◆ Ask if the linking relation between nodes in each proposition is valid (Novak & Gowin, 1984).
- ◆ Ask if the relation in each proposition clear and descriptive.
- ◆ If the net is hierarchical, determine how many levels are represented. Ask if each subordinate concept is more specific than the concept above it (Novak & Gowin, 1984).
- ◆ Determine if the direction of links with arrows conveys a hierarchical or causal relationship between nodes in propositions (McClure & Bell, 1990).
- ◆ Assess the validity and synthesis of crosslinks between concepts in different propositions (Novak & Gowin, 1984).
- ◆ Assess the number and accuracy of linked concept pairs and number of insightful links between concept pairs (White & Gunstone, 1992).
- ◆ Determine the ratio of instances to concepts (integratedness or embeddedness of concepts).
- ◆ Check the centrality of each node. (How many other concepts is a node linked to directly and indirectly?)
- ◆ Evaluate the number of different link types. Links should be parsimonious. The law of parsimony pertains to the economy with which you express yourself. If six different links will describe all of the relationships in the network, then do not use more than six (i.e., don't use three different links that mean the same thing, such as "attribute of," "property of," and "characteristic of").

◆ Use enough links to discriminate meaningful differences. Overreliance on one or two particular types of links shows a narrowness in thinking. Look at the proportions of link types used in the network. Calculate (roughly at least) the proportions of inclusion, characteristic, action, process, and temporal relations.

◆ Evaluate the network's salience, that is, the number of valid links in the map divided by the total number of links in the map (Hoz, Tomer, & Tamir, 1990).

◆ Determine the consistency in use of links.

◆ Determine the ratio of the number of links to the number of nodes.

◆ Use links consistently throughout the network. The meaning of any link should be the same each time it is used.

◆ Look at the number of dead-end nodes, that is, those that are linked to only one other concept. Such nodes are thought to be on the edge of the network; they prevent the browser from traveling to any node other than the one they came from.

◆ Make sure that the ratio of the number of types of links to the number of nodes is low. It is not appropriate to develop a different type of link for each concept (see earlier comments on parsimony).

◆ Check the accuracy of the information included in the network. This, of course, is the most important criterion. Are learners making meaningful connections? Is the text in nodes correct, that is, is the information in the network correct?

Evaluating Semantic Networks

The richness, elaborateness, and complexity of a network, as described in the assessment criteria just given, are only measures of the meaningfulness of a network. Once you assess the students' concept maps, you will probably want to evaluate their *quality*. How good are the networks that the students created? Evaluation requires standards against which to compare the networks. A few methods for evaluating the quality of networks are presented next.

1. *Compare* a learner's network with the expert's (teacher's). Research has shown that during the process of learning, the learner's knowledge structure begins to resemble the knowledge structures of the instructor, and the degree of similarity is a good predictor of classroom performance on examinations (Aidman & Egan, 1998; Diekhoff, 1983; Shavelson, 1974; Thro, 1978). Instruction, then, may be conceived of as the mapping of subject-matter knowledge (usually that possessed by the teacher or expert) onto the learner's knowledge structure. Semantic networks are a way of measuring that convergence. The closer a student's network resembles the teacher's, the more that student has (presumably) learned. This use of semantic networks represents a traditional notion of learning (i.e., the purpose of instruction is to get the learner to think like the teacher). The constructivist ideas on which this book is based, however, would argue that this is not an appropriate use of semantic networks. Nevertheless, learners do come to think like teachers, so semantic networks are a means for evaluating that change in students.

2. *Determine* a learner's knowledge growth. The most significant problem with comparing a learner's knowledge with an expert's is that knowledge construction occurs in stages rather than in a single increment. Learners do not jump from novice to expert in a single bound. Therefore, basing an evaluation of a network on its lack of convergence with an expert's may not be fair. Instead, evaluate a learner's network when he or she begins studying and at different points during the learning process. The network should be a visible sign of how much has been learned.

The best semantic networks are very large. In fact, the best use of semantic networking is to spend the entire academic year contributing to a map of the ideas studied throughout the course. Very large networks help learners see the complexity of knowledge and how all knowledge is interrelated. Construction of a network with thousands of nodes requires collaboration. The entire class can work on a network, as can a group of three or more students. From a constructivist perspective, an important goal of semantic networking is for learners to recognize that there are multiple perspectives for any content. Creating visual maps of ideas helps students compare how they think with how others think.

3. *Accept* a learner's different perspectives. Multiple perspectives in knowledge representation often result from the variety of perspectives an individual can have on a particular content domain (e.g., thinking about Newtonian concepts like a scientist versus like a race car driver). It is useful and informative to have learners create multiple networks on the same content. Each time students begin a network, ask them to also assume a different perspective. You can also analyze a group of ideas in different classes so that learners think about the same ideas from varied perspectives, for example, as social scientists, mathematicians, or writers.

4. *Compare* a learner's networks to course goals. Semantic networks have been shown to be related to examination performance (Goldsmith et al., 1991). More research is needed to verify a consistent relationship between particular criteria for evaluating networks and traditional measures of course performance, such as exams, research papers, and case studies.

ADVANTAGES AND LIMITATIONS OF SEMANTIC NETWORKING FOR MODELING

There are several advantages to integrating semantic networking into learning activities.

◆ Semantic networking tools are easy to use. Most learners gain proficiency with most semantic networking software in less than an hour.
◆ Semantic networking tools provide for spatial representations of content, which helps memory.

♦ Semantic networking tools enhance comprehension and retention of the ideas being studied by helping learners build structural knowledge. In addition to improving comprehension, structural knowledge improves retention of content being studied.

♦ Semantic networks demonstrate the interconnectedness of ideas from different subjects and different courses.

♦ Semantic networking should improve problem-solving performance in learners.

Semantic networks also have limitations:

♦ Semantic networks have a limited ability to represent causal relationships. A semantic network can define a causal link, but it does not provide the implications and inferences that accompany causal relationships. Concept maps convey semantic relationships, not causal ones. They can convey the semantic meaning of a causal relationship, but they cannot demonstrate the effects of cause on effect, because causal relationships are dynamic.

♦ Semantic networks can be too readily thought to reify the structures of the mind. The implication is that our semantic stores of information can be cognitively mapped and literally searched, just as a computer searches its memory stores. Semantic networks are not truly maps of the mind; rather, they are representations of what we think is in the mind.

♦ The knowledge that semantic networks represent is dynamic; that is, it changes depending on the context, the experiences, and the backgrounds of those producing the networks. Structural knowledge also changes over time. To truly and accurately represent knowledge, semantic networking tools would need to enable minute-by-minute, context-by-context changes in the concepts, relationships, and structures that are represented in them.

♦ Many educators overestimate the capabilities of concept maps for representing what students know. The propositional networks in the mind, in whatever form they really exist, are far more complex than anything that can be represented in a concept map. Concept maps are *not* identical to the semantic networks in the mind. The ideas that we know are interrelated and multiply encoded in rich, redundant networks of ideas. These networks are multidimensional, not two dimensional as represented in concept maps. Beware of educators who oversell the importance of concept maps.

SUMMARY

Semantic networking programs provide a set of graphic conceptualization tools for creating concept maps. These concept maps represent the structure of ideas in memory or in a content domain. Concept maps are representations of learners' structural knowledge, the knowledge of the semantic relationships between concepts. Structural knowledge is the basis of meaning making.

Semantic networking engages learners in an analysis of content domains that helps them organize their knowledge for better comprehension and retention. Semantic networking is also effective for planning other kinds of productions and knowledge bases. Semantic networks, which are used in schools around the world, are among the most versatile of the Mindtools described in this book.

REFERENCES

Aidman, E. V., & Egan, G. (1998). Academic assessment through computerized concept mapping: Validating a method of implicit map reconstruction. *International Journal of Instructional Media, 25*(3), 277–294.

Besterfield-Scare, M., Gerchak, J., Shuman, L. J., & Wolfe, H. (2004). Scoring concept maps: An integrated rubric for assessing engineering education. *Journal of Engineering Education, 93*(2), 105–115.

Brandt, L., Elen, J., Hellemans, J., Heerman, L., Couwenberg, I., Volckaert, L., & Morisse, H. (2001). The impact of concept-mapping and visualization on the learning of secondary school chemistry students. *International Journal of Science Education, 23*(12), 1303–1313.

Chang, K. E., Sung, Y. T., & Chen, S. F. (2001). Learning through computer-based concept mapping with scaffolding aid. *Journal of Computer Assisted Learning, 17*(1), 21–33.

Daley, B. J., Shaw, C. R., Balistrieri, T., Glasenapp, K., & Piacentine, L. (1999). Concept maps: A strategy to teach and evaluate critical thinking. *Journal of Nursing Education, 38*(1), 42–47.

DeSimone, C., Schmid, R. F., & McEwan, L. A. (2001). Supporting the learning process with collaborative concept mapping using computer-based communication tools and process. *Educational Research and Evaluation, 7*(2–3), 263–283.

Diekhoff, G. M. (1983). Relationship judgments in the evaluation of structural understanding. *Journal of Educational Psychology, 75,* 227–233.

Feghali, A. A.(1991). A study of engineering college students' use of computer-based semantic networks in a computer programming language class (Doctoral dissertation, Purdue University, 1991). *Dissertation Abstracts International, 53*(3), 701.

Goldsmith, T. E., Johnson, P. J., & Acton, W. H. (1991). Assessing structural knowledge. *Journal of Educational Psychology, 83,* 88–96.

Gordon, S. E., & Gill, R. T. (1989). *The formation and use of knowledge structures in problem solving domains* (Tech. Report AFOSR-88-0063). Washington, DC: Bolling AFB.

Hoz, R., Tomer, Y., & Tamir, P. (1990). The relations between disciplinary and pedagogical knowledge and the length of teaching experience of biology and geography teachers. *Journal of Research in Science Teaching, 27,* 973–985.

Jegede, O. J., Alaiyemola, S., & Okebukola, P. A. (1990). The effect of concept mapping on students' anxiety and achievement in biology. *Journal of Research in Science Teaching, 27*(10), 951–960.

Jonassen, D. H. (1987). Assessing cognitive structure: Verifying a method using pattern notes. *Journal of Research and Development in Education, 20*(3), 1–14.

Jonassen, D. H., Beissner, K., & Yacci, M. A. (1993). *Structural knowledge: Techniques for representing, conveying, and acquiring structural knowledge.* Hillsdale, NJ: Lawrence Erlbaum.

Jonassen, D. H., & Grabowski, B. L. (1993). *Handbook of individual differences, learning, and instruction.* Hillsdale, NJ: Lawrence Erlbaum.

Mansfield, H., & Happs, J. (1991). Concept maps. *Australian Mathematics Teacher, 47*(3), 30–33.

Marra, R. M., & Jonassen, D. H. (2002). Transfer effects of semantic networks on expert systems: Mindtools at work. *Journal of Educational Computing Research, 26*(1), 1–23.

McClure, J. R., & Bell, P. E. (1990). *Effects of an environmental education-related STS approach to instruction on cognitive structures of preservice science teachers.* University Park, PA: Pennsylvania State University. (ERIC Document Reproduction Service No. ED 341 582)

Novak, J. D., & Gowin, D. B. (1984). *Learning how to learn.* New York: Cambridge University Press.

Okebukola, P. A. (1992). Can good concept mappers be good problem solvers in science? *Educational Psychology, 12*(2), 113–129.

Preece, P. F. W. (1976). Mapping cognitive structure: A comparison of methods. *Journal of Educational Psychology, 68*, 1–8.

Robertson, W. C. (1990). Detection of cognitive structure with protocol data: Predicting performance on physics transfer problems. *Cognitive Science, 14*, 253–280.

Schvaneveldt, R. W. (1990). *Pathfinder associative networks: Studies in knowledge organization.* Norwood, NJ: Ablex Publishing.

Shavelson, R. J. (1972). Some aspects of the correspondence between content structure and cognitive structure in physics instruction. *Journal of Educational Psychology, 63*, 225–234.

Shavelson, R. J. (1974). Methods for examining representations of subject matter structure in students' memory. *Journal of Research in Science Teaching, 11*, 231–249.

Thro, M. P. (1978). Relationships between associative and content structure of physics concepts. *Journal of Educational Psychology, 70*, 971–978.

West, D. C., Pomeroy, J. R., Park, J. K, Gerstenberger, E. A., & Sandoval, J. (2000). Critical thinking in graduate medical education: A role for concept mapping assessment? *Journal of the American Medical Association, 284*(9), 1105–1110.

White, R., & Gunstone, R. (1992). *Probing understanding.* London: Falmer Press.

CHAPTER 11

Modeling with Spreadsheets

Spreadsheets are computerized, numeric record-keeping systems. They were originally designed to replace paper-based ledger systems. Accountants would enter all of the expenses and income from their business in different columns of the ledger and sum, subtract, and balance the assets of the company. Ledgers required performance of all the accounting operations by hand. When a single mistake was found, the entire ledger had to be recalculated. Spreadsheets have automated all of these processes.

SPREADSHEET COMPONENTS AND FUNCTIONS

Essentially, a spreadsheet is a grid (or table or matrix) of empty cells, with columns identified by letters and rows identified by numbers (see Figure 11-1)—a ledger sheet spread in front of the user. The information included in any cell may consist of text, numbers, formulas to manipulate the numeric contents of any other cells,

◇	A	B	C	D	E	F	G	H
1		Receipts				Expenditures		
2		Tuition	48000			Salary	43200	
3		Public	18233			Taxes	2344	
4		Gifts	7895			Utilities	1179	
5						Rent	2365	
6		Total	SUM (c2..c4)			Misc	466	
7								
8		Profit	c6-g8			Total	SUM (g2..g6)	
9								
10								

Figure 11-1
A simple profit and loss sheet.

and mathematical or logical functions to manipulate the contents of any other cells. For example, cells B2, B3, and B4 in Figure 11-1 contain text that is used to label the contents in cells C2, C3, and C4. Cell C2 contains the number 48,000. A user can change that number by moving to that cell and rekeying. Formulas consist of numeric relationships between the contents of different cells. For example, the formula B6 + (C7/C6) would tell the program to go to cell B6, retrieve the value of the number in it, divide the contents of cell C7 by the contents of cell C6, then add that value to the contents of cell B6. Formulas may refer to numeric values placed anywhere in the grid and may refer to any other cells by name.

Functions are mathematical or logical operations that may be performed on the values in a set of specified cells. For example, the function in cell C6 tells the program to retrieve the values in cells C2 to C4 and SUM them. AVG (B9 . . . B12) would calculate the average of the values in those cells. More sophisticated functions, such as ITERATE, perform operations a set number of times in a sequence. Functions are also logical, such as IF, MATCH, LOOKUP, or INDEX. These may be included in formulas, such as IF B9 < E10,B9 * E6 (if the value in cell B9 is less than that in E10, then multiply it by the value in E6). Other functions automatically match values in cells with other cells, look up values in a table of values, or create an index of values to be compared with other cells.

The primary differences among spreadsheets are the size of the grid, the number of functions available, and the graphic representations provided. Small spreadsheets, such as the first VisiCalc spreadsheets, provided a grid of approximately 250 by 400 cells, whereas Excel provides multiple grids that contain 10,000 cells. All spreadsheets provide the same basic functions, but more sophisticated ones provide more elaborate functions for interrelating content in the sheet and creating simulations.

Spreadsheets have three primary functions: storing, calculating, and presenting information. First, information, usually numeric, can be stored in a particular location (the cell), from which it can be readily accessed and retrieved. Second, and most importantly, spreadsheets support calculation functions such that the numeric contents of any combination of cells can be mathematically related in just about any way the user wishes. (Most spreadsheets also provide other mathematical functions, such as logarithmic, trigonometric, etc.) Third, spreadsheets present information in a variety of ways. All spreadsheets can display their contents in a two-dimensional grid, such as in Figure 11-2. All spreadsheets enable the user to display the numeric

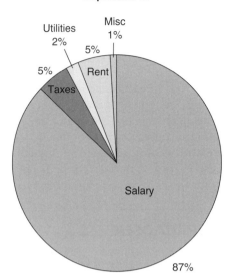

Figure 11-2
Graphic representation of amounts in Figure 11-1.

contents of any combination of cells graphically in the form of charts or graphs. The user identifies a series of cells, and the program automatically provides graphs and charts of those quantities. By merely highlighting a group of cells (such as G2 to G6 in Figure 11-3) and clicking on a chart type, the program produces a multicolored pie chart or a bar and line chart. Being able to visualize data instantaneously in several ways affords new ways of thinking with numbers.

Most spreadsheets provide advanced operations as well. For example, in the replication function, the program fills in formulas in cells by replicating a formula from another cell. During spreadsheet construction, the user is not required to copy a similar formula over and over again in different cells. Also, the spreadsheet can change the formula relative to the position of the cell. Many spreadsheet programs allow the user to write macros, which are miniprograms that identify a sequence of operations that the program should perform when a single, special key is struck. Macros are often used in spreadsheets for collecting information from the user. A macro can be included in a cell for getting the user to input a value (e.g., his or her age), which can then be related to other cells in the spreadsheet. Some spreadsheets enable the user to open several windows, each of which provides a different view of the spreadsheet. These functions are normally reserved for the "power user" who has become skilled in spreadsheet use. Most spreadsheet programs also enable users to produce graphic representations of data for the purpose of producing simulations. These will be described and illustrated later in the chapter.

Spreadsheets were originally developed, and are most commonly used, to support business decision making. The electronic spreadsheet was designed by a couple of graduate accounting majors as a tool to support accounting operations. Their professors assigned them problems based on balance sheets and profit and loss statements (see Figure 11-1) that would ask them what-if questions, such as, What if interest rates increased by 1%? Tired of having to recalculate all of the values that would be affected by the change, the students developed an electronic balance sheet where all of the values could be more easily manipulated. Changes had to be made in only one location; then the spreadsheet automatically recalculated all of the affected values. Use of this spreadsheet program, called VisiCalc, burgeoned immediately and triggered the phenomenal growth of microcomputers in business in the early 1980s.

Spreadsheets remain in common use today. Businesses use them not only for maintaining accounts but also for managing financial portfolios, determining service or interest rates, and modeling financial markets to support decision making. Spreadsheets are also popular for personal accounting and budgeting.

MODELING WITH SPREADSHEETS

Spreadsheets are an example of a cognitive technology that amplifies and reorganizes mental functioning. They have restructured the work of budgeting, thereby enabling the accountant to be a hypothesis tester (playing what-if games) rather than merely a calculator (Pea, 1985). This was the original purpose of spreadsheets, as just described. In the same way that they have qualitatively changed the accounting process, spreadsheets can change educational processes that require manipulation or speculation with numbers.

Spreadsheet construction and use engage a variety of mental processes that require learners to use existing rules, generate new rules describing relationships, and organize information. The emphasis in a spreadsheet is on identifying relationships and describing those relationships in terms of higher order rules. Therefore, if users learn to develop spreadsheets to describe content domains, they probably will be thinking more deeply.

Spreadsheets are rule-using tools that require users to become rule makers (Vockell & Van Deusen, 1989). To calculate values in a spreadsheet, users must identify relationships and patterns among the data they want to represent in the spreadsheet. Those relationships must be modeled mathematically using rules to describe the relationships. So building spreadsheets requires abstract reasoning. Although spreadsheets have been used most consistently in schools as management tools for accounting, they are being used increasingly as Mindtools to support higher order quantitative thinking. Spreadsheets have been used to model phenomena in at least four ways: computational reasoning for analyzing data, mathematics comprehension, visualization, and simulation modeling.

Computation, Analysis, and Reasoning

First and foremost, spreadsheets are calculators that off-load cognitive effort associated with computations. Whenever learners have a need to calculate, they can set up a spreadsheet to fulfill their purpose. Spreadsheets, therefore, support

◇	A	B	C	D	E	F	G	H	I	J	K
1	Vol. of 0.1 M HCl Added (mL)	PH	PH								
2	0	14	14	0	Strength	1					
3	10	13.9	13.9	14	Conc (M)	0.14					
4	20	13.8	13.8	28							
5	30	13.7	13.7	42							
6	40	13.6	13.6	56							
7	50	13.5	13.5	70							
8	60	13.4	13.4	84							
9	70	13.3	13.3	98							
10	80	13	13	112							
11	90	12.7	12.7	126							
12	95	12.4	12.4	133							
13	99	11.7	11.7	138.6							
14	99.9	10.7	10.7	139.86							
15	99.99	9.7	9.7	139.986							
16	100	7	7	140							
17	100.01	4.3	4.3	140.014							
18	100.1	3.3	3.3	140.14							
19	101	2.3	2.3	141.4							
20	105	1.6	1.6	147							
21	110	1.4	1.4	154							
22	120	1	1	168							
23	130	0.88	0.88	182							
24	140	0.77	0.77	196							
25	150	0.7	0.7	210							
26	160	0.68	0.68	224							
27	170	0.67	0.67	238							
28	180	0.66	0.66	252							
29	190	0.65	0.65	266							
30	200	0.64	0.64	280							
31											
32											
33											
34											

Figure 11-3
Spreadsheet used in calculating and illustrating the effects of titration.

problem-solving activities. In a problem situation with quantitative relationships, spreadsheets can be used to represent those relationships. For example, the spreadsheet in Figure 11-3 illustrates the effects of titrating a base. Because learners off-load cognitive effort to the computer, they are able to apply more of their effort to understanding the relationships being calculated and represented graphically by the spreadsheet. There are many examples of spreadsheets being used to help learners calculate and reason with quantities. Spreadsheets have been used to

♦ function as a calculator to demonstrate multiplicative relationships in elementary mathematics (Edwards & Bitter, 1989);

♦ solve complex chemistry problems such as wet and dry analysis of flue gases, which may be expanded to include volumetric flow rate, pressure, humidity, dew point, temperature, and combustion temperature, in a mass and energy balances course (Misovich & Biasca, 1990);

♦ calculate the force needed to lift assorted weights in various lever problems (Schlenker & Yoshida, 1991);

♦ solve a number of science problems, including problems involving an incline plane and conversion of protein into energy (Goodfellow, 1990);
♦ calculate the dimensions of a scale model of the Milky Way to demonstrate its immensity (Whitmer, 1990);
♦ solve elementary mathematical story problems (Verderber, 1990);
♦ support decision analysis by helping users find the best use of available information as well as evaluate any additional information that can be obtained (Sounderpandian, 1989);
♦ facilitate student grading of peer speech performances, thereby providing a high level of motivation for students (Dribin, 1985);
♦ estimate and compare the relative velocities of various dinosaurs (Karlin, 1988);
♦ implement Polya's problem-solving plan with arithmetic problems (Sgroi, 1992);
♦ solve rate equation chemical kinetics problems in a physical chemistry course (Blickensderfer, 1990); and
♦ solve multiloop circuit problems (Hart, 1995).

In these applications, the spreadsheet calculates relationships among the numeric variables; the learners reason about those relationships *with* the spreadsheet. To support higher level thinking skills such as collecting, describing, and interpreting data, Niess (1992) provided students with a spreadsheet with wind data for different towns. Wind directions (NE, SW, WSW) described rows of data, and the percentage of days in each month of the year was represented in the columns. Niess asked students to use the spreadsheets to answer queries such as the following:

♦ Are the winds more predominant from one direction during certain months? Why do you think this is the case?
♦ In which months is the wind the calmest?
♦ Which wind direction is the most stable throughout the year?

One of the best applications of spreadsheets is as a tool to enter and calculate the results of an experiment. Spreadsheets have been used to

♦ analyze lunchroom trash and project annual waste for an Earth Day project (Ramondetta, 1992);
♦ analyze field data on the ecology of tree species (Sigismondi & Calise, 1990);
♦ solve problems in physics laboratory experiments on time, displacement, and velocity and their interrelationships using a free-fall apparatus (Krieger & Stith, 1990);
♦ analyze and graphically represent data collected on the distribution and abundance of different kinds of trees in the forest (Silvius, Sjoquist, & Mundy, 1994);
♦ analyze the results of an experiment on microbial growth rates using simple fermentation equipment (Mills & Jackson, 1997); and
♦ analyze experimental data on salt concentrations and state changes in water (Goodwin, 2002).

Mathematics Comprehension

Spreadsheets support numeric thinking. When learning to perform mathematical processes, learners can get bogged down in the manipulation of numbers. Even after a great deal of practice, learners can lose sight of what they were trying to solve (Dubitsky, 1988). Spreadsheets are a powerful manipulation tool for representing values and developing formulas to interrelate them. Spreadsheets enhance learners' understanding of the algorithms used to compare values and the mathematical models used to describe content domains. Students understand calculations (both antecedents and consequents) because they are actively involved in identifying the interrelationships between the components of the calculation. This is a substantively different activity than sitting through countless math drill-and-practice programs, which can actually impair math performance, according to a study by the Educational Testing Service (Matthews, 1998). The study concluded that simulations and real-life applications of math concepts on computers improved math scores and improved the learning climate for eighth graders.

Spreadsheet construction requires learners to identify all steps of numeric solutions, that is, the progression of calculations as they are performed in an algorithm. The spreadsheet models the mathematical logic that is implied by calculations, thereby making the underlying logic obvious to learners, which should improve learners' understanding of the interrelationships and procedures. Spreadsheets have been used to

- root-find in precalculus using synthetic division, the bisection method, and Newton's method (Pinter-Lucke, 1992);
- help children understand the meaning of large numbers (a million) by comparing quantities to everyday things (Parker & Widmer, 1991);
- implement linear system-solving algorithms, that is, advanced mathematical formulas (Watkins & Taylor, 1989);
- enable elementary students to refine estimates and see patterns while learning to solve long-division problems, which helps them to better understand numbers (Dubitsky, 1988);
- help students to develop conceptual understanding of relationships between variables while solving problems such as planning a party, holiday shopping, and calculating interest (Hoeffner, Kendall, Stellenwerf, Thames, & Williams, 1990);
- help 10-to-11-year-old children in Mexico and Britain to symbolize relations and rules in algebra problems and think in general mathematical relationships (Sutherland & Rojano, 1993).

Visualization

The capabilities of modern spreadsheets to visualize and animate numeric phenomena make them a powerful alternative to visualization tools (see Chapter 15). Although they cannot visualize phenomena as completely as some visualization tools, they are more flexible because they can visualize a large range of phenomena. For example,

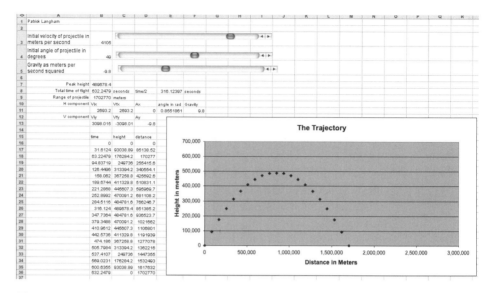

Figure 11-4
Spreadsheet used to graph a physics experiment.

the spreadsheet in Figure 11-4 illustrates the effects of gravity, angle, and initial velocity on the trajectory of an object. Spreadsheets have also been used for helping learners to

◆ animate sine waves (Sharp, 2003); and
◆ construct three-dimensional maps, including contour and topographic maps, to understand spatial relationships (Feicht, 1999).

Simulation Modeling

Simulating phenomena using spreadsheets provides a "direct and effective means of understanding the role of various parameters and of testing different means of optimizing their values" (Sundheim, 1992, p. 654). Students are more engaged if they construct simulations than if they simply use simulations that teachers developed. For example, my students developed a cognitive simulation (see Figure 11-5) of the effects of motivation factors (i.e., subject complexity, amount of task assigned, time allotted, help provided, and level of self-efficacy) on motivation. This simulation enabled the students to test their assumptions about motivation and the relationships of variables to each other by manipulating the values of the factors. Barnes (1997) showed how the following dynamic systems (systems that change over time as described by variables), could be modeled in spreadsheets: chaos and the butterfly effect, population growth, the ecology of predator-prey relationships, and Newton's Law of Cooling. Other examples of simulation modeling are listed next:

◆ Tracking portfolio performance in a stock training simulation (Crisci, 1992)
◆ Modeling stoichiometric relationships in chemical reactions and calculating how many bonds are broken, the energy required to break bonds, and the new

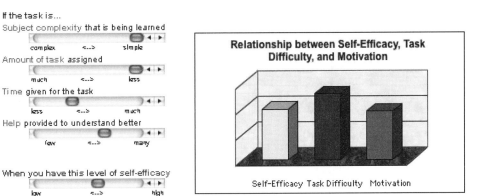

Figure 11-5
Cognitive simulation of motivation.

masses and densities of the products and reagents in the reactions (Brosnan, 1990)

◆ Representing Keynesian versus classical macroeconomic models, such as savings-investment and inflation-unemployment (Adams & Kroch, 1989)

◆ Interrelating demographic variables in population geography courses using population templates (Rudnicki, 1990)

◆ Calculating and graphing quantum mechanical functions such as atomic orbitals to simulate rotational and vibrational energy levels of atomic components in a physical chemistry class (Kari, 1990)

◆ Creating and manipulating economic models (e.g., balance of payments, investment appraisal, elasticity, cost-benefit analysis) in an economics course (Cashien, 1990)

◆ Representing different experiments on Archimedes' law and potential energy (Silva, 1998)

◆ Simulating electrical circuitry: students are required to predict the results of changing parameters, qualitatively analyze what happens when changes are introduced, and quantitatively verify different laws (Silva, 1994)

◆ Identifying factors affecting population growth, and determining the factors and interrelationships that should be included in a simulation of population growth (Wells & Berger, 1985/1986)

◆ Modeling planetary orbits (Bridges, 1995)

◆ Modeling a thermostated water bath and graphing heat distributions (Sundheim, 1992)

◆ Using Excel to represent two cognitive models: an associative learning model for representing contingency and causal learning, and a multinomial processing tree, signal-detection model to simulate a series of experiments. The use of arrays and the libraries of statistical and engineering functions enables the construction of sophisticated cognitive models (Macho, 2002).

Coaching Construction of Spreadsheets

Imagine that for Earth Day, your elementary school students want to calculate and represent the impact of a new recycling policy on the city in which they live. Identification of all of the disposable and recyclable products, the quantities discarded in each part of the city, and the costs (short term and long term) of burying or recycling those products requires extensive investigation. Then building a model to interrelate all of the products, costs, and savings on a spreadsheet requires activities of extensive synthesis, which would provide your students with feelings of satisfaction and accomplishment. Rather than having your students read about experiments in their science books, have them conduct the experiments and use spreadsheets to record and analyze the results. Or, have your students construct a survey about the attitudes of students in different grades, administer the survey, and use spreadsheets to record and analyze the results. There are many applications for spreadsheets in all grades.

Performing the kinds of content analysis required to set up and describe such problem situations and build spreadsheets requires many new skills. The ultimate goal for your students is two fold: (1) to independently analyze a new problem situation by identifying the problem variables and interrelationships among those variables and (2) to create formulas and use functions to calculate and manipulate the quantities in those variables. The ability to create quantitative models of problem situations is a powerful, transferable skill. To develop this skill, several stages of learning must occur. The following steps introduce a series of stages and learning activities for preparing your students.

STEP 1. Students are given a spreadsheet template. To introduce the structure and functions of spreadsheets, you may want to have students complete some exercises using an existing spreadsheet. Begin with a spreadsheet template (a spreadsheet with formulas entered but no values) and require students to fill in the gaps. For example, conduct a simple science experiment and have students enter the data collected in particular cells. Or, start with a familiar spreadsheet, perhaps a spreadsheet of personal information (height, weight, shoe size, age, parent data) about students in the class. Ask students to input their personal information in the spreadsheet, then calculate high, low, and averages of these values and other quantities, such as density (weight/height). Later, use a content spreadsheet that contains formulas and have students look up information from almanacs, tables, or other reference materials to enter into the spreadsheet. Make sure that students trace all of the calculations that are completed by the spreadsheet. These activities familiarize learners with spreadsheet functions and structure.

STEP 2. Students make a plan. Before they develop a spreadsheet, students need to make a plan for their spreadsheet. What are they interested in representing? Do they want to build a simulation? What points do they want to make? What kind of structure and information is required to make those points? What learning goals will they work toward?

STEP 3. Students adapt existing spreadsheets or design new spreadsheets for other students to complete. Start with familiar content and require students to adapt existing spreadsheets, such as adding nutritional information and relationships to the personal variables in the classroom information spreadsheet. Or, ask students to design new spreadsheets that they can fill in collaboratively. Topics such as local sports teams, dating patterns, and television shows are popular. Students can add data, construct graphs and charts to represent the data, and add variables.

STEP 4. Students create and complete a problem-oriented spreadsheet. Increase the complexity of the spreadsheet content by relating it to classroom studies. Start with concrete activities such as geographic or demographic features in social studies or mathematical formulas in algebra. Assign students to work in small, collaborative groups, and ask them to determine what values, formulas, and functions are required. Have them start with small phenomena first. For example, students should model the output of a single farm or business before trying to develop models of national economies. What gets modeled depends on what kinds of questions students want answered, that is, what kinds of relationships should be compared in the spreadsheet. This is perhaps the most difficult part of the instruction process. Compare the student-constructed spreadsheets in class and discuss the relationships portrayed in terms of how completely and accurately they reflect the content domain. Construction of a spreadsheet requires learners to identify variables and information needs, develop formulas and functions, complete the spreadsheet, and use the spreadsheet to answer questions.

STEP 5. Students extrapolate from spreadsheets. Students can create new formulas, variables, and graphs in an existing spreadsheet to support other applications. For example, students might start with a spreadsheet on geographic information, and add political and economic variables and relationships to support questions about geopolitical relationships.

STEP 6. Students reflect on the activity. Reflection should not start when the project is completed. Rather, students should continuously review their progress during the project. Are we achieving our goals? What changes are necessary? How do we compare with other groups? Are we answering questions and making the points that we set out in our plan? After the project is completed, the students should reflect further. What have we learned about math? What have we learned about spreadsheet construction, and can spreadsheets be used to represent knowledge? What have we learned about working with each other? You may choose to provide students with some or all of the criteria for evaluating their spreadsheets (presented in the next section). The activity of constructing spreadsheets engages meaningful thinking, and reflection cements the knowledge that learners construct.

EVALUATING SPREADSHEETS

What makes an effective spreadsheet? That depends on the kind of spreadsheet that is being constructed and the age and abilities of the learners who are constructing the spreadsheet. Figure 11-6 presents a number of criteria that you may use to evaluate the spreadsheets that students construct as their knowledge and skills move

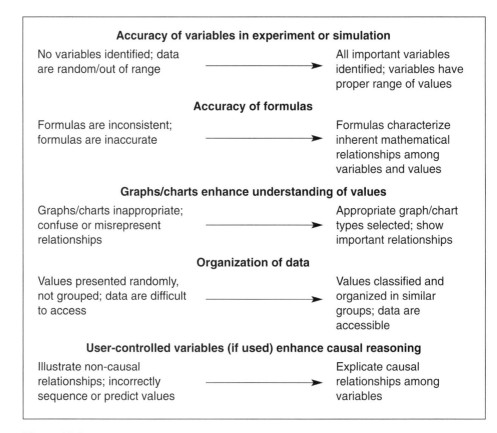

Figure 11-6
Evaluation rubrics for assessing student-constructed spreadsheets.

from emergent to mastery. Most likely, you will adapt these or add your own criteria as you evaluate your students' projects.

ADVANTAGES AND LIMITATIONS OF SPREADSHEETS FOR MODELING

A spreadsheet will always perform the calculations that are embedded into its cells.
Therefore, if one value in the grid is changed, all of the values in the spreadsheet
that are related to it are automatically recalculated. This capability frees the user
from reentering all of the values in a formula if one value changes, which is required by most calculators. Perhaps the major logistical advantage of spreadsheets is
that they are easy to adapt and modify.

A spreadsheet is, in essence, a computer program for making multiple calculations. But spreadsheets do not require the use of a complex programming language,
so they reduce the proliferation of syntax and logical errors that are common with
such languages (Misovich & Biasca, 1990). If you like computer languages, many of
the more powerful spreadsheet packages provide simple programming languages to
enhance the capabilities of the spreadsheet. Nevertheless, you can always access
the power of programming without learning to program.

Spreadsheets support speculation, decision making, and problem solving.
Given a problem with complex quantitative relationships, the experienced spreadsheet user can quickly create a spreadsheet to represent those relationships. Spreadsheets are often used in what-if analyses (e.g., What will be the effect on accounts
payable and debt ratio if interest rates increase 1%? What will happen if the population of an emerging country increases at 7% rather than 5%?). This type of thinking
is best supported by spreadsheets and is essential to decision analysis (Sounderpandian, 1989). Such questioning requires learners to consider the implications of
various conditions or options, which entails higher order reasoning.

Spreadsheets explicitly demonstrate values and relationships in any problem or
content domain in numeric form. Identifying values and developing formulas to interrelate them enhances learners' understanding of the algorithms used to compare
them and of the mathematical models used to describe content domains. Students
understand calculations (both antecedents and consequents) because they are actively involved in identifying the interrelationships among the components of the
calculation. Spreadsheet construction and use demonstrate all steps of problem
solutions and show the progression of calculations as they are performed. The
spreadsheet process models the mathematical logic that is implied by calculations.
When the underlying logic becomes obvious to learners, their understanding of the
interrelationships and procedures improves.

Spreadsheets integrate graphics with computation. What makes modern spreadsheet programs so powerful is their ability to visualize in different ways quantitative
relationships. Early spreadsheets could only show the grid of cells, but modern
spreadsheets can easily create graphs, charts, and models of phenomena. Research

has shown that even children as young as 6 years are able to enter and graphically display information (Goodfellow, 1990). This graphic capability enables spreadsheets to be used as simulation modeling and visualization tools.

Although the spreadsheet is a versatile tool, it is most effective in solving quantitative problems. Modern spreadsheets are able to represent a variety of data types, but they are intended primarily to manipulate and represent quantitative information. Therefore, they are most useful in mathematics, science, and in some social science applications (e.g., economics, psychology, and sociology). Spreadsheets are generally not as useful for humanities instruction, although there are a few types of analyses that can be quantified and are amenable to spreadsheet use (e.g., metric analysis of poems).

SUMMARY

Spreadsheets were developed as an electronic replacement for paper-based ledger systems. They automated accounting operations and enabled accountants to test hypotheses in addition to calculating. Similarly, spreadsheets can qualitatively change educational processes that require manipulation or speculation with numbers.

Construction and use of spreadsheets engages users in mental processes that require them to use existing rules, generate new rules describing relationships, and organize information. Many studies show how spreadsheets have been used to model phenomena in four ways: computational reasoning, comprehension, visualization, and simulation modeling.

Spreadsheets are easy to adapt and modify. They support speculation, decision making, and problem solving, and they are often used in what-if analyses. Spreadsheets demonstrate values and relationships in a problem or content domain in numeric form. When students learn to construct spreadsheets, they are learning the underlying logic implied by the calculations. Spreadsheets are versatile tools that are most effective in solving quantitative problems.

REFERENCES

Adams, F. G., & Kroch, E. (1989). The computer in the teaching of economics. *Journal of Economic Education, 20*(3), 269–280.

Barnes, J. A. (1997). Modeling dynamical systems with spreadsheet software. *Mathematics and Computer Education, 31*(1), 43–55.

Blickensderfer, R. (1990). Learning chemical kinetics with spreadsheets. *Journal of Computers in Mathematics and Science Teaching, 9*(4), 35–43.

Bridges, R. (1995). Fitting planetary orbits with a spreadsheet, *Physics Education, 30*(5), 266–271.

Brosnan, T. (1990). Using spreadsheets in the teaching of chemistry: Two more ideas and some limitations. *School Science Review, 71*(256), 53–59.

Cashien, P. (1990). Spreadsheet investigations in economics teaching. *Economics, 26*(Pt. 2, 110), 73–84.

Crisci, G. (1992, January). Play the market! *Instructor, 102,* 68–69.

Dribin, C. I. (1985, June). Spreadsheets and performance: A guide for student-graded presentations. *The Computing Teacher, 12,* 22–25.

Dubitsky, B. (1988, November). Making division meaningful with a spreadsheet. *Arithmetic Teacher, 36,* 18–21.

Edwards, N. T., & Bitter, B. G. (1989, October). Changing variables using spreadsheet templates. *Arithmetic Teacher, 37,* 40–44.

Feicht, L. (1999). 3-D graphing, contour graphs, topographical maps, and matrices using spreadsheets. *Mathematics Teacher, 92*(2), 166–174.

Goodfellow, T. (1990). Spreadsheets: Powerful tools in science education. *School Science Review, 71*(257), 47–57.

Goodwin, A. (2002). Using a spreadsheet to explore melting, dissolving and phase diagrams. *School Science Review. 83*(304), 105–108.

Hart, F. X. (1995). Solving multi-loop circuit problems with a spreadsheet. *The Physics Teacher, 33,* 542.

Hoeffner, K., Kendall, M., Stellenwerf, C., Thames, P., & Williams, P. (1993, November). Problem solving with a spreadsheet. *Arithmetic Teacher, 41,* 52–56.

Kari, R. (1990). Spreadsheets in advanced physical chemistry. *Journal of Computers in Mathematics and Science Teaching, 10*(1), 39–48.

Karlin, M. (1988, February). Beyond distance = rate * time. *The Computing Teacher, 15,* 20–23.

Krieger, M. E., & Stith, J. H. (1990, September). Spreadsheets in the physics laboratory. *The Physics Teacher, 28,* 378–384.

Macho, S. (2002). Cognitive modeling with spreadsheets. *Behavior Research Methods, Instruments, & Computers, 34*(1), 19–36.

Matthews, J. (1998, September). Retrieved from http://www.washingtonpost.com/wp-srv/washtech/daily/sept98/tech093098.htm

Mills, J., & Jackson, R. (1997). Analysis of microbial growth data using a spreadsheet. *Journal of Biological Education, 31*(1), 34–38.

Misovich, M., & Biasca, K. (1990). The power of spreadsheets in a mass and energy balances course. *Chemical Engineering Education, 24,* 46–50.

National Curriculum Commission. (1990). *Technology in the national curriculum.* London: Author.

Niess, M. L. (1992, March). Winds of change. *The Computing Teacher, 19,* 32–35.

Parker, J., & Widmer, C. C. (1991, September). Teaching mathematics with technology. *Arithmetic Teacher, 38/39,* 38–41.

Pea, R. D. (1985). Beyond amplification: Using the computer to reorganize mental functioning. *Educational Psychologist, 20*(4), 167–182.

Pinter-Lucke, C. (1992). Rootfinding with a spreadsheet in precalculus. *Journal of Computers in Mathematics and Science Teaching, 11,* 85–93.

Ramondetta, J. (1992). Learning from lunchroom trash. *Learning Using Computers, 20*(8), 59.

Rudnicki, R. (1990). Using spreadsheets in population geography classes. *Journal of Geography, 89*(3), 118–122.

Schlenker, R. M., & Yoshida, S. J. (1991). A clever lever endeavor: You can't beat the spreadsheet. *The Science Teacher, 58*(2), 36–39.

Sgroi, R. J. (1992, March). Systematizing trial and error using spreadsheets. *Arithmetic Teacher, 38/39,* 8–12.

Sharp, J. (2003). Simple animated spreadsheets. *Micromath, 19*(2), 35–39.

Sigismondi, L. A., & Calise, C. (1990). Integrating basic computer skills into science classes: Analysis of ecological data. *The American Biology Teacher, 52*(5), 296–301.

Silva, A. A. (1994). Simulating electrical circuits with an electronic spreadsheet. *Computers in Education, 22*(4), 345–353.

Silva, A. A. (1998). Archimedes' law and potential energy: Modelling and simulation with a spreadsheet. *Physics Education, 33*(2), 87–92.

Silvius, J. E., Sjoquist, D. W., & Mundy, D. D. (1994). Vegetation analysis using a computer spreadsheet, *The American Biology Teacher, 56*(1), 41–43.

Sounderpandian, J. (1989). Decision analysis using spreadsheets. *Collegiate Microcomputer, 7*(2), 157–163.

Sundheim, B. R. (1992). Modelling a thermostatted water bath with a spreadsheet. *Journal of Chemical Education, 69*(8), 650–654.

Sutherland, R., & Rojano, T. (1993). A spreadsheet approach to solving algebra problems. *Journal of Mathematical Behavior, 12*, 353–383.

Verderber, N. L. (1990). Spreadsheets and problem solving with AppleWorks in mathematics teaching. *Journal of Computers in Mathematics and Science Teaching, 9*(3), 45–51.

Vockell, E., & Van Deusen, R. M. (1989). *The computer and higher-order thinking skills.* Watsonville, CA: Mitchell Publishing.

Watkins, W., & Taylor, M. (1989). A spreadsheet in the mathematics classroom. *Collegiate Microcomputer, 7*(3), 233–239.

Wells, G., & Berger, C. (1985/1986). Teacher/student-developed spreadsheet simulations: A population growth example. *Journal of Computers in Mathematics and Science Teaching, 5*(2), 34–40.

Whitmer, J. C. (1990). Modeling the Milky Way. *The Science Teacher, 57*(7), 19–21.

CHAPTER 12

Modeling with Expert Systems

Expert systems are computer programs designed to simulate expert reasoning in order to facilitate decision making for all sorts of problems. The first expert system, MYCIN, was developed to help physicians diagnose unfamiliar bacterial infections. Physicians consulted the expert system, which asked them questions about the patient's symptoms and then provided a diagnosis. Expert systems have also been developed to help geologists decide where to drill for oil, firefighters decide how to extinguish different kinds of fires, computer sales technicians configure computer systems, bankers decide on loan applications, and employees choose among a large number of company benefits. Problems whose solutions include decisions or prediction based on a variety of factors are good candidates for expert systems.

FUNCTIONS OF EXPERT SYSTEMS

Expert systems evolved from research in the field of artificial intelligence. Artificial intelligence (AI) is a specialty in computer and cognitive sciences that focuses on the development of programming techniques that enable machines to perform tasks that are regarded as intelligent when done by people. *Artificial* means simulated and *intelligence* is the capacity to learn, reason, and understand; so, AI researchers and expert system builders attempt to develop programs that simulate the human capability to reason and to learn. *Simulated* means imitating a real object or event. For example, flight simulators look real and feel real to flight trainers; however, a flight simulator is an artificial airplane that never actually flies and could not replace an airplane's primary function—to fly.

AI programs, including expert systems, may perform functions that simulate human thinking, such as decision making. In reality, though, AI programs merely imitate what we believe to be human mental activity. Why can't computers replicate human reasoning? Because human intelligence is generalizable and transferable to new situations, but most forms of computer intelligence are not, and that includes expert systems. For example, a computer that is programmed to play chess cannot transfer that capability to play Monopoly.

An expert system, then, is a computer program that attempts to simulate the way human experts solve problems; it is an artificial decision maker. For example, when you consult an expert (e.g., doctor, lawyer, teacher) about a problem, the expert asks for current information about your condition, searches his or her knowledge base (memory) for existing knowledge to which elements of the current situation can be related, processes the information (thinks), arrives at a decision, and presents a decision or solution. Similarly, an expert system is approached by an individual (novice) with a problem. The system queries the individual about the current status of the problem, searches its knowledge base (which contains previously stored expert knowledge) for pertinent facts and rules, processes the information, arrives at a decision, and reports the solution to the user.

COMPONENTS OF EXPERT SYSTEMS

Figure 12–1 diagrams the seven components of an expert system. Each component is essential in constructing an expert system.

User

Like a human expert, an expert system cannot put its knowledge and skills to use unless a need arises. The computer must await input from a user with a need or problem. For example, imagine that a novice loan officer in a bank is asked by an individual for a personal, unsecured loan. There are many factors to consider when making the decision (e.g., applicant's income and past credit record, amount of loan, reason for the loan, size of monthly payment)—so many factors that it may take months or years of training to prepare the loan officer to consider all of the parameters involved. An alternative is to build an expert system that asks the loan officer to input all data necessary for making an informed decision. The expert system is composed of a knowledge base of facts and rules that an experienced or expert

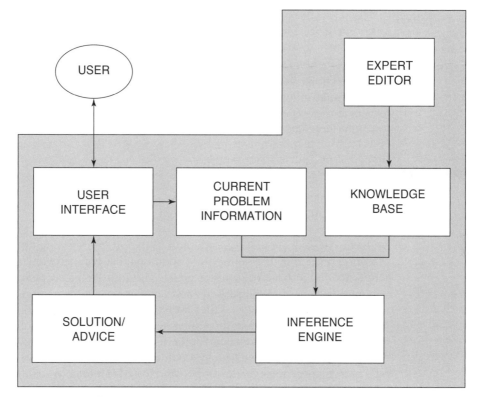

Figure 12-1
Components of an expert system.

loan officer uses in making a decision. The expert system compares the information provided by the loan applicant to the knowledge base and presents a decision that provides valuable advice to the loan officer. In this way, the expert system increases productivity, because it saves both analysis time and training time.

Current Problem Information

Because an expert system is based on programming techniques derived from AI, it is designed to deal with changing conditions in the problem situation it was designed to help. To handle these changing conditions, data about the current situation are collected from the user and entered into computer memory to help guide the expert system to a solution. For example, an expert system designed to help an undergraduate student select courses for the current semester might ask the student the following questions:

◆ What is your major?
◆ What courses have you completed?

◆ Do you have a job that prevents you from taking classes at certain times?

◆ When do you expect to graduate?

◆ Do you plan to take summer school courses?

The questions asked by the expert system through the user interface (described next) results in information that will change with each individual situation. The answers to these questions are integrated within an existing knowledge base of information (facts and rules).

User Interface

The user interface facilitates the expert system's communication with the user. The communication process gathers current problem data from the user, explains the expert's reasoning, and presents the solution or advice for the problem being solved. The user provides information to the program through the interface by answering questions that define the conditions that will be evaluated by the rules in the knowledge base (discussed next). The interface also provides explanations about the questions being asked and the decisions being made. Typically, the interface allows users to ask why they were asked for information or why the program made a particular decision; the expert system will retrieve that information from the knowledge base and display it for the user. The expert system must carry on a dialogue with the user; therefore, the nature of the dialogue, as well as the format of the presentation, must be developed and tested carefully to ensure easy input of the information sought.

Knowledge Base

Information that is programmed into the knowledge base (analogous to long-term memory) is relatively stable. It is composed of facts about objects and rules about the relationships among those objects that represent knowledge structures used by a human expert to reach a decision. Facts simply state given conditions (e.g., Calculus 1 is offered at 8 a.m., 10 a.m., and 2 p.m. on Monday, Wednesday, and Friday), and rules consist of conditions and decisions. Rules state that IF a set of conditions exists, THEN some decision is reached. Conditions can be combined in a number of ways into sets. Sets of IF conditions are combined using conjunctions (condition 1 AND condition 2 must exist), disjunctions (condition 1 OR condition 2 must exist), and negations (condition 1 but NOT condition 2 must exist) for a decision to be reached. A decision may be an action or it may state another condition, which is then combined with other conditions to reach another decision. In the case of an expert system advising students about course selection, a knowledge base would store lists of required courses for every major, as exemplified by the following rules:

◆ IF student's major is mechanical engineering, THEN Differential Equations is required.

◆ IF student's major is mechanical engineering OR student's major is electrical engineering, THEN Calculus 2 is required.

◆ IF Differential Equations is NOT taken AND Calculus 3 has been completed AND Differential Equations is offered at a time student is available, THEN advise student to sign up for Differential Equations.

Variables may be used to carry current problem information (e.g., whether student has completed Calculus 2) or to carry a preliminary decision value on through the process. The knowledge base also may contain explanations for why questions are being asked and why certain rules are activated, that is, why certain decisions are reached.

Expert Editor

Most expert systems provide an editor that enables the expert or the knowledge engineer to enter information into the knowledge base. Editors consist of text editors and parsers. The text editor allows the engineer to input facts and rules into the knowledge base in a prespecified format. The parser checks the syntax of information that is input as well as the validity or logic of the information. For example, the parser usually decides if rules are consistent and mutually exclusive or whether redundancy exists.

Inference Engine

The inference engine is the part of an expert system that functions intelligently while querying the knowledge base. This component is not usually accessible to an expert system designer. Instead, it is built into the system that the designer uses. The inference engine is constructed of AI programming techniques that act on the knowledge base and current problem data to generate solutions. In an expert system, the inference engine does its work after the user poses a specific problem and enters current problem information. The inference engine contains the logical programming to examine the information provided by the user, as well as the facts and rules specified within the knowledge base. It evaluates the current problem situation and seeks rules that will provide advice about that situation.

Inference engines are usually of two types: backward chaining and forward chaining. The backward-chaining engine (goal-driven model) starts with a solution or decision and searches the knowledge base for rules containing the conditions necessary to fulfill that solution. If sufficient conditions are not found, it asks the user to supply information or searches the knowledge base for subgoals that contribute to the solution. The forward-chaining engine (data-driven model) starts by trying to match existing data with a condition or conditions stated in the rules; then it examines the knowledge base to see if a solution is viable with only that information. It successively acquires information in an effort to make a decision.

Solution/Advice

The final feature of an expert system is its presentation of a solution generated by the inference engine based on the permanent knowledge base and current problem information. For example, the student advisor system considers all of the data entered by the student, relates those data to the rules in the knowledge base, and presents a solution, such as the following: Recommend Calculus 2, Section 2, 10–11, MWF.

MODELING WITH EXPERT SYSTEMS

Expert systems have been used primarily in business to control manufacturing processes and assist people with decision making. However, there are also many applications of expert systems in education. The primary use of expert systems is to provide intelligent advice to novices who request it. For this application, knowledge engineers work with subject matter experts to record their expertise about a knowledge domain. Users query the knowledge base to get help in making a decision. Most educational applications of expert systems have focused on developing expert systems to provide advice. For example, expert systems have been developed to help educators and psychologists clinically diagnose students with learning disabilities or other special needs. They have also been used to model experts' and students' thinking in intelligent tutoring systems. Expert system advisors have also been developed to guide novices through the instructional development process (Tennyson & Christensen, 1991) and to assist students in selecting the correct statistical test (Karake, 1990; Saleem & Azad, 1992). Grabinger and Pollock (1989) used expert systems to guide students through self-evaluation of their own projects. This form of feedback was as effective in enhancing learning as instructor-provided feedback. Using expert systems as a feedback method may be more useful than using expert systems to walk learners through required decision-making sequences. Despite the many experiences with expert systems, consulting an expert system knowledge base does not necessarily engage users as deeply as building a knowledge base that reflects their own thinking.

Level of intellectual engagement is an important issue in expert system use. How much knowledge can learners gain using expert systems? Surprisingly little research has been reported on this topic. Students who used an expert system to select the most appropriate statistical analysis procedure were more accurate in their selections and retained the information better than students who used traditional computer-assisted instruction (Marcoulides, 1988). In another study, students who followed expert systems queries for deducing research hypotheses learned to break the task into small steps, which helped them to better understand the process. If the questions of the expert system model the kind of thinking that users need to learn, and if the users practice that sequence consistently, how much will they learn about the process? We really don't know.

We do know that negative consequences can result from relying on the expertise of expert systems. When using expert systems to resolve chemical spill scenarios, chemical process operators tended to overestimate their performance capabilities when using the expert system (Su & Lin, 1998). Such overconfidence could prove to be dangerous if the operators were required to solve problems in real time without the use of the expert system.

Based on the equivocal results of using expert systems, I argue that students gain more understanding from building expert systems. Trollip, Lippert, Starfield, and Smith (1992) were among the early advocates who argued that learner construction of expert systems results in deep understanding, because the construction process provides an intellectual environment that demands the refinement of domain knowledge, supports problem solving, and monitors the acquisition of knowledge. Building expert systems is a knowledge-modeling process that enables people to represent their conceptual models of domain knowledge (Adams-Webber, 1995). Modeling domain knowledge requires identifying declarative knowledge (facts and concepts), structural knowledge (knowledge of interrelationships among ideas), and procedural knowledge (how to apply declarative knowledge) that an expert (or at least a knowledgeable person) possesses. The expert system is the most common way to represent procedural knowledge (Gagné, 1985). As learners identify the IF–THEN structure of a decision-making problem, they tend to understand the nature of decision-making tasks better. This deeper understanding should make subsequent practice opportunities more meaningful. Nevertheless, mere development of an expert system does not necessarily lead learners to acquire the compiled procedural knowledge of a domain. For example, a student project may correctly identify many of the IF–THEN rules involved in flying an airplane, but actual acquisition of procedural expertise would require extended practice flying an airplane.

Trollip et al. (1992) believe that learning environments, whether computer based or not, should provide a mechanism for helping learners monitor their knowledge growth. This requires learners to have metacognitive awareness of their knowledge, which is a necessary component of problem solving (Flavell & Wellman, 1977). Clearly, building expert systems requires learners to synthesize knowledge by making explicit their own reasoning, thereby improving retention, transfer, and problem-solving abilities. Although these requirements sound complex and beyond the grasp of most students, experience has indicated otherwise. Using simple expert system shells, most students begin building simple rule bases within an hour. Many of the shells are free or inexpensive. My preferred expert system shell (editor) is WinExpert, which is bundled with the book, *How to Model It* (Starfield, Smith, & Bleloch, 1990).

A small amount of research has validated the effectiveness of learner construction of expert systems:

◆ Lippert (1987) found that the subject matter analysis that is required to develop expert systems is so deep and so incisive that learners develop a greater comprehension of the subject matter. Building expert system rule bases engages learners in analytical reasoning, elaboration strategies such as synthesis, and metacognitive strategies.

◆ Lippert (1988) found that having learners construct small knowledge bases is a valuable method for teaching problem solving and knowledge structuring to students from the sixth-grade level to adults. Learning is more meaningful because learners evaluate not only their own thinking processes but also the product of those processes, the resulting knowledge base.

◆ Lai (1989) found that when nursing students developed medical expert systems to perform diagnoses, they developed enhanced reasoning skills and acquired a deeper understanding of the subject domain.

◆ Six first-year physics students used an expert system to create questions, decisions, rules, and explanations pertaining to classical projectile motion. The students developed more refined, domain-specific knowledge as a result of the greater degree of elaboration required during encoding and the greater quantity of material processed in an explicit, coherent context, and therefore in greater semantic depth (Lippert & Finley, 1988).

◆ High school students with hearing impairments constructed rule bases in current events and geographic continents. The students learned significant amounts of content and spontaneously used categorization and conditional reasoning while building the expert systems (Wilson, 1997).

◆ Lippert (1988) described physics students' development of rule bases to solve problems about forces. Students identified factors such as kind of force acting on an object (gravitational, centripetal, etc.), motion of the object (free fall, circular, sliding, etc.), velocity of the object, and so on. The decisions that students reached included the laws that affect the motion, the formulas that should be applied, and so on. Students reported meaningful learning from evaluating their own thought processes, more enthusiasm for learning, and learning of content that they were not expected to master.

◆ Knox-Quinn (1992) reported that MBA students who developed knowledge bases on tax laws in an accounting course were consistently engaged in higher order thinking, such as classifying information, breaking down content, organizing information, and integrating and elaborating information. All of the students who developed rule bases showed substantial gains in the quantity and quality of declarative and procedural knowledge and improved their problem-solving strategies. Students who built expert systems reasoned more similarly to experts.

◆ Dezman, Trninic, and Dizdar (2001) developed expert systems to help them predict the quality of basketball players. They found that stable factors were difficult to identify and that quality often depends on the quality of the opponents. This finding may be obvious to experienced coaches, but it was a significant discovery for the authors.

Coaching Construction of Expert Systems

Expert system rule bases are reflective tools that can be used in a variety of classroom situations. Imagine that you have just completed a science lab. As a way of reviewing what was learned, have the students construct a rule base that reflects the decisions they had to make to complete the lab. In a social studies class, have students create a rule base that will predict who will win an election, or whether a health care reform bill will pass through Congress, and explain why. For any content, expert systems require you to consider how students should use that content to predict outcomes, explain results, or infer reasoning. For most students, this will represent a new way of thinking, so you will have to coach them. The process that you should coach includes the following activities.

STEP 1. Students make a plan. Before beginning, students need to make a plan for their expert system. What are they interested in representing? What points do they want to make? What kinds of structure and information are required to make those points? What learning goals will they work toward?

STEP 2. Students identify the purpose for building the expert system and the problem domain. This activity will determine the overall approach students take in seeking information to fill in the knowledge base. If your goal is to understand students' current mental models, then students will do little outside research to create the knowledge base (Knox-Quinn, 1988). However, if your goal is student mastery and problem solving of new content, then student research may be integral to the process. Your decision will depend, to a large degree, on students' current level of knowledge about the subject domain.

Regardless of students' age or amount of prior subject knowledge, they will need help in developing the skills needed for constructing expert systems. Getting them to understand the IF–THEN logic of rules and the syntax of even simple expert system shells is not easy, so start with familiar content. For example, have students develop rule bases on which fast-food restaurant to eat in, what kind of person to ask out on a date, or which popular music groups are best. Students will be surprised by how much they know, how much they don't know, and how difficult it is to articulate what they do know.

STEP 3. Students specify problem solutions or decisions. Once students have determined the problem domain, they work to identify the solutions, decisions, or outcomes the expert system is expected to provide. In the atomic bomb example (see Figure 6–7), there are only four decisions (threaten to drop the bomb, drop the bomb, do not drop the bomb, and a general statement of advice about using fission for peaceful purposes). Decisions are not necessarily mutually exclusive; that is, you may want to provide more than one recommendation to the same individual.

There are several reasons for beginning with solutions or decisions. Most problems suitable for implementation in an expert system have many alternative solutions, so the first part of the goal-identification stage involves generating all possible solutions within the defined problem area. "All possible solutions" refers to all those students can think of. It is important not to make judgments about the feasibility or value of each solution (brainstorming can help here). It is critical that students identify as many alternative solutions as possible so that none are overlooked.

After they have identified all possible solutions, students may want to limit the options, because in most cases it is neither practical nor necessary to deal with each one. Students can identify the most probable solutions or develop classes of solutions that have common attributes. For example, a decision could be made to reject any goal with less than a 25% likelihood of happening. How important is a particular solution and is it worth including in the knowledge base?

STEP 4. Students isolate problem attributes, factors, or variables. The problem attributes compose the set of factors an expert considers when making a decision. They are decision points used during the problem-solving process to determine the most appropriate solution. The expert gathers and analyzes information, then decides what other information is needed to solve the problem. Each decision point adopts a value that is called an attribute value. In other words, each problem attribute used in an expert system must have at least two alternatives or options to help direct the process to a solution. For example, in the course-selection advisor described earlier, the goal was to schedule each student into appropriate classes. The problem attributes in this case are the required courses for the student's curriculum, courses completed, available times, etc. Problem attributes, then, are those arguments used by an expert when arriving at a decision (you need this course; it is available at 8:00 a.m., so take it).

The three major steps to identifying the primary problem attributes used in an expert system are (1) identify the problem factors or attributes used when making the decision (the questions that will be asked by the expert system); (2) separate the critical problem attributes from the trivial attributes; and (3) assign the significant values for each attribute (i.e., the answers to the questions).

STEP 5. Students generate rules and examples. Rules represent the knowledge or expertise in an expert system. They are used to arrive at a decision. Consider this example: IF the consumer makes $1,200 per month and has a job and has a good credit rating and is older than 24, THEN a loan of $10,000 is permitted. Rules are a series of IF–THEN statements that describe the means of reaching a specific decision in narrative form. They set forth the conditional relationships among the problem attribute values.

Rules consist of two essential elements: the premise (antecedent) and the conclusion (consequent). The premise begins with the word *if* and states the conditions that are compared with the situation or the desires of the user. Conditions are combined logically using the logical operators *and* and *or*. If conditions are connected by *and*, both conditions must be met for the rule to be true. If the conditions are connected by *or*, one or both conditions must be true for the rule to be true. Conclusions are signaled by the word *then*.

Rules in expert systems vary in complexity and certainty (confidence levels). Rule complexity refers to the number of premises that must be satisfied before reaching a decision for solving the problem. The number of antecedents may vary, as well as the number of consequents. A rule that must meet only one condition is simple:

IF the subject in a picture is more than 40 yards away

THEN use a 400-millimeter lens.

The only condition in that rule is the subject's distance from the camera. A rule that meets more than one condition or a rule that contains alternative solutions is complex:

IF the purpose of the car is commuting

AND IF number of commuters is less than four

AND IF distance to work is greater than 25 miles

OR IF more than one return trip per day is made

THEN buy a two-door sedan

ELSE take the bus.

The conditions or attributes in this rule for helping consumers to select an appropriate car include the purpose of use, number of commuters using the car, distance to work, and number of trips per day. Given a particular combination of these conditions, the alternative solutions are buying a two-door sedan or taking the bus. Complex rules are appropriate when there are a number of conditions and alternatives. A few simple rules do not justify the development time involved in creating an expert system, nor will they be able to provide advice on any significant problem.

STEP 6. Students refine logic and efficiency of decision making. To make construction of the rule base easier, you may want to advise students to generate interim decisions and use those as factors rather than writing complex rules with eight or more factors. For example, in the car selection example, a student may want to make an interim decision about the size of car (compact, midsize, or luxury) and use selection factors to first determine the size of the car needed:

IF the purpose of the car is commuting

AND IF number of commuters is less than three

AND IF distance to work is greater than 25 miles

AND IF the roads are good

THEN size needed is compact.

This conclusion can then be combined with other factors to make the final decision:

IF size needed is compact

AND IF price must be below $10,000

AND IF status need is low

THEN buy a Smart Car.

Interim decisions help the flow of knowledge base development by avoiding long, complex rules. Also, students can collaborate with others: Break the final decision up into a set of subdecisions and assign the subdecisions to different groups.

STEP 7. Students test the system. The purpose of building a Mindtool knowledge base is not absolute fidelity of the knowledge base to real-world occurrences. Nevertheless, it is useful to ensure that the system works. Have different students query the system and note any improper conclusions or sets of conditions that do not produce a conclusion. As the number of factors increases, the number of possible combinations of rules increases geometrically. Writing a rule for every possible combination of circumstances may not be feasible or even desirable. However, if users' queries lead to dead ends, a rule should probably be generated for those combinations.

STEP 8. Students reflect on the activity. Reflection should not start when the project is completed. Rather, students should continuously review their progress during the project. Are we achieving our goals? What changes are necessary? How do we compare with other groups? Are we answering questions and making the points that we set out in our plan? After the project is completed, the students should reflect further. What have we learned about content? What have we learned about expert systems and causal relationships among variables? What have we learned about working with each other? You may choose to provide students with some or all of the criteria for evaluating their expert systems (presented in the next section). The activity of constructing expert systems engages meaningful thinking, and reflection cements the knowledge that learners construct.

EVALUATING EXPERT SYSTEMS

What makes a meaningful expert system simulation? That depends on the kind of expert system that is being constructed and the age and abilities of the learners who are constructing it. You must consider the age and ability of your students. Figure 12–2 presents a number of criteria for assessing the expert systems that your students construct as their knowledge and skills move from emergent to mastery. Most likely,

Quality of decisions/solutions/advice

Advice would never be given
(implausible); solutions
missing or not elaborated;
conclusions not useful

$\longrightarrow$

Advice is plausible; all
solutions identified;
meaningful conclusions

Explanations meaningful

Explanations of results
are vague; do not explain
reasoning or enhance
learning

$\longrightarrow$

Explanations of advice explain
reasoning, enhances user's
understanding

Sensitivity of factors (questions)

Factors do not
discriminate solutions;
variables and factors
missing; factors overlap

$\longrightarrow$

Factors ask important questions;
identify all variables that pertain
to solution; each factor elicits
different information

Rules logical and complete

Running system results in
dead ends; combinations
not anticipated; not
enough rules; rules
poorly organized

$\longrightarrow$

All combinations of factors
represented by a rule; all dead
ends blocked; rules well
organized

Meaningful representation of thinking

Poorly simulates thought;
poor models of activity;
represents associative
thinking

$\longrightarrow$

Simulates coherent thinking;
models meaningful activity;
represents causal/predictive
reasoning

Figure 12-2
Criteria for assessing student-constructed expert systems.

you will adapt these or add your own criteria as you evaluate your students'
projects.

ADVANTAGES AND LIMITATIONS OF EXPERT SYSTEMS
FOR MODELING

A number of advantages result from using expert systems to model phenomena:

◆ More than other Mindtools, except for systems modeling tools (Chapter 13),
expert systems focus thinking on causal reasoning and problem-solving
activities.

◆ Expert systems engage learners in metacognitive reasoning. Reflecting on and representing the thinking involved in problem solving provides valuable insights to learners.

◆ Expert systems emphasize inferential and implicational reasoning. Few activities in schools stress going beyond existing information to infer why something happened or to consider the implications of what might happen if a set of conditions exists. Building expert systems engages learners in this form of deeper processing.

◆ Expert systems highlight the natural complexity that exists in most problem-solving situations. Becoming aware of how complex problems can really be is enlightening.

In contrast, there are some potential drawbacks to using expert systems to model phenomena:

◆ The process of building coherent knowledge bases requires novel thinking for many learners, so the work is difficult. Some students will likely protest the requirements to think more deeply.

◆ Formal operational reasoning is required, so expert systems will be difficult for students younger than 13. Lippert (1988) reports that expert systems may be used with children as young as sixth grade.

◆ Wideman and Owston (1991) found that development of expert systems most benefited learners with higher abstract reasoning ability; students with lower abstract reasoning ability were not affected as much or as capable. However, in an earlier study (Wideman & Owston, 1988) they found that seventh graders built rule bases enthusiastically, even though they had to use rigorous, systematic thinking and metacognitive skills. The ability of students to construct expert systems depends on their intellectual development and motivation to perform.

SUMMARY

Expert systems are computer programs designed to simulate the reasoning of experts. The knowledge bases of expert systems represent causal, procedural knowledge about content domains. Expert systems are especially effective in representing problem-solving tasks that require decision making. Expert systems represent inferential thinking about the implications of findings.

Building an expert system involves working with seven components. The *user* provides the need or problem situation. Data about the *current situation* are collected from the user and entered into computer memory to guide the expert system to a solution. A *user interface* facilitates communication between the user and the expert system. The *knowledge base* consists of the facts and rules that lead to a decision. In most systems, an *expert editor* allows facts and rules to be entered into the knowledge base in a specific format. The *inference engine* functions intelligently while querying the knowledge base; this component of building an expert system is built into the software the builder is using. Finally, a *solution* (or advice) is generated by the inference engine based on the knowledge base and current problem information.

Students who build expert system rule bases are engaged in reflective thinking about the dynamic, causal relationships among concepts in any knowledge domain. The thinking required to build expert systems may be the most difficult of any Mindtool because of the need for formal, logical reasoning. Building expert systems is intellectually engaging and challenging. However, if your goal as an educator is to support students' causal reasoning, introduce them to the process of constructing expert systems.

REFERENCES

Adams-Webber, J. (1995). Constructivist psychology and knowledge elicitation. *Journal of Constructivist Psychology, 8*(3), 237–249.

Dezman, B., Trninic, S., & Dizdar, D. (2001). Models of expert system and decision-making systems for efficient assessment of potential and actual quality of basketball players. *Kinesiology, 33*(2), 207–215.

Flavell, J. H., & Wellman, H. M. (1977). Metamemory. In R. V. Kail & J. W. Hagen (Eds.), *Perspectives on the development of memory and cognition.* Hillsdale, NJ: Lawrence Erlbaum.

Gagné, E. (1985). *The cognitive psychology of school learning.* Boston: Little, Brown.

Grabinger, R. S., & Pollock, J. (1989). The effectiveness of internally-generated feedback with an instructional expert system. *Journal of Educational Computing Research, 5*(3), 299–309.

Karake, Z. A. (1990). Enhancing the learning process with expert systems. *Computers and Education, 14*(6), 495–503.

Knox-Quinn, C. (1988). A simple application and a powerful idea: Using expert systems shells in the classroom. *Computing Teacher, 16*(3), 12–15.

Knox-Quinn, C. (1992, April). Student construction of expert systems in the classroom. Paper presented at the annual meeting of the American Educational Research Association, San Francisco, CA.

Lai, K. W. (1989, March). Acquiring expertise and cognitive skills in the process of constructing an expert system: A preliminary study. Paper presented at the annual meeting of the American Educational Research Association, San Francisco, CA. (ERIC Document Reproduction Service No. ED312986)

Lippert, R. (1987). Teaching problem solving in mathematics and science with expert systems. *School Science and Mathematics, 87,* 407–413.

Lippert, R. C. (1988). An expert system shell to teach problem solving. *Tech Trends, 33*(2), 22–26.

Lippert, R., & Finley, F. (1988, April). Students' refinement of knowledge during the development of knowledge bases for expert systems. Paper presented at the annual meeting of the National Association for Research in Science Teaching, Lake of the Ozarks, MO. (ERIC Document Reproduction Service No. ED 293872)

Marcoulides, G. A. (1988). An intelligent computer-based learning program. *Collegiate Micro-computer, 6*(2), 123–126.

Saleem, N., & Azad, A. N. (1992). Expert systems as a statistics tutor on call. *Journal of Computers in Mathematics and Science Teaching, 11*, 179–191.

Starfield, A. M., Smith, K. A., & Bleloch, A. L. (1990). *How to model it: Problem solving for the computer age.* New York: McGraw-Hill.

Su, Y. L., & Lin, D. Y. (1998). The impact of expert-system-based training on calibration decisions confidence in emergency management. *Computers in Human Behavior, 14*(1), 81–194.

Tennyson, R. D., & Christensen, D. L. (1991). Automating instructional systems development. Proceedings of selected research presentations at the annual convention of the Association for Educational Communications and Technology. (ERIC Document Reproduction Service No. ED335018)

Trollip, S., Lippert, R., Starfield, A., & Smith, K. A. (1992). Building knowledge bases: An environment for making cognitive connections. In P. Kommers, D. H. Jonassen, & T. Mayes (Eds.), *Cognitive tools for learning.* Heidelberg, Germany: Springer-Verlag.

Wideman, H. H., & Owston, R. D. (1988). Student development of an expert system: A case study. *Journal of Computer-Based Instruction, 15*(3), 88–94.

Wideman, H. H., & Owston, R. D. (1991, April). Promoting cognitive development through knowledge base construction. Paper presented at the annual meeting of the American Educational Research Association, New Orleans, LA.

Wilson, L. M. (1997). The effects of student created expert systems on the reasoning and content learning of deaf students. Unpublished doctoral dissertation, University of Minnesota, Minneapolis.

CHAPTER 13

Modeling with Systems and Population Dynamics Tools

Systems modeling is the most complex and engaging of all the modeling tools described in this book. Learning to model systems will require considerable effort on the part of students. Nevertheless, systems modeling is learnable, and it has been accomplished successfully and regularly by junior high school and high school students.

SYSTEMS THINKING

Systems dynamics attempts to show the causal interrelatedness of the components of a system. Systems are dynamic when their components are related to changes in other components; that is, components of a system affect other components which, in turn, affect the original or other components. The components of systems can be modeled using causal loops, or feedback loops (see Figure 13-1). Causal loops are used to describe the influences of system components on each other. They do not

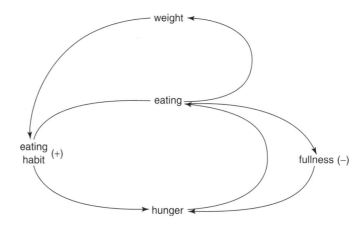

Figure 13-1
Causal (feedback) loop diagram.

assume, for instance, that hunger causes eating. Rather, hunger has a causal relationship to eating, which then feeds back to influence hunger.

The influences of system components on each other can be positive or negative. Positive influences are those in which a directional change in one component causes a similar change in another. The relationships are reciprocal. Eating influences the habit of eating, which influences hunger, which influences eating. However, dynamic changes result from the interplay of factors, both positive and negative. Negative influences are regulatory. Eating influences fullness, which negatively influences (or regulates) hunger. A system in which positive factors and negative factors increase or decrease a factor equally is in balance. For instance, eating habits and fullness counterbalance each other. If these forces are equal, there will be no change in eating and, therefore, no change in weight. When one force exerts a greater influence, eating and weight will rise or fall.

Causal loops provide a formalism for diagramming relationships in dynamic systems. However, causal loops have limitations when used to represent systems. They may specify relationships and specify predictions, but they do not describe the operations of the system and they lack quantitative information, so they cannot be used to simulate the systems they describe (Mandinach & Cline, 1994). An underlying assumption of the tools described in this chapter is that most systems can be modeled by causal loops (Steed, 1992) but that those systems need more powerful tools to simulate them. Those tools are the subject of this chapter.

SYSTEMS MODELING/DYNAMIC SIMULATION CONSTRUCTION TOOLS

Complex learning requires that students solve complex and ill-structured problems and develop complex mental models of the world to do so. Formation of mental models results from conceptual change. Because systems thinking is so important to understanding complex, real-world systems and for building mental models of those systems, students need to be familiar with the tools for simulating systems that are now available.

Building models of real-world phenomena is at the heart of scientific thinking and requires diverse mental activities such as planning, data collecting, collaborating and accessing information, data visualizing, modeling, and reporting (Soloway, Krajcik, & Finkel, 1995). The process for developing the ability to model phenomena requires defining the model, using the model to understand some phenomena, creating a model by representing real-world phenomena and making connections between its parts, and finally analyzing the model for its ability to represent the world (Spitulnik, Studer, Finkel, Gustafson, Laczko, & Soloway, 1995).

This chapter describes computer tools for developing dynamic simulations of systems. What the students construct are referred to in different places as dynamic models, dynamic simulations, or systems models. What are they? A *model* is a conceptual representation of something, described verbally, visually, or quantitatively. A *simulation* is a resemblance of a phenomenon that imitates the conditions and actions of it. These are sometimes referred to as computer models. *Dynamic* is characterized by action or change in states. So a dynamic simulation model is one that conceptually represents the changing nature of system phenomena in a form that resembles the real thing. These simulations are only abstractions or models of reality. They are not faithful, actual simulations of things.

There are two classes of systems modeling tools, according to Wilensky (1999), aggregate modeling tools and population dynamics tools.

Aggregate Modeling Tools

The class of computer tools called aggregate modeling tools include Stella, VenSim, PowerSim, and a tool developed for students called Model-It (Jackson, Stratford, Krajcik, & Soloway, 1996). These tools, which help learners build dynamic simulation models of systems that elaborate causal loops, use accumulations and flows as the primary means of modeling. For example, the systems model in Figure 13-2 was built using Stella and represents the factors that contribute to the formation of smog. The models use simple algebra to convey the strength of relationships. When the model is run, it becomes a simulation that is driven by an engine based on differential equations, which emphasize change over time.

The most popular systems modeling tool for education is Stella. Stella is a powerful and flexible tool for building simulations of dynamic systems and processes. It uses a simple set of building-block icons to construct a map of a process: stocks, flows, converters, and connectors (see Figure 13-2). Stocks illustrate the level of something in the simulation. In Figure 13-2, *moisture, fumes, pollutants*, and *gas* are stocks. Flows control the inflow or outflow of material to stocks. *Emitting after combustion, evaporating, absorbing,* and *demanding* are flows. Flows often counterbalance each other, like positive and negative influences in causal loops. For example, *emitting after combustion* has a positive influence on *fumes*, which causes a positive influence on *pollutants*. Converters convert inputs into outputs. They are factors, or ratios, that influence flows. *Efficiency rate of gas* is a converter that controls both

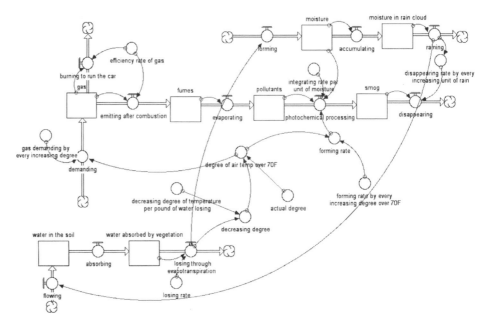
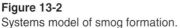

Figure 13-2
Systems model of smog formation.

emitting after combustion and *burning to run the car.* Converters are used to add complexity to the models to better represent the complexity in the real world. Finally, connectors are the lines that show the directional effect of factors on each other by the use of arrows. Students generate equations in the stocks and flows for numerically representing relationships between the variables identified on the map.

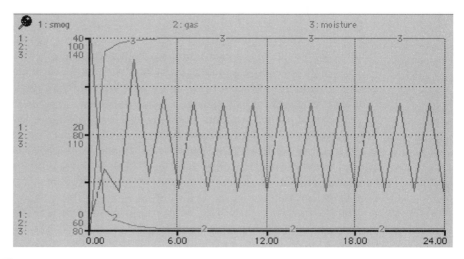

Figure 13-3
Graphic output of smog model in Figure 13-2.

Once a model has been built, Stella enables learners to run the model that they have created and observe the output in graphs, tables, or animations (as shown in Figure 13-3). That is, Stella enables students to create simulations of their models. At the run level, students can change the variable values to test the effects of parts of a system on the other parts. If the results are inconsistent with expectations, students must examine their models to find the equations that are out of balance. Students may search the Internet for real-world statistics to use in their models, or they may use data from experiments that they have conducted. The use of real-world data makes the modeling process all the more authentic and engaging.

Simulation-modeling tools like Stella are extremely powerful Mindtools, and they require more intensive effort to learn than any of the other Mindtools described in this book. Students need considerable practice to master tools such as Stella. In an effort to afford students the ability to model systems while reducing the difficulty of the modeling process, the Highly Interactive Computing (HI-C) group at the University of Michigan developed a simpler modeling tool called Model-It. It is a systems modeling tool designed for middle-school students. Although it does not have the power of modeling tools like Stella, it is easy to learn and use.

To build a model in Model-It, students are required to identify the measurable, quantifiable factors that are used to predict the outcome they are simulating, in this case a tomato garden. The factors in Figure 13-4 show the beginnings of a

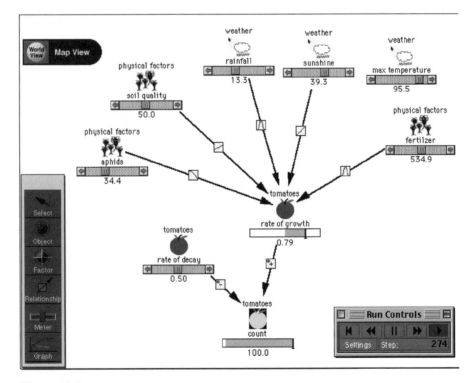

Figure 13-4
Factors in tomato garden simulation (Model-It) with meters turned on.

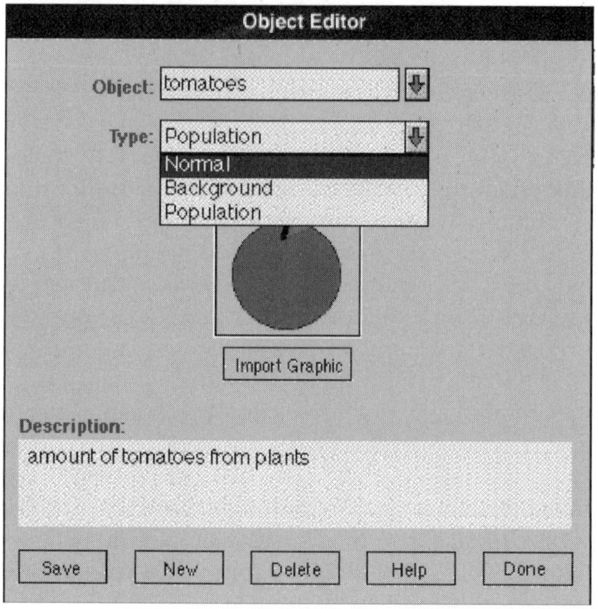

Figure 13-5
Object Editor in Model-It.

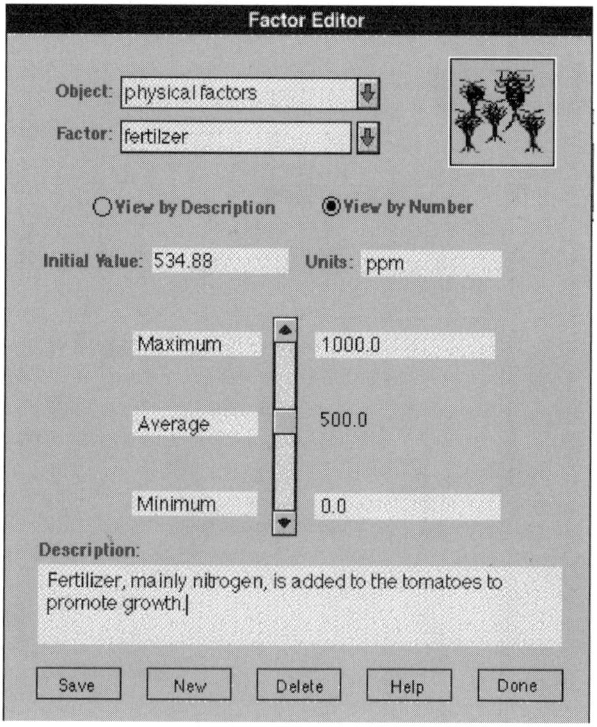

Figure 13-6
Factor Editor in Model-It.

simulation of a tomato garden. Each object in the simulation can be described using the Object Editor (see Figure 13-5). In the Object Editor, the type of object is defined and the factors affecting and affected by the object are defined. Each factor may be further described in terms of its measurement unit, initial value, and maximum, average, and minimum values in the Factor Editor (see Figure 13-6). Students build factor maps (see Figure 13-4) that show the interactive effects of factors on each other. Students then must define the relationships between those factors using the Relationship Editor (see Figure 13-7). When the model is complete, it may be tested; results are shown either by meters or in a graph (see Figure 13-8). Model-It is easy to use and usually requires no more than an hour to learn.

Remember that Model-It was designed for use by middle-school students, who have not mastered advanced mathematics. The Relationship Editor in Model-It scaffolds students' use of mathematics by providing a range of qualitative relationships that describe the quantitative relationship between the factors or by allowing them to enter a table of values that they have collected. So students use pull-down menus to describe relationships such as this: As fertilizer use increases, the number of tomatoes decreases/increases by about the same/a lot/a little/more and more/less and less, or (as in this case) a bell-shaped curve. Through inferring and speculating about the effects of variables on each other, students are thinking like

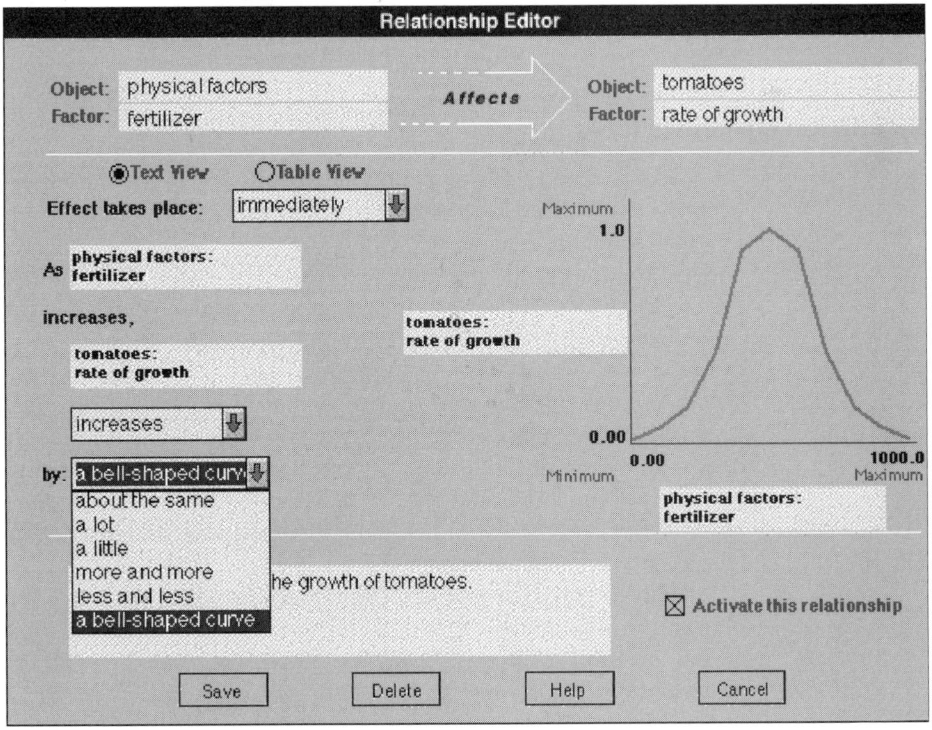

Figure 13-7
Relationship Editor in Model-It.

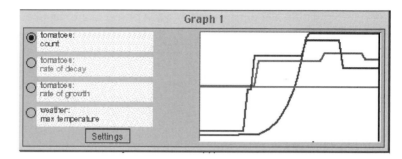

Figure 13-8
Graphs of Model-It output.

scientists; that is, students are building working models of phenomena and testing them against the real world.

   Systems modeling enables students to engage in scientific decision making, thereby treating science as a process rather than facts and concepts to memorize. Providing students with the responsibility of making decisions should be the goal of scientific literacy. To make a decision, a student must (1) determine his or her own opinion and state a position based on scientific knowledge; (2) comprehend the implications, advantages, and disadvantages of that position; and (3) understand the effects of such a position (Spitulnik et al., 1995).

Population Dynamics Tools

   The second class of systems modeling tools, according to Wilensky (1999), represents systems in terms of population dynamics. These are object-based modeling languages that are represented by tools such as NetLogo (formerly Star Logo), Agent Sheets (Repenning, 1993), and Cocoa (Smith, Cypher, & Spohrer, 1994). These tools enable learners to describe rules related to populations of entities. Object-based modeling tools enable learners to model systems by identifying individual elements of the system and describing their behavior. For example, a deer population consists of a herd of deer, and each deer has a probability of reproducing or dying. Wilensky (1999) argues that it is easier for students to produce rules for individual deer than it is to describe the flow of deer populations. In Figure 13-9, the student sees each of the individual entities in a population. Wilensky argues that thinking in terms of the behavior of individual entities is more intuitive, especially for students who lack mathematical skills.

   The most popular population modeling tool is NetLogo. NetLogo is a cross-platform, multiagent programmable modeling environment that can be used to model any kind of population. The model illustrated in Figure 13-9 depicts the growth of a virus. Users can input the infectious rate, recovery chances, duration, and number of people in the population. When run, the model shows the growth of the virus in a graph (at lower left) and in the population window. Different colors depict those who are sick, immune, and healthy. Visualizing a population in two ways

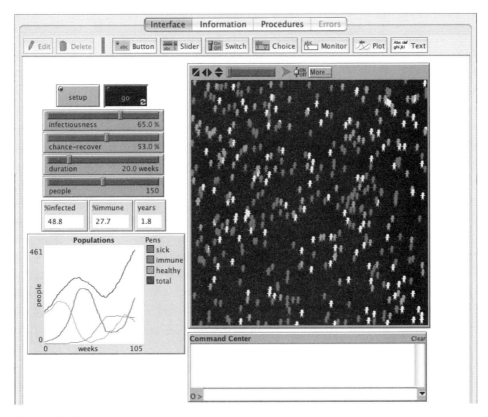

Figure 13-9
NetLogo model of a virus growth.

increases the likelihood of comprehension of population dynamics. The most effective use of these tools is to have students build the model to represent the systems they are studying (see Chapter 5).

Another special-purpose population modeling tool is EcoBeaker, which simulates an environment for teaching subjects such as ecology. Figure 13-10 shows the growth of mold in bathrooms.

MODELING WITH SYSTEMS DYNAMICS TOOLS

Systems modeling tools enable students to represent the complexity of dynamic systems. Students can build models of those systems and test them. These systems modeling tools are probably the most powerful Mindtools available to students. Observing the systems that students create is perhaps the most powerful way to assess the viability and comprehensiveness of their mental models.

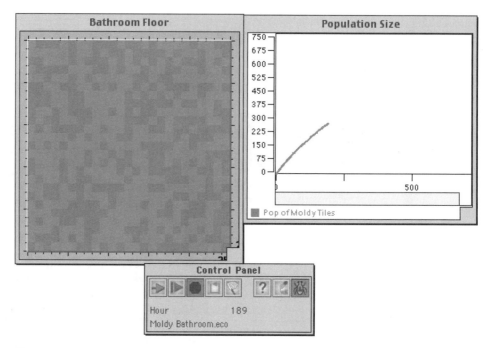

Figure 13-10
Model of the growth of mold in a bathroom, created with EcoBeaker.

Little systematic research is available on the effects of building dynamic systems models on learning and thinking, although there has been plenty of experience. The Cross-Curriculum Systems Thinking and Dynamics Using Stella (CC-STADUS) project, funded by the National Science Foundation, trained a couple of hundred junior high and high school teachers to use Stella in their classrooms. All of their experience indicates that developing systems models significantly enhances learning (Fisher, 1994). Other studies of systems modeling include the following:

♦ Niedderer, Schecker, and Begthe (1991) showed how Stella can be used in physics classes.
♦ Hopkins (1992) developed a Stella model that analyzes Hamlet's motivation to avenge the death of his father by killing Claudius. Students use the model to follow the action of the play and to speculate about a variety of possible responses. Hopkins also shows how Stella could be used for literary analysis and for writing short stories and plays.
♦ Blankenship and Tumlinson (1995) showed how Stella can be used to represent action potentials (eating doughnuts, drinking milk, writing a story). Building simulation models makes action theory come alive.
♦ Hogan and Thomas (2001) found that the best systems modelers focused on the whole picture of model: They modeled outputs and interactions rather than inputs and individual relationships while building and testing models; they

explored dependencies and implications of positive and negative feedback rather than components; and they used variables in continuous relationships rather than constants to control model outputs.

◆ In a graduate course, students constructed systems models of mariculture systems (Dooley & Neill,1999). Although students found Stella challenging, most of them regarded systems modeling as a new way to learn.

◆ Using case study analysis, Steed (1995) showed how Stella modeling portrayed diverse dimensions of information and helped high school students shift their thinking by allowing them to compare different representations (different models).

◆ Zaraza and Fisher (1999) described how they have trained teachers in Oregon to engage students in physics, biology, and mathematics classes to model a variety of phenomena using Stella.

Coaching Construction of Systems Models

Diane Fischer, the director of the CC-STADUS project mentioned earlier, recommended that students be introduced to modeling by having the teacher demonstrate how to develop a model, then allowing the students to manipulate the model and make predictions (Fisher, 1994). Later, students develop models as a classroom activity while being guided by the teacher. As they become more independent, students select a topic that interests them, identify the system parameters, work with a resource person to develop a model, and present the model to their class. Coaching the development of modeling skills in learners may include the following steps. The rate of progress depends on the age, intelligence, and interest of the students.

STEP 1. Students run and test an existing model. Provide simulation templates with predefined components and connections that work. Students make predictions and generate hypotheses, thereby testing their predictions using the model while they test the model.

STEP 2. Students manipulate existing model. Create a diagram but leave some of the "between" variables unspecified. Students are required to deduce their own relationships. The models in Step 1 and this step could represent an experiment that students have conducted; or, they could represent a local phenomenon with which the students would be familiar.

STEP 3. Students create a group model. Working as a class, with your guidance as the teacher, students work together to create a model of some familiar phenomenon. This is especially useful if you have only one computer in your classroom. Students are supported by you and by each other. Probe students' understanding, ask leading questions to help the students articulate their model, and encourage students to make predictions and hypotheses about the results before running the model. When the students test their model, you may need to provide hints about why the model may not be producing the output they expected.

STEP 4. Students make a plan for their own models. Before developing their own model, students need to make a plan for their systems model. What are they interested in representing? What points do they want to make? What kinds of structure and information are required to make those points? What learning goals will they work toward?

STEP 5. Students create their own models. Working in groups, students attempt to model an experiment, a chapter, some real-world phenomenon, or some other system being studied. They must test their own model.

STEP 6. Students demonstrate their models to the class. The class discusses and evaluates students' models or helps their peers to troubleshoot difficulties.

STEP 7. Students create their own theories. Based on their working models, students attempt to generalize their results into a theory that describes the behavior of a larger class of objects or events.

STEP 8. Students reflect on the activity. Reflection should not start when the project is completed. Rather, students should continuously review their progress during the project. Are we achieving our goals? What changes are necessary? How do we compare with other groups? Are we answering questions and making the points that we set out in our plan? After the project is completed, the students should reflect further. What have we learned about content? What have we learned about model building and about our own mental models? What have we learned about working with each other? You may choose to provide students with some or all of the criteria for evaluating their models (presented in the next section).

Hogan and Thomas (2001) provide additional advice on how to help learners become systems modelers. For them, it is important to emphasize to students why scientists use models, that is, to support theories, generate hypotheses, and explain systems behavior. Hogan and Thomas also recommend that students become familiar with the system and concepts that they are modeling. When they are, it is important to focus on the behavior of the system, not the behavior of isolated components. In addition, Hogan and Thomas recommend provision of emotional as well as cognitive scaffolding to students, because systems modeling can be frustrating.

EVALUATING SYSTEMS MODELS

What makes an effective systems model? That depends on the kind of model that students are constructing and the age and abilities of those constructing the model. Viewing a student model created with a systems modeling tool provides perhaps the clearest and most definitive evidence of student intellectual activity available. I have experienced considerable excitement viewing student models.

Some of the criteria that you might use to evaluate those models include the following:

- Does the model include all of the important components or objects?
- Are the values of each component appropriately defined?
- Are the direction and dimension of the relationships between components viable or accurate?
- Do the graphic outputs of the model convey viable relationships?
- Are the important variables represented as graphs?

Figure 13-11 presents a number of rubrics that you may use to evaluate the models that students construct as their knowledge and skills move from emergent to

	Quality of factors	
Factors are irrelevant; insufficient factors identified; important factors are missing	→	Factors are important; enough factors identified to represent complexity of system
	Relationship quality	
Relationships are associative; use incorrect mathematic functions; connected to incorrect objects	→	Relationships are causal; use appropriate mathematic functions; flow between appropriate objects
	Quality of model	
Inaccurately simulates systems; represents naive student understanding; makes incorrect assumptions; cannot support predictions or hypotheses	→	Simulates real-life system; simulates appropriate student understanding of system; makes appropriate assumptions; supports predictions/hypotheses
	Appropriate objects	
Objects (concepts) too advanced or too simple for target audience	→	Objects (concepts) appropriate for target audience (challenging but not impossible)
	User testing	
Provides restricted range of tests; enables manipulation of limited variables or values	→	Enables users to test a range of hypotheses by manipulating appropriate variables or values

Figure 13-11
Possible rubrics for evaluating student models.

mastery. Most likely you will adapt these or add your own criteria as you evaluate your students' projects.

ADVANTAGES AND LIMITATIONS OF SYSTEMS MODELING

Fischer (1994) suggests a number of advantages of systems modeling, including these:

◆ Affords students the ability to visualize functional relationships among system components, illustrating all of the components and their dependent relationships (Stella refers to this as "laying out the plumbing")
◆ Requires mathematical rigor by defining the dynamic relationships between components

Steed (1992) also identified advantages and benefits of systems modeling:

◆ Building dynamic simulations is useful when performing the real experiments would be impossible, too dangerous, or require too long a time.
◆ Simulations allow manipulation of one variable at a time, which is often impossible in the real world.
◆ Students are required to make explicit their assumptions, generate hypotheses, and make predictions about how their model will perform.
◆ Models reflect the mental models that learners have of the systems that they are studying.
◆ Systems modeling tools are laboratories for scientific inquiry, exploration, explanation, and testing.
◆ Models are highly symbolized; they use meaningful icons to represent ideas.
◆ Modeling makes fuzzy causal relationships less ambiguous. By explicitly diagramming connections between system components, students clarify their understanding.
◆ Modeling makes concrete the relationship between a system's processes and its structure.
◆ Models enable real-world phenomena to be explored without sophisticated mathematical knowledge.
◆ Simulations can help to identify hidden, causal factors in systems.
◆ Modeling engages metacognitive reasoning.

Joy and Zaraza (1997), experienced CC-STADUS teachers, have provided perhaps the most eloquent description of the power of systems modeling in classrooms:

As the modeling reaches deeper realms, the teacher and student explore together—a student's curiosity and imagination teamed with a teacher's wisdom and experience. This intellectual intimacy, brief on a daily basis, but profound over time, conjures the master–apprentice models of earlier times. For the students of average ability, this relationship bears much fruit. Many of these students have languished through course work, doing what's required but retaining little over time, just enough to pass or a bit better; many of these students are lost in the vast crowds of American education. But the visual aspect of system dynamics engages students both conceptually and pragmatically so that many more students are drawn into this question-rich learning. This dialectic mode of instruction is far more endearing to these students for whom teachers were oft viewed as authoritarians rather than mentors. Because the computer model makes explicit what heretofore was unknown in a student's mind, the teacher and student now have very clear venues for questions and suggestions. The best teaching and the best learning still take place at this primary level—the intellectual intimacy of teachers and students breeds trust, curiosity, imagination. It is not that this didn't happen before; it was just rare. System dynamics creates more possibilities for this as it enjoins minds in deep ways: students solve complex problems and teachers instruct directed minds. (p. 10)

Many implementation issues arise when moving toward systems modeling. Based on longitudinal case studies, Mandinach and Clive (1994) identified several concerns, including these:

◆ Administrative support (most principals were supportive)
◆ Adequate and appropriate hardware (newer software demands more powerful computers)
◆ Technical expertise (supporting Stella and the hardware)
◆ Relatively expensive software
◆ Orientation of the curriculum (accommodating systems modeling)
◆ Expertise and training
◆ Changing role of teachers (constructivist perspective; more to follow)

Hogan and Thomas (2001) found that students experience difficulties choosing and defining factors and representing rates of change. They tend to think in terms of concrete objects rather than variables. Also, students tend to think in terms of linear causal thinking (one cause to one effect) rather than about the dynamic interplay of variables on each other. These misconceptions can mitigate the effectiveness of systems modeling.

Systems modeling, like all Mindtools, requires new approaches to teaching. Teachers must relinquish some of their intellectual authority to students and allow them to explore the limits of their own understanding. Joy and Zaraza (1997) identify some of the obligations:

The nature of system dynamics demands some measure of independence for its devotees. If we wish students to fully study, then we must grant them some intellectual independence and allow their curiosity to lead them. In this new setting, the teachers grant the questioners primacy. A teacher might introduce some conceptual material on acceleration, and then allow students to work through a series of increasingly difficult models that test some of the conceptual material as well as some equations and precise data. More advanced students are free to experiment and test their own well-educated notions, each time receiving immediate feedback that redirects their personal search. Likewise, the struggling student can receive such thoughtful, prolonged attention from the teacher who knows the other students are well engaged. No longer one question for the many, but a myriad of questions, each appropriate, for the multitude.

It is not easy for many teachers to teach this way. Before systems modeling can be successfully implemented in classrooms, teachers must adopt a more constructivist pedagogy.

As with most other Mindtools, systems modeling will not allow teachers to "cover" as much of the curriculum. This remains the major issue related to constructivist pedagogies, and it is a complex issue given the pressures of high-stakes testing. Students must master any content about which they construct systems models and will surely perform better on any tests about that content. However, when students are constructing models, they may bypass other important content. The key question is this: How meaningful is the learning experience?

SUMMARY

Causal loops provide a formal mechanism for diagramming relationships in dynamic systems. Although most systems can be modeled by causal loops, they cannot be simulated by them. To simulate systems, more powerful tools are necessary.

There are two classes of systems modeling tools: aggregate modeling tools and population dynamics tools. Aggregate modeling tools, such as Stella, help learners build dynamic simulations of their models using stocks, flows, converters, and connectors as the primary means of modeling. Population dynamics tools, such as Net-Logo, represent systems in terms of population entities and their behaviors. Systems modeling tools enable students to build models of complex, dynamic systems and test the models.

Model building is a clear indicator of the depth and breadth of student understanding. If your students can build reasonable models of the systems they are studying, then you may rest assured that they understand the content deeply. Systems modeling, like all Mindtools, asks teachers to allow students to explore the limits of their understanding.

REFERENCES

Blankenship, V., & Tumlinson, J. (1995). A Stella-II teaching simulation of the dynamics of action model. *Behavior Research Methods, Instruments, and Computers, 27*(2), 244–250.

Dooley, K. E., & Neill, W. H. (1999). Systems modeling by interdisciplinary teams: Innovative approaches to distance education. *Journal of Natural Resources and Life Sciences Education, 28,* 3–8.

Fisher, D. M. (1994). *Teaching system dynamics to teachers and students in 8–12 environment.* Paper presented at the International Systems Dynamics Conference, Edinburgh, Scotland.

Hogan, K., & Thomas, D. (2001). Cognitive comparisons of students' systems modeling in ecology. *Journal of Science Education and Technology, 10*(4), 319–345.

Hopkins, P. L. (1992). Simulating Hamlet in the classroom. *Systems Dynamics Review, 8*(1), 91–98.

Jackson, S., Stratford, S., Krajcik, J., & Soloway, E. (1996). A learner-centered tool for students building models. *Communications of the ACM, 39*(4), 48–49.

Joy, T., & Zaraza, R. (1997). *Fundamental changes in how we teach: A narrative about teaching systems dynamics and the art of learning.* Paper presented at the International Systems Dynamics Conference, Turkey.

Mandinach, E. B., & Cline, H. F. (1994). *Classroom dynamics: Implementing a technology-based learning environment.* Hillsdale, NJ: Lawrence Erlbaum.

Niedderer, H., Schecker, H., & Begthe, T. (1991). The role of computer-aided modeling in learning physics. *Journal of Computer-Assisted Learning, 7,* 84–95.

Repenning, A. (1993). *Agent sheets: A tool for building domain oriented, dynamic, visual environments.* Unpublished doctoral dissertation, University of Colorado, Boulder.

Smith, D.C., Cypher, A., & Spohrer, J. (1994). Kidsim: Programming agents without a programming language. *Communications of the ACM, 37*(7), 55–67.

Soloway, E., Krajcik, J., & Finkel, E. A. (1995). *Science project: Supporting science modeling and inquiry via computational media and technology.* San Francisco: American Educational Research Association.

Spitulnik, J., Studer, S., Finkel, E., Gustafson, E., Laczko, J., & Soloway, E. (1995). The River-MUD design rationale: Scaffolding for scientific inquiry through modeling, discourse, and decision making in community based issues. In T. Koschman (Ed.), *Proceedings of Computer Support for Collaborative Learning.* Hillsdale, NJ: Lawrence Erlbaum.

Steed, M. (1992). Stella, a simulation construction kit: Cognitive process and educational implications. *Journal of Computers in Science and Mathematics Teaching, 11*(1), 39–52.

Steed, M. (1995). *Effects of computer simulation construction on shifts in cognitive representation: A case study using Stella.* Unpublished doctoral dissertation, University of Massachusetts, Amherst.

Wilensky, U. (1999). GasLab—An extensible modeling toolkit for connecting micro- and macro-properties of gases. In W. Feurzig & N. Roberts (Eds.), *Modeling and simulation in science and mathematics education* (pp. 151–178). New York: Springer-Verlag.

Zaraza, R., & Fisher, D.M. (1999). Training systems modelers: The NSF CC-STADUS and CC-SUSTAIN projects. In W. Feurzig & N. Roberts (Eds.), *Modeling and simulation in science and mathematics education* (pp. 38–69). New York: Springer-Verlag.

CHAPTER 14

Modeling with Teachable Agents and Direct Manipulation Environments

A new class of modeling tools is emerging. These tools, teachable agents and direct manipulation environments, provide domain-specific environments for building models of phenomena within those domains. These tools are not as commonly known as others, and their utility will depend on your interest and willingness to be alert to new environments as they become available. Your efforts will be rewarded, because these environments are very powerful.

INTELLIGENT AGENTS

An agent is someone who acts on your behalf for some purpose. Travel agents interact with airlines and book business or vacation trips. A real estate agent mediates the sale or purchase of a home. Agents are useful because they have learned about their markets. In one sense, you pay them a fee to benefit from their knowledge. In the cyberworld, we will increasingly use agents to act on our behalf to find information, move files, complete transactions, and so on. Apple Computer's video, *Knowledge Navigator*, developed in 1987, showed how agents would find information, book meetings, locate and communicate with other people, and perform various other tasks. The agents become capable only if we teach them; that is, they have to learn how to do their jobs.

The growth of agents in personal computing is amazing. A variety of information searching agents, Web agents, shopping agents, and virtual assistants can help you perform an infinite number of tasks. The Software Agents Group at the MIT Media Lab is experimenting with agents such as GloBuddy2, which uses a vast knowledge base of commonsense facts and relationships to help people in foreign countries use appropriate words and phrases in languages related to their situation. GloBuddy2 is an intelligent phrase book that adapts to a user's needs and context. In the future, intelligent agents will increasingly do our bidding.

TEACHABLE AGENTS

Intelligent agents must be taught; so the user must instruct them. An example of an agent that is taught is Mondrian (Lieberman, 1992), an object-oriented graphic editor that has a learning agent. The agent records drawing procedures that are generated by the teacher. Mondrian can then apply those recorded procedures to other drawings. In this case, Mondrian learned drawing procedures from a user. Thousands of other such agents exist.

A fine line exists between intelligent agents and teachable agents. In one sense, all agents are teachable. However, an emerging class of agents is being designed to help students learn by being taught by students. Teachable agents are based on the premise that the quickest way to learn something is to have to teach it. Graduate students, faced with the responsibility of teaching, reported using strategies to gain deeper understanding of material to be taught and to develop better conceptual organizations, and questions from students prompted deeper reflection (Biswas, Schwartz, Bransford, & The Teachable Agents Group at Vanderbilt, 2001).

A teachable agent has specific requirements (Huffman & Laird, 1995). It must comprehend instructions and map them onto some object or activity. So the agent must be able to internally represent a set of actions and be able to translate commands into those actions. The agent must also support interactive dialogue between the teacher (the person who programs the agent) and the object. That dialogue should be able to support initiation by either the teacher or the agent. The agent must also be able to learn instructions and transfer them to different situations. Huffman and Laird (1995) describe INSTRUCTO-SOAR, a robotic agent that moves, picks up objects, and so on. However, not all agents are robotic.

Among the most researched teachable agents is Betty's Brain. Betty provides a concept map interface where the links convey a constrained set of causal relationships or dependency relationships. For example, in Figure 14-1, students are teaching

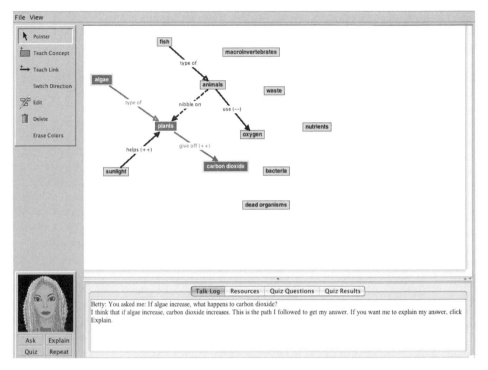

Figure 14-1
Teaching Betty's Brain.

Betty using an influence diagram that looks like a concept map (see Chapter 10). This diagram contains two types of links between the concepts. The most commonly used link illustrates a causal relationship in which one concept increases or decreases another concept. The second type of link is a dependency relationship, where one concept necessitates (but does not change) another concept.

After teaching Betty, students can quiz her to see how much she knows. Students generate questions based on the entities in the concept map (see Figure 14-2). Betty responds with the answer if the students have taught her adequately. If not, she claims that she doesn't know and needs to be taught the answer, which students can then do. Studies show that students who programmed Betty's Brain reported significantly more relationships among concepts than students who summarized a passage, and students who asked Betty questions generated better maps (Leelawong, Wang, Biswas, Vye, Bransford, & Schwartz, 2001). Betty also seems to facilitate reflection among students, who realized after programming Betty that they had been thinking in terms of correlation and not causation. Most of those students did not realize how much things changed when studying exercise physiology. That is, Betty influenced their understanding.

Another agent, which was created by the AAA Lab at Stanford University (aaalab.Stanford.edu), is Moby, who can learn logic rules based on the presence or absence of objects, the states of one or two factors, and a set of rules (see Figure 14-3).

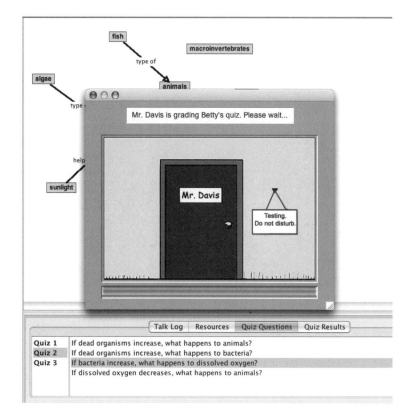

Figure 14-2
Quizzing Betty's Brain.

Quiz 1	If dead organisms increase, what happens to animals?
Quiz 2	If dead organisms increase, what happens to bacteria?
Quiz 3	If bacteria increase, what happens to dissolved oxygen?
	If dissolved oxygen decreases, what happens to animals?

Figure 14-3
Teaching Moby by defining objects, states, and rules.

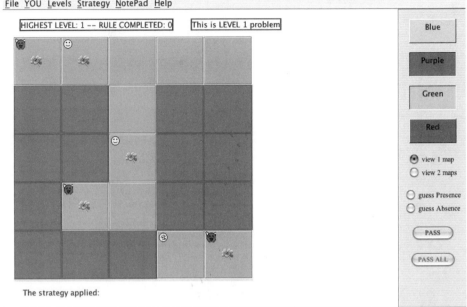

Figure 14-4
Playing a game in Moby: trying to guess rules.

The rules are developed to construct a game for others to play, such as (1) guess where the flowers are based on the factor map or (2) guess if certain factors are present in each cell (see Figure 14-4). Students learn how to play different games and then transfer that knowledge to teaching Moby, who then performs.

Students use the Script Creator in Moby to create new problems or edit existing ones. They generate logic rules, such as these: (1) One factor is necessary and sufficient for the flower, and (2) The flower is always with the factor and never anywhere else. The gaming environment is engaging for students who learn to use different forms of logic to stump their classmates. Most likely, suites of teachable agents will be developed to support a variety of kinds of thinking. The little bit of research on teachable agents to date confirms the adage that the fastest way to learn something is to have to teach it. While that belief is endemic in every Mindtool, teachable agents exploit the belief better than most.

DIRECT MANIPULATION ENVIRONMENTS

Direct manipulation environments (DMEs) engage students in building models of specific phenomena. When doing so, learners are directly manipulating parameters that are included within the environment. Because of the immediacy of modeling, DMEs provide a sense of reality to the learners. Learners feel like they are working directly with objects, which in many cases, they are. Some DMEs resemble systems dynamic tools; however, they are domain specific, so they can be used for only a single purpose.

The use of direct manipulation tools for learning by modeling is probably best articulated by the Concord Consortium (www.concord.org) in their initiative titled Modeling Across the Curriculum. The consortium has created direct manipulation modeling tools in biology (BioLogica: a model of genetics built on various inheritance patterns at the level of molecules, genes, and individuals) and physics (Dynamica: for introducing vectors, kinematics, and dynamics in physical science and beginning physics courses) as well as a visualization tool in chemistry (see Chapter 15). DMEs are being introduced all the time, so you must be alert for new releases.

GenScope

The predecessor of BioLogica is GenScope (Horwitz, 1996). Genscope is a direct manipulation environment for investigating Mendelian genetics. Learners may select different animals to model genetically. In Figure 14-5, students have chosen

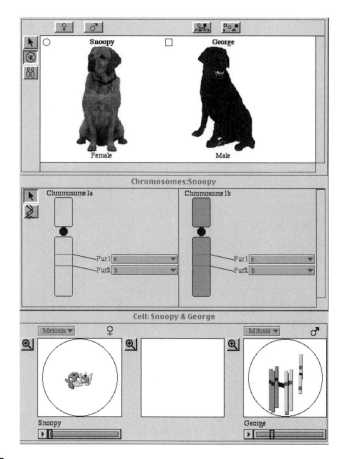

Figure 14-5
Genscope environment for genetic modeling of Labrador retrievers.

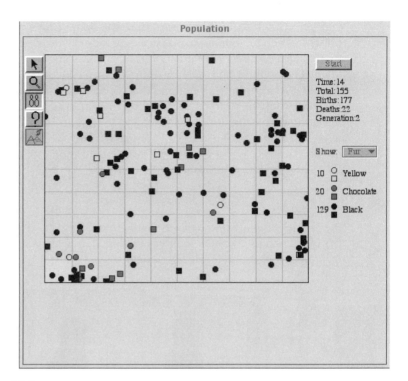

Figure 14-6
Population growth of Labrador retrievers represented in GenScope.

Labrador retrievers to model from a list that includes dragons, birds, and other animals. After naming two dogs, the students can click on each dog with the chromosome tool to reveal each dog's chromosomes. Other tools reveal the DNA structure of the chromosomes, and the cell view (at the bottom of Figure 14-5) reveals the cell and provides an animation of cell division (meiosis or mitosis). Figure 14-6 shows the growth of Labrador populations starting with Snoopy and George; the color of the dogs is represented as shapes and colors. The Concord Consortium analyzed research data from 43 high schools over a three-year period and found that student ability to reason about genetics improved after using GenScope. The consortium also found that GenScope helped bring about a fundamental, qualitative change in student thinking. Genscope and other modeling tools from the Concord Consortium are excellent examples of DMEs.

Interactive Physics

Interactive Physics is a DME that enables students to design, test, and illustrate their own problems in mechanics. Figure 14-7 illustrates a projectile motion problem. Students drag and drop objects from the left side of the screen into the experimental space. They then determine initial conditions, (e.g., gravity, air resistance)

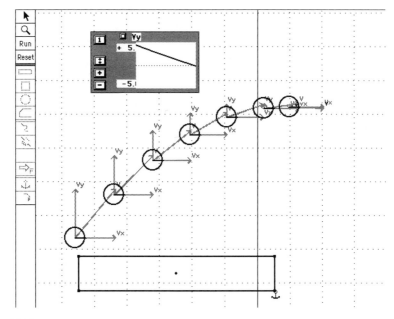

Figure 14-7
Projectile motion experiment in Interactive Physics.

and run their simulation. By changing the values of the initial conditions, they can experiment with numerous causal relationships. Additionally, each experiment that they construct can be visualized by animated vectors of the process as well as graphic output, as illustrated in Figure 14-7. Stevenson (2002) used Interactive Physics to model mechanical systems by adding objects and defining the relationships between them.

RoboLab

RoboLab, from Lego Corporation, consists of software for programming and directing a small RCX computer (see Figure 14-8) to move about and use its sensors to collect data from the environment in order to conduct different types of investigations. For the investigation represented in Figure 14-9 and 14–10, RoboLab was programmed to use the light sensor and temperature sensor to collect values overnight to determine the degree of correlation between light and temperature. The program in Figure 14-9 uses simple icons to activate equipment, in this case by taking periodic measurements starting at 1:00 a.m. Figure 14-10 plots the correlation between temperature and light. The tools help students to build simple models of experiments and experimental results. The environment is simple for students to use because of its direct manipulation interface, but it is complex enough to support a wide range of experiments.

Figure 14-8
RCX computer module.

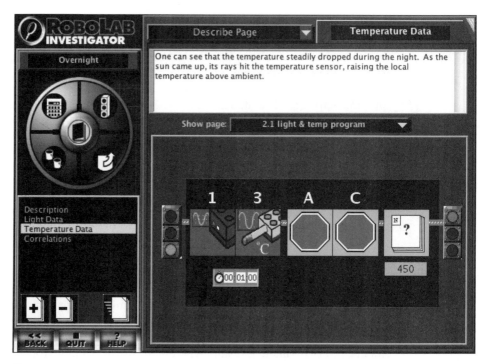

Figure 14-9
Programming the RCX to collect data.

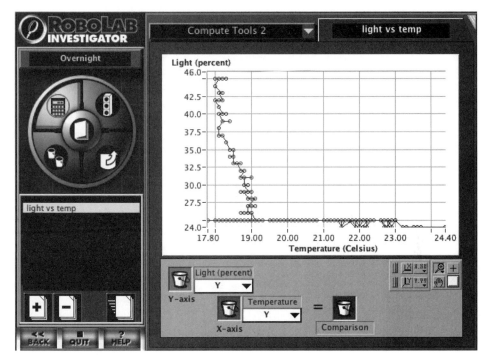

Figure 14-10
Illustrating results in RoboLab.

SUMMARY

This chapter introduced two new kinds of modeling tools, teachable agents and direct manipulation environments (DMEs). With both of these kinds of modeling tools, students learn by teaching the agent or the environment how to investigate some phenomenon and report the results in different ways. Teachable agent and DME software tend to be more specific in the kinds of modeling they can support. That is, they support modeling a limited range of phenomena, unlike other Mindtools that can model phenomena across domains. However, their ease of use makes teachable agents and DMEs powerful modeling tools in the domains they represent. More of these kinds of environments are being developed, so keep an eye out for them.

REFERENCES

Biswas, G., Schwartz, D., Bransford, J.D., & The Teachable Agents Group at Vanderbilt (2001). Technology support for complex problem solving: From SAD environment to AI. In K. D. Farbus & & P. J. Feltovoch (Eds.), *Smart machines in education: The learning revolution in educational technology.* Menlo Park, CA: AAAI/MIT Press.

Horwitz, P. (1996). Linking models to data: Hypermodels for scinecde education. *The High School Journal, 79*(2), 148–156.

Huffman, S. B., & Laird, J. E. (1995). Flexibly instructable agents. *Journal of Artificial Intelligence Research, 3*, 271–324.

Leelawong, K., Wang, Y., Biswas, G., Vye, N., Bransford, J., & Schwartz, D. (2001). Qualitative reasoning techniques to support learning by teaching: The teachable agents project. In G. Biswas (Ed.), *AAAI qualitative reasoning workshop*, San Antonio, TX.

Lieberman, H. (1992). Mondrian: A teachable graphical editor. *Cypher, 93.*

Stevenson, I. (2002). Microworlds and direct manipulation environments: The case of Newtonian mechanics. *Journal of Educational Computing Research, 27*(1–2), 167–183.

CHAPTER 15

Modeling with Visualization Tools

Humans are complex organisms who possess a well-balanced sensorimotor system. This system is counterbalanced with receptor and effector systems, which enables us to sense perceptual data and act on the data using complex motor systems. Likewise, humans have reasonably keen aural perception that allows us to hear a large range of sounds. Those sounds can be replicated or at least responded to orally by forcing air through the diaphragm, palette, and lips to create an infinite variety of sounds. In our most sophisticated sensory system, vision we receive the largest amount and variety of data. However, vision has no counterposing effector system. Humans can receive visual input but have no output mechanism for visually representing ideas, except in mental images and dreams, which cannot be easily shared with others. These mental images are powerful mediators of meaning making. Often we have to visualize something before we can make sense of it, but sharing those visions is problematic. Therefore, according to Hermann Maurer (an AI specialist from Austria), humans need visual prostheses to help them visualize ideas and share those images with others.

NATURE OF VISUALIZATION TOOLS

To some extent, draw-and-paint software packages provide the visual prostheses that allow us to visually represent what we know. They contain sophisticated tools that enable us to draw and paint objects electronically. To represent our mental images using such programs, however, we have to translate our images into a series of motor operations. (It is not yet possible to dump our mental images directly from our brains into a computer.) Skilled artists commonly use these sophisticated tools to visualize ideas, which can help others to interpret ideas. But what we need are tools that help most of us, who are unskilled artists, to visualize ideas.

This chapter describes a new but rapidly growing class of tools that allows people to reason and represent ideas visually without need of the artistic skills required to produce original illustrations. These tools help to interpret and represent visual ideas and to automate some of the manual processes for creating images. Currently, most of these tools are being used for visualizing scientific ideas in geography, meteorology, chemistry, and physics. Researchers in geography are especially interested in visualization tools to enhance reading of maps and interpreting ideas in physical geography.

Unlike the generalized representational capabilities of most Mindtools, visualization tools tend to be fairly task and domain specific. That is, there are no general-purpose tools for visualizing ideas across domains, except for draw-and-paint programs. Rather, visualization tools closely mimic the ways in which different images must be interpreted or created to make sense of the ideas.

Visualization tools have two major uses, interpretive and expressive (Gordin, Edelson, & Gomez, 1996). Interpretive tools help learners view and manipulate visuals to extract meaning from the information being visualized. Interpretive illustrations help to clarify difficult-to-understand text and abstract concepts (Levin, Anglin, & Carney, 1987). Expressive visualization helps learners visually convey meaning to communicate a set of beliefs. Crayons-and-paper or paint-and-draw programs are powerful expressive tools that learners use to express themselves visually. However, these tools rely on graphic talent. Visualization tools go beyond paint-and-draw programs by scaffolding, or supporting, some form of expression. They help learners to visualize ideas in ways that make the ideas more easily interpretable by other viewers.

MODELING WITH VISUALIZATION TOOLS

Because of the abstractness of mathematics, visualization has been an important strategy in helping learners to understand mathematical concepts. For example, Cotter (2000) showed that using Asian forms of visualization (abacus, tally sticks, and place cards) advanced the concepts of place value, addition, and subtraction.

Mathematics educators have promoted the use of manipulables and similar visual comparative devices for many years.

Snir (1995) argues that computers can make a unique contribution to the clarification and correction of commonly held misconceptions about phenomena by visualizing those ideas. For example, the computer can be used to form a representation for a phenomenon in which all the relational and mathematical wave equations are embedded within the program code and reflected on the screen in graphics and visuals. Thus, the computer acts as an efficient tool to clarify scientific understanding of waves. By using computer graphics, a scientist, for example, can shift attention back and forth from local to global properties of a phenomenon and train the mind to integrate the two aspects into one coherent picture (Snir, 1995).

Many visualization tools provide reasoning-congruent representations that enable learners to reason about objects that behave and interact (Merrill, Reiser, Bekkelaar, & Hamid, 1992). Visualization tools have been developed primarily for mathematics and the sciences.

Mathematical Visualization

Mathematics is an abstract field of study. Understanding equations in algebra, trigonometry, calculus, and virtually all other fields of math is aided by seeing plots of the equations. Understanding the dynamics of mathematics is aided by manipulating formulas and equations and observing the effects of that manipulation. Programs such as Mathematica, Maple, and MathLab, and Statistical Analysis System (SAS), and Statistical Package for the Social Sciences (SPSS) are often used to visually represent mathematical relationships in problems so that learners can *see* the effects of any manipulation (e.g., manipulation of the values of a sine function in Figure 15-1).

Porzio (1995) found that calculus students who used Mathematica were better able to make connections between numeric, graphic, and symbolic representations than students who used calculators or students who learned through traditional methods. Engineering mechanics students who used Mathematica solved problems that required calculus more conceptually than traditional students who focused only on the procedures (Roddick, 1995). The ability to interrelate numeric and symbolic representations with their graphic output helps learners to understand mathematics more conceptually. Students in math classes and in science classes who use different forms of math can learn mathematical functions more effectively by seeing them.

I do not mean to imply that Mathematica, Maple, and MathLab, SAS, and SPSS are merely visualization tools. They are much more than that: They are powerful calculators, computers, storehouses of mathematical algorithms and handbooks, analyzers of data input, and systems modeling tools as well. These programs support students in every aspect of mathematics and statistics learning. However, for the purposes of this chapter, they are powerful visualization tools. A variety of other mathematics visualization tools are also available. For example, the graphic proof tree representation in Geometry Tutor (Anderson, Boyle, & Yost, 1986) visualizes problem solution sequences.

In[6]:=

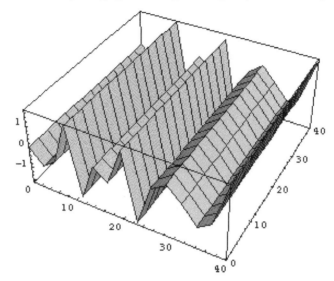

Plot3D[Sin[x] + Sin[1.6 x], {x, 0, 40}, {y, 0, 40}]

Out[6]= - SurfaceGraphics -

Figure 15-1
Mathematica visualization of a sine function.

Scientific Visualization

A number of visualization tools have been developed for the sciences, especially chemistry. Figure 15-2 illustrates a molecule of androsterone. Not only does the Mac-Spartan program enable learners to visualize molecules using five different representations (wire, ball and wire, tube, ball and spoke, and space filling), but it also enables them to test different bonds and create ions and new molecules (Figure 15-3). Notice the phosphorus ion that has been added to the androsterone molecule on the left.

Students' understanding of molecular chemistry is greatly facilitated by visualizing the complex processes. High school students used eChem to build molecular models and view multiple representations of molecules. Students who used the visualization tool were able to generate better mental images of chemicals, which aided their understanding (Wu, Krajcik, & Soloway, 2001). Students who engaged in discussions while building models benefited the most. Provision of extra visualization, including colored drawings of experiments and ionic representations of reactions, facilitated concept acquisition in chemistry (Brandt et al., 2001).

Another powerful chemistry visualization tool from the Concord Consortium (www.concord.org) is Molecular Workbench. Students use Molecular Workbench to create visual models of the interactions among atoms and molecules. The program

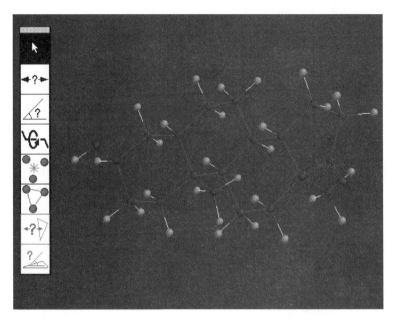

Figure 15-2
Visualization of a molecule of androsterone.

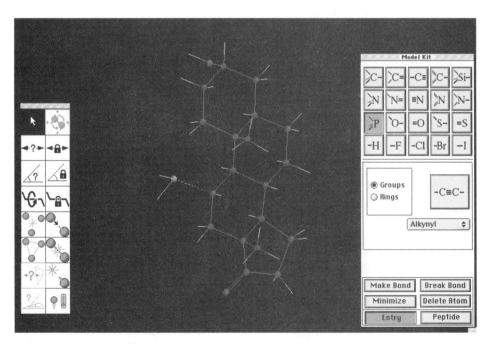

Figure 15-3
Manipulating molecules in MacSpartan.

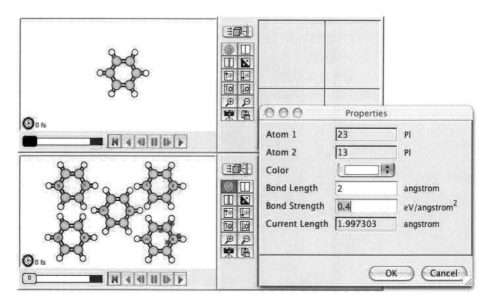

Figure 15-4
Benzene molecule represented in Molecular Workbench.

also provides learning activities to help clarify what is happening at the atomic level. Molecular Workbench is especially effective for representing molecular problems. Figure 15-4 illustrates how benzene molecules may be used instead of proteins.

General scientific concepts may also be aided by use of visualization tools. Students in a collaborative problem-solving process who were provided with a content-specific visualization tool (CoStructure) consisting of a theoretical plane and an empirical plane, improved their risk taking and conceptual learning (Fischer, Bruhn, Grasel, & Mandl, 2002). Although more research is needed, the case for visualization tools is easy to make.

Coaching Use of Visualization Tools

Visualization tools are normally used to support some kind of investigation or larger learning activity. They are not used, as are many Mindtools, to produce a final model. Rather, they are used to help learners to interpret ideas or to represent ideas while conducting a study and investigating a topic. For instance, chemical visualization tools should be used as part of solving chemical problems.

Because visualization tools are not used in a consistent manner, it is impossible to make generalizations about how to use them. Coaching the use of visualization tools for modeling phenomena varies considerably with the tools and the content. Modeling with visualization tools is probably most effective in the context of the larger, investigative project.

EVALUATING VISUALIZATION MODELS

It is difficult to evaluate the effectiveness of visualization tools outside the context of the project in which they are being used. The same tools may be used in different ways in different projects. Visualization tools are intended to support other activities. In reality, visualization tools are a good example of computer-supported scaffolding of learning; that is, the tools help learners comprehend ideas and perform tasks that they otherwise would be unable to do.

There is a direct way to evaluate students' use of visualization tools. Ask one group of students to perform project activities without the use of visualization tools. Compare their performance with that of students who used visualization tools to perform the same activities.

ADVANTAGES AND LIMITATIONS OF VISUALIZATION TOOLS FOR MODELING

When learners use visualization tools for modeling, the tools perform these functions:

◆ Clarify and correct commonly held misconceptions of phenomena by visualizing those ideas (Snir, 1995)
◆ Support specific kinds of reasoning
◆ Enable learners to manifest visual ideas more easily and accurately

Sometimes problems occur when visualization tools are used for modeling learner knowledge. The tools can become an intellectual crutch if used too consistently, and often the tools require high-resolution computers, which may not be readily available.

SUMMARY

Humans receive visual input but they have no output mechanism for visually representing ideas, except for mental images that are not easily shared with others. A rapidly growing class of tools allows people to reason and represent ideas visually without the need of artistic skills. Currently, most of these tools are being used to visualize scientific ideas in disciplines such as geography, meteorology, chemistry, and physics.

Visualization tools can help students understand mathematical and scientific concepts. Programs such as Mathematica visually represent mathematical relationships in problems. In chemistry, programs such as MacSpartan and eChem help students visualize complex processes.

Visualization tools are commonly used to help students interpret or represent ideas while they are involved in a larger learning activity, such as conducting a study or investigating a topic. Visualization tools support learning activities.

REFERENCES

Anderson, J. R., Boyle, C. F., & Yost, G. (1986). The geometry tutor. *Journal of Mathematical Behavior, 5,* 5–19.

Brandt, L., Elen, J., Hellemans, J., Heerman, L., Couwenberg, I., Volckaert, L., et al. (2001). The impact of concept-mapping and visualization on the learning of secondary school chemistry students. *International Journal of Science Education, 23*(12), 1303–1313.

Cotter, J. A. (2000). Using language and visualization to teach place value. *Teaching Children Mathematics, 7*(2), 108–114.

Fischer, F., Bruhn, J., Grasel, C., & Mandl, H. (2002). Fostering collaborative knowledge construction with visualization tools. *Learning and Instruction, 12*(2), 213–32.

Gordin, D. N., Edelson, D. C., & Gomez, L. (1996, April). *Supporting students' science inquiry through scientific visualization.* Paper presented at the annual meeting of the American Education Research Association, New York.

Levin, J. R., Anglin, G. J., & Carney, R. N. (1987). On empirically validating functions of pictures in prose. In D. M. Willows & H. A. Houghton (Eds.), *The psychology of illustration: Vol. 1. Basic research.* New York: Springer-Verlag.

Merrill, D. C., Reiser, B. J., Bekkelaar, R., & Hamid, A. (1992). Making processes visible: Scaffolding learning with reasoning-congruent representations. In C. Frasson, C. Gauthier, & G. I. McCall (Eds.), *Intelligent tutoring systems: Proceedings of the second international conference, ITS '92* (pp. 103–110). (Lecture Notes in Computer Science, No. 608.) Berlin: Springer-Verlag.

Porzio, D. T. (1995). *Effects of differing technological approaches on students' use of numerical, graphic, and symbolic representations and their understanding of calculus.* (ERIC Document Reproduction Service No. ED391665.)

Roddick, C. S. (1995). *How students use their knowledge of calculus in an engineering mechanics course.* (ERIC Document Reproduction Service No. ED389546.)

Snir, J. (1995). Making waves: A simulation and modeling computer tool for studying wave phenomena. *Journal of Computers in Mathematics and Science Teaching, 8*(4), 48–53.

Wu, H. K., Krajcik, J. S., & Soloway, E. (2001). Promoting understanding of chemical representations: Students' use of a visualization tool in the classroom. *Journal of Research in Science Teaching, 38*(7), 821–842.

CHAPTER 16

Modeling with Hypermedia

Hypermedia is simply the marriage of multimedia and hypertext. Hypertext is based on the term *hyper*—meaning above, beyond, super, excessive, more than normal. Hypertext is beyond normal text. Normal text is linear, which means it is constructed to be read from beginning to end. The author uses a structure and a sequence to influence the reader's understanding of the topic. Hypertext refers to a nonsequential, nonlinear method for organizing and displaying text (Jonassen, 1989) that was designed to enable readers to access information from text in ways that are most meaningful to them (Nelson, 1981). Hypertext is supertext because the reader has much greater control of what is read and the sequence in which it is read. Hypertext is based on the assumption that the organization the reader imposes on a text is more personally meaningful than that imposed by the author. Hypermedia is hypertext with multiple representation forms (text, graphics, sounds, video, etc.).

CHARACTERISTICS OF HYPERMEDIA

The most pervasive characteristic of hypermedia is the *node*, which consists of chunks of text, sound, graphics, animation, video, and images. The most common example of a node is a Web page. Nodes are the basic unit of information storage in hypermedia. While reading hypermedia, you can access any node (screen) in the hypermedia knowledge base, depending on your interests. The World Wide Web (WWW) is a huge hypermedia program that is distributed among computers all over the world.

In a hypermedia system, the nodes are accessed by following *links* that connect them. Links in hypermedia systems typically describe associations between the nodes that they connect. That is, while reading one node, you have links (usually identified as hot buttons or hot spots) that will take you to another node of information. At any node you may have access to hundreds of other nodes, or only one or two. Links are usually indicated by highlighted words that you click on in order to navigate to the page that contains the information identified by the link. The structure of nodes and links forms a network of ideas.

Hypermedia systems, like the WWW, permit users to determine the sequence in which to access information (browsing); they are random access systems. Hypermedia systems also enable users to add information (e.g., personal Web pages). Hypermedia information systems provide interactivity by permitting dynamic user control of the information in the knowledge base.

The organization or architecture of hypermedia systems is open. The same set of nodes can be organized in many different ways to reflect many different conceptual orientations or perspectives. The hypermedia author may create a tight structure that restricts access to information in ways to make it most easily understood. In contrast, a structure may be completely open, with immediate access to any node in the knowledge base.

Hypermedia systems afford users many options. Nevertheless, significant problems have plagued hypertext users while they browse through existing hypermedia knowledge bases. The most commonly acknowledged problem is that of navigation. Hypermedia documents can contain millions of nodes, each with multiple links to other nodes. Therefore, it is easy for users to lose track of where they are or where they came from; that is, users can become disoriented.

Perhaps the most significant problem related to using hypermedia to facilitate learning is how learners integrate the information they acquire in the hypertext into their own knowledge structures (Jonassen, 1989). Once information has been found in a hypermedia document, it needs to be related to what the learner already knows. Then learners must reorganize what they know to accommodate the new information. However, when learners are busily browsing hypermedia, they often try to take in more than they can accommodate.

A solution to this problem of integration is to think of hypermedia not as a source of knowledge to learn *from*, but rather as a Mindtool to construct and learn *with*. Learners can create their own hypermedia knowledge bases that reflect their own perspectives or understanding of ideas as they collaborate with other learners.

The primary belief of this book is that students learn more by constructing instructional materials than by studying them.

MODELING WITH HYPERMEDIA

Learners' production of their own hypermedia knowledge bases is an example of *constructionism*. Papert (1990) coined the term to describe "the theory that knowledge is built by the learner, not supplied by the teacher" and "that this happens especially felicitously when the learner is engaged in the construction of something external or at least sharable . . . a sand castle, a machine, a computer program, a book" (p. 3). Constructionism claims that learners construct knowledge most naturally and completely while they are constructing some artifact. Although all Mindtools support knowledge construction, hypermedia is an especially constructionist tool.

The rationale for constructionism is "knowledge as design" (Perkins, 1986), the belief that knowledge acquisition is a process of design that is facilitated when learners are actively engaged in designing knowledge rather than in interpreting and encoding it. Learners become designers when they focus on the purpose for acquiring information, identify its underlying structure, generate model cases, and use the arguments entailed by the subject matter to justify the design. When constructing hypermedia, learners are actively engaged in perceiving different perspectives and organizing their own representations, which reflect their sense of the communities to which they belong. Learners participate and interact with the hypermedia environment to invent and negotiate their own views of the subject (Jonassen, Myers, & McKillop, 1996). Hypermedia is a powerful tool for engaging and supporting knowledge construction. So let students become designers rather than learners, and knowledge constructors rather than knowledge users. They will learn more in the process.

A number of researchers have illustrated the power of hypermedia construction:

◆ Hays, Weingard, Guzdial, Jackson, Boyle, and Soloway (1993) found that as students' experiences with hypermedia construction increased, their documents became more integrated rather than merely annotated text. Students were enthusiastic about hypermedia production and believed that they were learning more because they understood the ideas better.

◆ Spoehr (1995) showed that students who built hypermedia apparently developed a proficiency to organize knowledge about a subject in a more expert-like fashion; they represented multiple linkages between related ideas and organized concepts into meaningful clusters. Superior knowledge representations support more complex arguments in written essays. Most importantly, the conceptual organization skills acquired through building hypermedia are robust enough to generalize to material that students acquire from many other sources.

◆ Learning Spanish was facilitated by building hypermedia presentations in Spanish, because the presentations were personal representations of student knowledge (Toro, 1995).

◆ Fifth graders who built hypermedia systems that compared the lifestyles of American colonists with their own supported their inference-making skills (Lehrer & Romberg, 1996).

Coaching Construction of Hypermedia

Five major processes form a framework for constructing a hypermedia system (Lehrer, 1993).

STEP 1. Students *make* a plan. Planning requires that students make decisions about (1) the major goals of the knowledge base (who is the audience, what they should learn), (2) the topics and content to include in the knowledge base, (3) the relationships among topics (how they will be linked), and (4) the look of the interface (what functions should be provided to the learner). You, the teacher, must guide but not control this planning process. Probably the most important thing that you can do is give the students a meaningful task, such as to design and develop some instruction for their peers. For example, students were assigned to produce a multimedia program that would be used to guide visitors through a zoo. The task was meaningful because it was real world. Ask questions; don't give directions. Lehrer (1993) suggests questions such as the following:

• How are you going to organize your presentation, and why?
• How are you going to decide on what to include and what to leave out?
• Can you draw a map of the flow of your program? Does it seem logical?
• Which stories do you want to include, and what do they represent?
• Which are the most important themes in describing your content? How did you determine that they were the most important?

If students are missing a crucial part of the plan, make sure they know about it. Students also need to decide how they will collaborate to complete all of the tasks required to construct the program.

STEP 2. Students *access, transform,* and *translate* information into knowledge. This is the heart of the learning process. This is where students construct their own understanding of the content. Be sure not to transmit your own understanding. Students must search and collect relevant information to fulfill their planned presentation, select the most important information and interpret it for whatever media they are using, develop and represent new perspectives, and allocate their interpretations to nodes. This interpretive process requires that students decide how information will be represented (e.g., text, graphics, pictures, video, audio) and how the information will be linked to provide access to the readers. Students are usually considerate of the viewers of their programs; they want their products to be desirable.

STEP 3. Students *evaluate* the knowledge base. Students must evaluate the effectiveness of their production. Has it met its goals? Will the readers like it? Student producers must assess how they represented and organized the information. They then need to try out the program with users and solicit their feedback.

STEP 4. Students *revise* the knowledge base. Based on the feedback they get during tryouts, students should correct any content errors that may have been reported. Then the students should reorganize the program to make it more accessible or meaningful for users.

STEP 5. Students *reflect* on the activity. After the project is completed, students should reflect on the project by asking questions such as these: What have we learned about the content we represented? What have we learned about hypermedia production for representing what we know? What have we learned about working with each other? You may choose to provide students with some or all of the criteria for evaluating student hypermedia presentations (presented in the next section). The activity of constructing hypermedia engages a range of meaningful learning. Reflection cements the knowledge that learners construct.

EVALUATING HYPERMEDIA MODELS

Designing hypermedia presentations is a complex process that requires many skills of learners. Carver, Lehrer, Connell, and Erickson (1992) listed some of the major thinking skills that learners need to use as designers, including the following:

- ◆ **Project management skills:** creating a time line for the completion of the project; allocating resources and time to various segments of the project; assigning roles to team members
- ◆ **Research skills:** determining the nature of the problem and how the research should be organized; posing thoughtful questions about the structure; searching for information using textual, electronic, and pictorial sources; developing new information with surveys, interviews, questionnaires, and other sources; analyzing and interpreting all of the information collected to find and interpret patterns

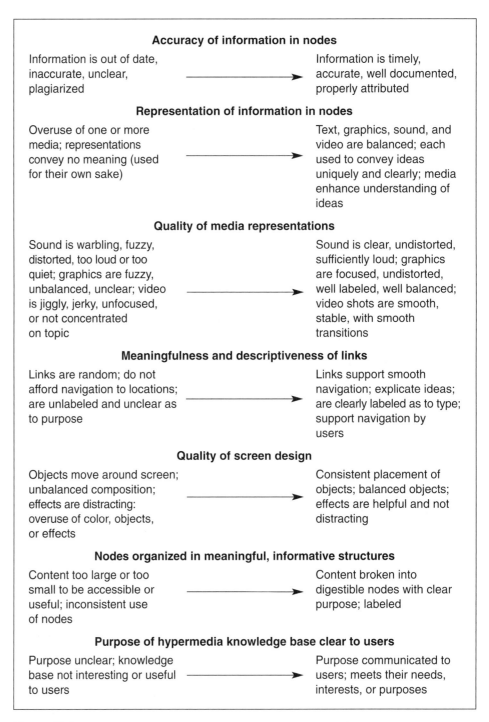

Accuracy of information in nodes

Information is out of date, inaccurate, unclear, plagiarized

⟶

Information is timely, accurate, well documented, properly attributed

Representation of information in nodes

Overuse of one or more media; representations convey no meaning (used for their own sake)

⟶

Text, graphics, sound, and video are balanced; each used to convey ideas uniquely and clearly; media enhance understanding of ideas

Quality of media representations

Sound is warbling, fuzzy, distorted, too loud or too quiet; graphics are fuzzy, unbalanced, unclear; video is jiggly, jerky, unfocused, or not concentrated on topic

⟶

Sound is clear, undistorted, sufficiently loud; graphics are focused, undistorted, well labeled, well balanced; video shots are smooth, stable, with smooth transitions

Meaningfulness and descriptiveness of links

Links are random; do not afford navigation to locations; are unlabeled and unclear as to purpose

⟶

Links support smooth navigation; explicate ideas; are clearly labeled as to type; support navigation by users

Quality of screen design

Objects move around screen; unbalanced composition; effects are distracting: overuse of color, objects, or effects

⟶

Consistent placement of objects; balanced objects; effects are helpful and not distracting

Nodes organized in meaningful, informative structures

Content too large or too small to be accessible or useful; inconsistent use of nodes

⟶

Content broken into digestible nodes with clear purpose; labeled

Purpose of hypermedia knowledge base clear to users

Purpose unclear; knowledge base not interesting or useful to users

⟶

Purpose communicated to users; meets their needs, interests, or purposes

Figure 16-1
Rubrics for evaluating student hypermedia productions.

◆ **Organization and representation skills:** deciding how to segment and sequence information to make it understandable; deciding how to represent information (e.g., in text, pictures, or video); deciding how to organize the information (e.g., in a hierarchy or in sequence) and link it
◆ **Presentation skills:** mapping the design onto the presentation; implementing the ideas in multimedia; attracting and maintaining the interest of the audience
◆ **Reflection skills:** evaluating the program and the process used to create it; revising the design of the program based on feedback

In your evaluation of students' hypermedia productions, assess students' use of project management skills, research skills, organization and representation skills, presentation skills, and reflection skills, and their use of critical, creative, and complex thinking skills. Figure 16–1 presents a number of rubrics that you may use to evaluate the hypermedia programs and Web sites that your students construct as their knowledge and skills move from emergent to mastery. You will probably want to adapt these or add your own criteria as you evaluate your students' projects.

ADVANTAGES AND LIMITATIONS OF HYPERMEDIA FOR MODELING

When learners construct hypermedia programs, including Web pages, many positive outcomes occur:

◆ Learners are much more mentally engaged when they develop materials than when they study materials. The search for information supports more meaningful learning when students plan to publish their products.
◆ Multimedia presentations permit concrete representations of abstract ideas and enable multiple representations of ideas (Hays et al., 1993).
◆ Students constructing multimedia and hypermedia presentations are actively engaged in creating representations of their own understanding through use of their own modes of expression. Multimedia presentations afford more creative expression than text-only presentations.
◆ Students are highly motivated by the construction activity because they have ownership of the product. Usually they are proud of their productions.
◆ Building multimedia and hypermedia presentations orients teachers and students away from the notions that knowledge is information and that the teacher's role is transmitter of it (Lehrer, 1993).
◆ Designing knowledge in the form of multimedia presentations promotes the development of critical theories of knowledge (not every design is successful) and critical thinking, such as defining the nature of the problem and executing a program to solve it (Lehrer, 1993).

On the other hand, constructing hypermedia knowledge bases has some disadvantages:

♦ Students often devote too much effort to the decorative effects of presentations and no improvement in knowledge acquisition occurs (Orion, Dubowski, Dodick, 2000).
♦ Construction of multimedia and hypermedia presentations is a time-consuming process.
♦ Hardware and software requirements are more significant for multimedia construction than for other Mindtools. Integration of audio, graphics, and video into presentations requires a scanner, an audio/video capture card, a larger-than-normal color monitor, speakers, a video camera, and sophisticated multimedia software. The software tools are not terribly expensive, but the hardware can be costly. Usually only one or two multimedia production machines are needed per school, so this limits the cost somewhat.

SUMMARY

Hypermedia is hypertext with multiple representation forms such as graphics, sounds, and video. Hypermedia systems are interactive; that is, they permit users to determine the sequence in which to access information and to add information.

Learners can create their own hypermedia knowledge bases that reflect their own understanding of ideas. Remember, students learn more by constructing instructional materials than by studying them. Students become designers of knowledge rather than interpreters and encoders. They participate and interact with the hypermedia environment to invent and negotiate their own views of a subject. Hypermedia is a powerful tool for engaging and supporting knowledge construction.

Design of hypermedia presentations is a complex process that involves skills such as project management, research, organization and representation, presentation, reflection, and critical, creative thinking.

REFERENCES

Carver, S. M., Lehrer, R., Connell, T., & Erickson, J. (1992). Learning by hypermedia design: Issues of assessment and implementation. *Educational Psychologist, 27*(3), 385–404.
Hays, K. E., Weingard, P., Guzdial, M., Jackson, S., Boyle, R. A., & Soloway, E. (1993, June). *Students as multimedia authors*. Paper presented at the Ed Media Conference, Orlando, FL.
Jonassen, D. H. (1989). *Hypertext/hypermedia*. Englewood Cliffs, NJ: Educational Technology Publications.

Jonassen, D. H., Myers, J. M., & McKillop, A. M. (1996). From constructivism to construction-ism: Learning *with* hypermedia/multimedia rather than *from* it. In B. G. Wilson (Ed.), *Constructivist learning environments: Case studies in instructional design* (pp. 9–106). Englewood Cliffs, NJ: Educational Technology Publications.

Lehrer, R. (1993). Authors of knowledge: Patterns of hypermedia design. In S. P. LaJoie & S. J. Derry (Eds.), *Computers as cognitive tools*. Hillsdale, NJ: Lawrence Erlbaum.

Lehrer, R., & Romberg, T. (1996). Exploring children's data modeling. *Cognition and Instruction, 14*(1), 69–108.

Nelson, T. (1981). *Literary machines*. Swarthmore, PA: Author.

Orion, N., Dubowski, Y., & Dodick, J. (2000). The educational potential of multimedia au-thoring as a part of the earth science curriculum: A case study. *Journal of Research in Science Teaching, 37*(10), 1121–1153.

Papert, S. (1990). Introduction by Seymour Papert. In I. Harel (Ed.), *Constructionist learning*. Boston: MIT Laboratory.

Perkins, D. N. (1986). *Knowledge as design*. Hillsdale, NJ: Lawrence Erlbaum.

Spoehr, K. T. (1995). Enhancing the acquisition of conceptual structures through hypermedia. In K. McGilly (Ed.), *Classroom lessons: Integrating cognitive theory and classroom prac-tice*. Cambridge, MA: Bradford Books.

Toro, M. A. (1995). The effects of HyperCard authoring on computer-related attitudes and Spanish language acquisition. *Computers and Human Behavior, 11*(3/4), 633–647.

CHAPTER 17

Modeling with Structured Computer Conferences

Asynchronous communication is becoming more common than synchyronous communication. Electronic mail (e-mail) is one the most pandemic communication forms in the world. Information that used to be disseminated through live presentations, textbooks, or correspondence courses is now available immediately through bulletin board services. Asynchronous computer conferences, also called discussion boards, have become one of the main features of most distance learning projects.

CHARACTERISTICS OF DISCUSSION BOARDS

Discussion boards are asynchronous discussions, debates, or collaborative communications among a group of people. A common use of discussion boards is creation of virtual classrooms where students socially construct their understanding. The understanding that students reach through conversation represents a verbal model. Therefore, discussion boards can support model building.

Discussion boards support long-distance collaboration among learners. Whether on different continents or at schools on opposite sides of a town, learners can correspond, solve problems, conduct experiments, debate, or simply share ideas and perspectives. Discussion boards provide a communication space in which anyone who is a member of the conference can contribute ideas to the group's representation of the topic they are addressing. The most effective computer conferences are those with a specific purpose, such as solving a problem. So rather than challenging your class to discuss same-sex marriages, have them propose an ordinance for your community regarding the legality of same-sex marriages.

Discussion boards also support debates, simulations, role-playing, and collaborative construction of knowledge bases (Paulsen, 1994). Debates are natural applications of computer conferences in which teams of learners are assigned issues and positions to argue. The research skills engaged in developing arguments that will adequately present the group's position are considerable. Many business simulations are mediated by computer conferences in which individuals are assigned roles and interact with each other. Effective simulations require a well-structured set of activities and careful monitoring of the contributions, but the experience can be powerful.

Role-plays are like simulations in that learners may assume a variety of roles and attempt to reason like the individuals they represent. For example, the University of Michigan involved schools all over the world in an Arab–Israeli conflict simulation in which students were assigned roles as either the combatants, the United States, or the former Soviet Union (Goodman, 1992). Other students represented the religious interests of the Muslims, Christians, and so on. These types of interactions are more engaging than hearing only the teacher's perspective, and they enhance multicultural awareness among the participants. Students can also conduct experiments or observe the environment and collaboratively contribute to a common knowledge base (examples are described later in this chapter).

Discussion boards are commonly supported. Every online course management system (e.g., Blackboard, WebCT, First Class) supports asynchronous communication through discussion boards. These systems require users to log on to a remote computer to communicate with others. File sharing and shared workspaces enable conference participants to work collaboratively on documents and projects.

In most conferencing systems discussions may be held at the whole-group level or be broken up into more specific or user-focused discussions of subtopics. Individuals may comment on the original ideas or on comments by other participants, thus creating an open, electronic discussion of ideas. As Romiszowski and de Haas (1989) point out, these interactions are democratic because all students have the same tools for communicating their ideas. These authors also mention that there is increased potential for deeper or more thoughtful classroom interaction, because individuals can reflect on and think over ideas—or even look up information— before responding (typically not possible in real classrooms). In addition, learners end up with a complete record of the discussion; thus, their anxiety that they will miss something important while taking notes (which often disrupts the communication process) is reduced. The discussion record also functions as a model of social knowledge construction; that is, the conversation is a model of collaboration. The more effective the discussion, the better it will function as a model of social meaning making.

Common Uses of Discussion Boards

In most discussion boards, learners read a message created by another member of the conference and decide whether to respond, how to respond, and the likely consequences of a response. Harasim (1990) found that learners perceive themselves as reflecting more on their thoughts while participating in a computer conference than when engaging in face-to-face or telephone conversations. Jonassen and Kwon (2001) found that computer conference groups who were making decisions and solving problems made fewer social and off-task comments during the conference sessions than groups holding face-to-face conferences.

Carefully considering and constructing responses to issues involves analytical thinking. The "need to verbalize all aspects of interaction within the text-based environment can enhance such metacognitive skills as self-reflection and revision in learning" (Harasim, 1990, p. 49). These are important thinking skills. Perhaps no Mindtool described in this book better facilitates constructive, social learning than asynchronous discussion boards, because they support reflection on what one knows and, through communication about that with others, may lead to conceptual change.

Problems with Discussion Boards

A primary problem teachers and professors face in using discussion boards is lack of engagement, which results from a number of causes. First, instructors do not always convey meaningful expectations to students. Too often, instructors explain participation only in terms of a number of postings per time unit. So to fulfill posting requirements, students respond to messages with such illuminating comments as, "I agree with you. Good point." One of the most likely causes of such meaningless responses is poorly conceived or absent performance rubrics. Instead of specifying performance requirements in terms of the number of required postings per week, instructors must evaluate the quality of students' postings. Another problem results from the classroom culture, which prevents students from taking issue with each others' comments. According to many students, rebutting another student's beliefs is not fair. If there is no interest in critical reasoning, discussions remain shallow.

There are several antidotes to this lack of intellectual engagement. The most obvious is to specify more rigorous expectations in the form of performance criteria (such as those illustrated in Figure 17-4 later in this chapter). Use of performance criteria requires the teacher to actually read and evaluate student messages. This is problematic because a meaningful discussion can result in hundreds of responses, so a critical evaluation of all of the comments generated during a discussion can be time consuming.

Another way of enhancing engagement during discussion boards is to alter the nature of the task. Learner awareness and acceptance of the learning task impels their thinking processes more than any instructional intervention (Jonassen & Wang, 1993). Therefore, it is important to select or design activities that take the greatest advantage of online collaboration. Too many studies have examined the effects of collaboration on individual recall tasks instead of analyzing how learners were prepared to collaborate or examining the nature of the collaboration that occurred. Generating effective discussion topics is hard work. Too often the assignment is to "discuss the importance of" some topic. Such a challenge is too diffuse. Students don't know what that means. It is important to provide a specific topic, task, or purpose for discussion.

One potentially effective focus is a debate about some controversial topic. For example, when students debated for and against the use of technology in formal learning situations, they had to develop initial positions, critically evaluate others' opinions, and develop counterarguments (Bernard & Lundgren-Cayrol, 2001). Debates engage students in argumentation. Argumentation is an essential kind of informal reasoning that is central to the intellectual ability involved in solving problems, making judgments and decisions, and formulating ideas and beliefs (Kuhn, 1991). However, Gunawardena, Lowe, and Anderson (1997) examined interactions in a global online debate and found that the debate inhibited the co-construction of knowledge. Participants were committed to exploring common ground despite the moderators' attempts to continue the debate. Unwillingness to rebut or critique the positions of others makes debates problematic (Martunnen and Laurinen, 2001). Students actually revealed more disagreement and attacked more during role-playing activities than during debates, which lead the researchers to conclude that role-playing is more effective than debates for engaging higher level argumentative discussion.

My preferred purpose for conducting online discussions is problem solving. That is, provide the learners with a complex, multifaceted problem that requires some level of collaboration in order to solve. When students were engaged in conducting expeditions to solve real-life problems, their knowledge construction activities were focused by the expedition activities. Uribe, Klein, and Sullivan (2003) found that collaborative dyads worked harder and solved ill-defined problems better than individuals. Jonassen and Kwon (2001) found that communication patterns of online groups who were solving Harvard business cases more closely resembled the general problem-solving process of problem definition, orientation, and solution development as group interaction progressed. In contrast, face-to-face group interactions tended to follow a linear sequence of interactions.

Cho and Jonassen (2002) compared the effects of argumentation scaffolds on college students who were solving well-structured and ill-structured problems. Ill-structured problems produced more extensive arguments because of the need to generate and support alternative solutions. That is what students can and should do—provide multiple perspectives. Try to get students to generate different viewpoints. Another option is to break the class into different groups to tackle different parts of the problem, or have the entire group generate multiple perspectives on the whole problem. The problem should have a specific purpose. Rather than conducting a conference about the topic "are school funding formulas fair?", require your students to "develop a new funding formula and present it to the state legislature." Be sure to state some requirements for the formula, such as how it affects urban and rural schools, the effects on state income and local property tasks, and so on.

Structured Discussion Boards

One method for enhancing the quality of discussion in discussion boards is to structure the conversation; that is, require learners to make specific kinds of responses to each other. Collaboratively solving problems and other higher order tasks require that learners know how to use various kinds of discourse, particularly argumentation. When using argumentation, students are required to communicate in modes quite different from their normal social chatter and written assignments. Therefore, some discussion boards are designed to *constrain* different forms of communication and reasoning. Structures constrain the kinds of comments that students can post to a computer conference.

The most common kind of scaffold is argumentative, that is, support for student construction of online arguments. For example, the Collaboratory Notebook was a collaborative hypermedia composition system designed to support scientific conjecturing (Edelson, Pea, & Gomez, 1996). During a project, the teacher or any student could pose a question or a conjecture to which learners could only "provide evidence" or "develop a plan" to support that conjecture. The structure of the conference constrained student contributions to the conference. Belvedere, another system, provides a framework for organizing, displaying, and recording the argumentation process, so that students can easily develop their argument toward solving a problem as they work with group members. Specifically, Belvedere provides four predefined conversation nodes ("hypothesis," "data," "principle," and "unspecified") and three links ("for," "against," and "and"). Students can respond only with a hypothesis, data, or a principle that supports or rebuts someone else's comment. Students use these predefined boxes and links to develop their arguments during a problem-solving session. Figure 17-1 illustrates student construction of an argument about an economic problem in Belvedere. When responding to a message, the student must specify the kind of response (a question, a comment, a rebuttal, an alternative).

Another example of a structured discussion board is Convince Me, a domain-independent "reasoner's workbench" that supports argument development and revision and provides feedback about how coherent arguments are based on the theory of explanatory coherence (Ranney & Schank, 1998). Convince Me incorporates tools for diagramming an argument's structure and modifying one's arguments and belief ratings. Using Convince Me, individuals can (1) articulate their beliefs about a controversy; (2) categorize each belief as either evidential or hypothetical; (3) connect their beliefs to support or reject a thesis; (4) provide ratings to indicate the believability of each statement; and (5) run a connectionist simulation that provides feedback about the coherence of their arguments. This feedback makes Convince Me among the most powerful argumentation tools available.

At the University of Missouri, we designed and implemented a structured discussion board. The instructor enters a title and description for the discussion board and defines the message types from which the student will be able to choose

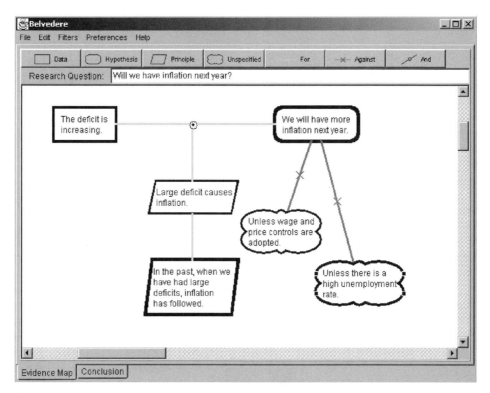

Figure 17-1
Illustration of an argument being constructed in Belvedere.

(e.g., Problem, Solution Proposal, Support Proposal). The instructor must define the name and provide the description for each message type (see Figure 17-2). For instance, we conducted a conference using the following message types:

◆ Solution Proposal
◆ Reason to Support
◆ Reason to Reject
◆ Modify Proposal
◆ Information or Facts
◆ Personal Opinion or Belief
◆ Personal Experience
◆ Research Findings

Next, the instructor must specify the relationships between message types (see Figure 17-3) by checking which message types are allowed to respond to other message types. We grouped the types of statements in the foregoing list into four levels: problem, proposal, warrant, and evidence. Our hierarchical structure constrains users' comments and response structures. At the problem level, the instructor posts a problem statement to which students only can respond using proposal-level

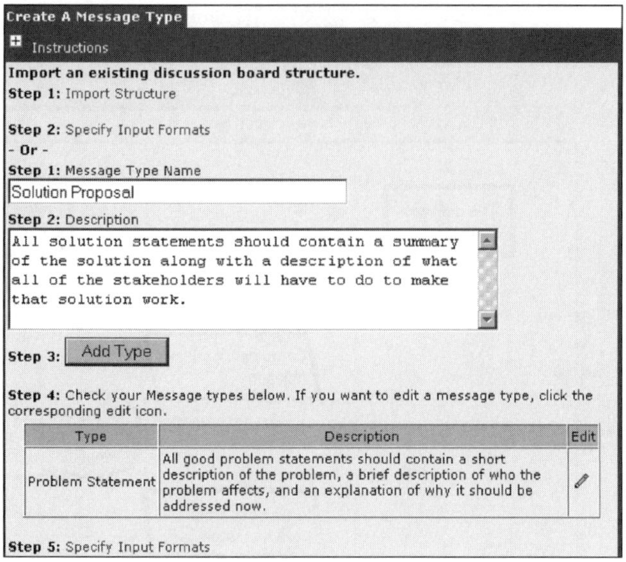

Figure 17-2
Creating message types in a structured discussion board.

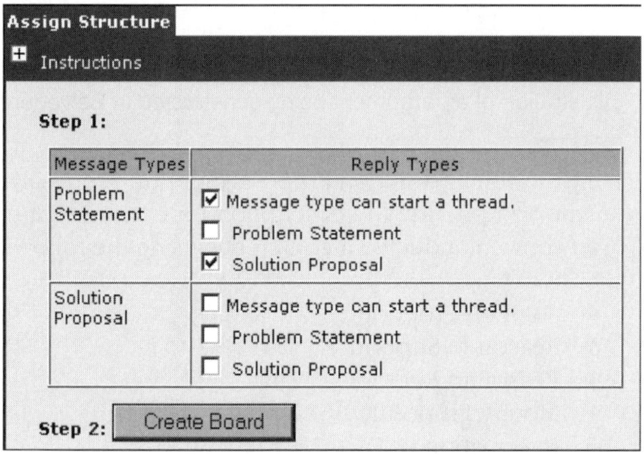

Figure 17-3
Defining relationships between message types in a structured discussion board.

statements. The only statement available at the proposal-level in our structure is the "Solution Proposal," and it can only be responded to with warrant-level statements. Warrant-level statements include "Reason to Support," "Reason to Reject," and "Modify Proposal." Warrant-level statements can only be responded to with evidence-level statements, which include "Information or Facts," "Personal Opinion or Belief," "Personal Experience," and "Research Findings." Although we defined a specific argumentation structure, the conferencing systems we are developing can be adapted to support multiple structures.

After specification of the relationships the message types can take, the next step is creation of the discussion board. In addition to supporting the creation of scaffolding structures, our system supports the ability to save, load, and share structures. Our structured discussion board was built to work within the ShadowNet Workspace, a Web-based work environment designed and developed to support K–12 schools and universities. Unfortunately, this system is no longer widely supported, so we are adjusting the environment to be open source.

MODELING WITH STRUCTURED DISCUSSION BOARDS

Discussion boards are not normally conceived of as modeling tools. However, in this chapter I argue that when a group of learners use constraint-based, structured discussion boards, they are collaboratively building a verbal model of the topic they are discussing. Some of the environments for constraining discussions, such as Belvedere and Convince Me, use visual representations of the discussion; nevertheless, the "meat" of the model is verbal.

Coaching the Use of Structured Discussion Boards

The facilitator or moderator of a structured discussion board plays an important role in ensuring the meaningfulness of an electronic discussion, just as a teacher manages a classroom discussion. As participants, the moderators must maintain a view of the structure of a discussion—that is, what are the issues and the positions on those issues—while avoiding definitive statements that may impede discussion. Teachers as moderators of structured discussion boards need to be coaches, not sources of knowledge. Several themes may emerge in a conference, and different aspects of the themes may be discussed by different individuals. The following activities (Romiszowski & de Haas, 1989; Romiszowski & Jost, 1989) are important for the moderators who are coaching student participation:

1. Assure students that they can really communicate with the system. Motivating learners and overcoming phobias and anxieties is a critical process. Welcome each new user to the conference.
2. Ensure that learners have access to the computer network through directly-connected computers or computers with modems so they can log on frequently.

3. Provide active leadership. Start by playing host: Welcome participants to the conference and establish a nonthreatening climate.

4. Periodically summarize the discussion and make sure that it does not drift off the theme or become too fragmented. Ask participants for clarification of their ideas; resolve disputes or differences in interpretation.

5. Periodically prompt nonparticipants to contribute ideas or reactions to the conference and reinforce their initial contributions. You may want to send students private mail that provides feedback or other interpretations.

6. Periodically ask engaging questions or submit issues that can clarify ideas or become a new focus for discussion.

We are just beginning to learn how to maximize the effectiveness of computer-mediated communication learning experiences. In the next few years, these processes should become well researched and reliable.

EVALUATING STRUCTURED DISCUSSION BOARDS

When students communicate about an issue or a problem, you need to evaluate the quality of their contributions. Remember, quality involves more than the quantity (number and length) of student messages sent to a discussion board. Figure 17-4 presents rubrics to evaluate student contributions to asynchronous computer conferences as their knowledge and skills move from emergent to mastery. You will probably want to adapt these or add your own criteria as you evaluate your students' projects.

ADVANTAGES AND LIMITATIONS OF STRUCTURED DISCUSSION BOARDS FOR MODELING

A number of advantages accrue to learners from using structured discussion boards for modeling:

◆ The primary goal of education, according to many theorists, is to socialize youth. Typically that process occurs only at a local level. Networked computers, however, are an even greater agent for the propagation and dissemination of social skills on a local, regional, national, and even international level (Margolies, 1991). In fact, people who perceive e-mail as important for their social life use it more.

Quality of student messages

Student messages confusing and disconnected; contain hearsay, unsupported remarks, and personal beliefs ⟶ Student messages contain clear communication, are supported by evidence, represent accepted theories

Coherence of student messages

Student messages not related to discussion topic, redundant, repeat other views; irrelevant comments ⟶ Student messages explain issues, provide new perspective, make significant contribution to discussion, elaborate on existing comments

Accuracy of student messages

Student messages misclassified: do not represent constraints consistently ⟶ Student messages consistently represent the constraint imposed by the discussion board

Relevance of student responses to messages

Student responses irrelevant, do not address issues; non sequiturs ⟶ Student responses elaborate, contradict, modify, or relate specifically to previous message

Figure 17-4
Rubrics for evaluating student contributions to structured discussion boards.

♦ Hiltz (1986) found that interchanges in computer conferences produced more interaction and involved more exchanges between students than did face-to-face interchanges. This is probably true because in computer conferences individuals have the ability to remain anonymous; therefore, the conferences reduce personal fears while enhancing academic efficacy. (Note that not all forms of conferencing afford anonymity.) Hiltz also found that undergraduates felt they had better access to the instructor through conferencing and that conference courses were more interesting than traditional courses.

♦ Structured discussion boards are likely to enhance the effectiveness of collaborative efforts among learners for these reasons: They improve access to other group participants, eliminate social distinctions and barriers between participants, contribute to a sense of informality, and foster a stronger group identity (Pfaffenberger, 1986).

♦ Berge and Collins (1993) discussed the independence of time afforded by asynchronous conferencing. Unlike face-to-face meetings, computer conferences are open and available 24 hours a day, 7 days a week. Time can also be allocated for reflecting on a message before responding in order to develop one's arguments or position. Students may do their work when it is convenient or when they are most alert.

◆ Students may argue and disagree without being involved in excessive conflict (Phillips & Santoro, 1989). This is especially helpful for introverted, shy, and reflective people.

◆ Discussion boards support collaborative learning. When working in groups, students accomplished more task objectives and participated more uniformly (Scott, 1993).

◆ Planning documents collaboratively enhances the writing of apprehensive and nonapprehensive writers (Mabrito, 1992). Conferencing is an effective means for teaching collaborative problem solving and other tasks.

◆ In a traditional classroom, the teacher contributes up to 80% of the verbal exchange. In contrast, computer conferencing shows instructor contributions to be 10% to 15% of the message volume (Harasim, 1987; Winkelmans, 1988). Allowing learners to generate questions, summarize content, clarify points, and predict upcoming events is applicable to many educational tasks. When performed online, these types of activities can facilitate the discussion of various structural relationships within the subject matter.

A number of disadvantages may also occur when using structured discussion boards for modeling:

◆ Users must be somewhat skilled as communicators; that is, they need facility with the language. Unfortunately, not all learners have this facility.

◆ The primary mode of input is text, which means that users must be moderately skilled as typists. That is problematic for many, particularly because the text editors for much conferencing software are comparatively primitive.

◆ Conferencing among individuals on different continents several time zones apart can appear to be delayed for hours or even days. The apparent delays may reduce the impact of certain messages or feedback.

◆ Participation within groups of users varies. Full participation in asynchronous conferences is as desirable as full participation in classroom discussions. Nevertheless, technophobia or communication anxieties may prevent some individuals from participating fully. People can become "lurkers" when they post an idea and nobody responds or even acknowledges it, or when they are treated harshly or rudely.

◆ In group decision-making situations, computer-mediated decision making can produce more polarized decisions than face-to-face situations (Lea & Spears, 1991). Decision making takes longer in conferences and may result in the use of stronger, more inflammatory, and more personalized expressions (Siegel, Dubrovsky, Kiesler, & McGuire, 1986). Moreover, anonymity may increase, rather than diffuse, anxiety.

◆ Conferencing may amplify social insecurities. Anxieties are especially common when communications are not acknowledged (Feenburg, 1987). Gunawardena (1995) argues that establishing a sense of social presence is necessary to improve effective instruction within computer conferences. When students have "the feeling that others are involved in the communication process" (Aragon, 2003), they become more engaged.

◆ The absence of social context cues can make discussion somewhat more difficult. Nonverbal communication is not available to help interpret the message.

◆ Hardware and communications lines and equipment are not 100% reliable, which may cause a loss of work or delays in communication. Such problems tend to frustrate users and may reduce participation.

SUMMARY

Asynchronous communication is changing the face of education. Asynchronous computer conferences are now one of the main features of most distance learning projects. In addition to disseminating information, these conferences, or discussion boards, support communication among the students in a course. Discussion boards engage learners in evaluating information, discussing options, solving problems, and justifying their decisions—all of which require critical thinking. These electronic learning communities may consist of a few people in a focused conference or thousands of students corresponding through global conference networks. Discussion boards usually focus on a project or problem, and learners co-construct meaning and collaboratively negotiate solutions. Those are meaningful outcomes for any student.

Problems such as lack of student engagement and a classroom culture that avoids debate do occur in discussion boards. However, there are antidotes for these problems. For example, instructors can specify rigorous performance criteria for students, design activities that take greatest advantage of online activities, and select controversial topics for debate. My preference is to provide learners with a complex, multifaceted task that requires collaboration to find a solution.

One way to enhance the quality of discussions is to structure the conversation. Software programs are available that require learners to make specific types of responses to each other; students are required to communicate in certain modes. When students use constraint-based, structured discussion boards, they are collaboratively building a verbal model of the topic they are discussing.

REFERENCES

Aragon, S. R. (2003) Creating social presence in online environments. *New Directions for Adult and Continuing Education, 100,* 57–68.

Berge, Z. L., & Collins, M. (1993). Computer conferencing and online education. *Electronic Journal on Virtual Culture.* Retrieved from ftp://byrd.mu.wvnet.edu.

Bernard, R. M., & Lundgren-Cayrol, K. (2001). Computer conferencing: An environment for collaborative project-based learning in distance education. *Educational Research and Evaluation, 7*(2/3), 241–261.

Cho, K.-L., & Jonassen, D. H. (2002). The effects of argumentation scaffolds on argumentation and problem solving. *Educational Technology Research and Development, 50*(3), 5–22.

Edelson, D. C., Pea, R. D., & Gomez, L. (1996). Constructivism in the collaboratory. In B. G. Wilson (Ed.), *Constructivist learning environments: Case studies in instructional design.* Englewood Cliffs, NJ: Educational Technology Publications.

Feenburg, A. (1987). Computer conferencing and the humanities. *Instructional Science, 16,* 169–186.

Goodman, F. L. (1992). Instructional gaming through computer conferencing. In M. D. Waggoner (Ed.), *Empowering networks: Computer conferencing in education.* Englewood Cliffs, NJ: Educational Technology Publications.

Gunawardena, C. (1995). Social presence theory and implications for interaction and collaborative learning in computer conferencing. *International Journal of Educational Telecommunications, 1*(2–3), 147–166.

Gunawardena, C. N., Lowe, C. A., & Anderson, T. (1997). Analysis of a global online debate and the development of an interaction analysis model for examining social construction of knowledge in computer conferencing. *Journal of Educational Computing Research, 17*(4), 397–431.

Harasim, L. (1987). *Computer-mediated cooperation in education: Group learning networks.* Paper presented at the meeting of the Second Guelph Symposium on Computer Conferencing, University of Guelph, Ontario, Canada.

Harasim, L. M. (1990). Online education: An environment for collaboration and intellectual amplification. In L. M. Harasim (Ed.), *Online education: Perspectives on a new environment.* New York: Praeger.

Hiltz, S. R. (1986). The virtual classroom: Using computer-mediated communication for university teaching. *Journal of Communication, 36*(2), 95–104.

Jonassen, D. H., & Kwon, H. I. (2001). Communication patterns in computer-mediated vs. face-to-face group problem solving. *Educational Technology: Research and Development, 49*(10), 35–52.

Jonassen, D. H., & Wang, S. (1993). Acquiring structural knowledge from semantically structured hypertext. *Journal of Computer-Based Instruction, 20*(1), 1–8.

Kuhn, D. (1991). *The skills of argument.* Cambridge, UK: Cambridge University Press.

Lea, M., & Spears, R. (1991). Computer-mediated communication, de-individuation and group decision making. *International Journal of Man-Machine Studies, 34,* 283–301.

Mabrito, M. (1992). Computer-mediated communication and high apprehensive writers: Rethinking the collaborative process. *Bulletin of the Association for Business Communication, 55*(4), 26–29.

Margolies, R. (1991, January). The computer as social skills agent. *THE Journal,* pp. 70–71.

Martunnen, M., & Laurinen, L. (2002). Quality of students' argumentation by e-mail. *Learning Environments Research, 5*(1), 99–123.

Paulsen, M. F. (1994). An overview of CMC and the online classroom in distance education. In Z. L. Berge & M. Collins (Eds.), *Computer-mediated communication and the online classroom in distance education.* Cresskill, NJ: Hampton Press.

Pfaffenberger, B. (1986). Research networks, scientific communication, and the personal computer. *IEEE Transactions on Professional Communication, 29*(1), 30–33.

Phillips, G. M., & Santoro, G. M. (1989). Teaching group discussion via computer-mediated communication. *Communication Education, 38,* 151–161.

Ranney, M., & Schank, P. (1998). Toward an integration of the social and the scientific: Observing, modeling, and promoting the explanatory coherence of reasoning. In S. J. Read & L. C. Miller (Eds.), *Connectionist models of social reasoning and social behavior* (pp. 245–274). Mahwah, NJ: Lawrence Erlbaum.

Romiszowski, A. J., & de Haas, J. A. (1989). Computer-mediated communication for instruction: Using e-mail as a seminar. *Educational Technology, 29*(10), 7–14.

Romiszowski, A. J., & Jost, K. (1989, August). *Computer conferencing and the distant learner: Problems of structure and control.* Paper presented at the Conference on Distance Education, University of Wisconsin, Madison.

Scott, D. M. (1993, January). *Teaching collaborative problem solving using computer-mediated communications.* Paper presented at the annual meeting of the Association for Educational Communications and Technology, New Orleans, LA.

Siegel, J., Dubrovsky, V., Kiesler, S., & McGuire, T. W. (1986). Group processes in computer-mediated communication. *Organizational Behavior and Human Decision Processes, 37,* 157–187.

Uribe, D., Klein, J. K., & Sullivan, H. (2003). The effect of computer-mediated collaborative learning on solving ill-defined problems. *Educational Technology Research and Development, 51*(1), 5–19.

Winkelmans, T. (1988). *Educational computer conferencing: An application of analysis methodologies to a structured small group activity.* Unpublished master's thesis, University of Toronto, Ontario, Canada.